Brecht on Performance

Brecht on Performance

Messingkauf and Modelbooks

Bertolt Brecht

Edited by
Tom Kuhn, Steve Giles and Marc Silberman

Translations by
Charlotte Ryland, Romy Fursland, Steve
Giles, Tom Kuhn and John Willett

BLOOMSBURY
LONDON • NEW DELHI • NEW YORK • SYDNEY

Bloomsbury Methuen Drama

An imprint of Bloomsbury Publishing Plc

50 Bedford Square	1385 Broadway
London	New York
WC1B 3DP	NY 10018
UK	USA

www.bloomsbury.com

Bloomsbury is a registered trademark of Bloomsbury Publishing Plc

British Library Cataloguing-in-Publication Data
A catalogue record for this book is available from the British Library.

ISBN: HB: 978-1-4725-5860-2
PB: 978-1-4081-5455-7
ePDF:978-1-4725-1543-8
ePub: 978-1-4081-5950-7

Library of Congress Cataloging-in-Publication Data
A catalog record for this book is available from the Library of Congress.

Typeset by Fakenham Prepress Solutions, Fakenham, Norfolk NR21 8NN
Printed and bound in India

Contents

Miscellaneous Texts

Plans and Appendices

Practice Pieces for Actors

Part Two   *Modelbooks*

Introduction

On *Life of Galileo* (1947–8) from *Constructing a Role: Laughton's*

Picture Credits

With the exception of the Neher design for *Antigone* from the Österreichisches Theatermuseum, Vienna, all the illustrations are courtesy of the Stiftung Akademie der Künste, Berlin (Bertolt Brecht Archive). Together with the archives we have done our utmost to identify and contact the relevant photographers and copyright holders. The publishers will be happy to include further acknowledgements at the first available opportunity.

The photographs accompanying the *Galileo* and *Antigone Modelbooks* between pages 160 and 179 are all by Ruth Berlau, © R. Berlau/Hoffmann. The Neher stage design on p. 180 is © Erbengemeinschaft Stoll-Neher.

The photographs accompanying the *Courage Modelbook* between pages 188 and 219 are mostly by Ruth Berlau, or prepared under her guidance. Of the numbered images (numbered in sequence as in the German publication of the *Couragemodell*), numbers 1, 5, 7, 11 and 18 can be ascribed unambiguously to Ruth Berlau, © R. Berlau / Hoffmann. Numbers 2, 3, 4, 6, 8, 9, 10, 13, 14, 15, 16 and 17 must be ascribed to Ruth Berlau and/or Hainer Hill (as both are known to have photographed that production), © R. Berlau/Hoffmann and Akademie der Künste. Number 12 cannot be ascribed with any certainty. Of the unnumbered images: 'Yvette's race' (p. 210), the four images 'The trader has haggled too long' and 'The mute scream' (pp. 211–12), 'The red shoes, Berlin' (p. 214) and 'Courage and the cook sing for their supper, Berlin' (p. 216) are by Hainer Hill, © Akademie der Künste; 'The red shoes, Munich' (p. 215), 'Courage and the cook sing for their supper, Munich' (p. 217) and 'The final image of Courage, Munich' (p. 219) are by Hildegard Steinmetz, © Steinmetz/Deutsches Theatermuseum Munich; 'The final image of Courage, Berlin' (p. 218) is by Willi Saeger, © Saeger/ Deutsches Theatermuseum Munich. The remaining, unnumbered images must again be ascribed to Ruth Berlau and/or Hainer Hill, © R. Berlau/ Hoffmann and Akademie der Künste.

The photographs of *Katzgraben* are by an unknown photographer (p. 252), by Hainer Hill (p. 260), © Akademie der Künste, by Percy Paukschta (p. 268), © Inge Steinert, and by Ruth Berlau (p. 270), © R. Berlau/Hoffmann.

Particular thanks are due to Anett Schubotz of the Brecht Archive and Hilda Hoffmann for their patient help in identifying photographers.

General Introduction

Brecht is widely known (and unjustly feared) as a theorist of the theatre. We have inherited from him a whole vocabulary of terms to articulate what he understood as a new 'theatre for the scientific age': *Verfremdung*, epic, gestus, the separation of the elements, *Haltung* (attitude), *Fabel* ('plot as playable argument' rather than 'plot as action') and so on.[1] He was, however, never just a theorist in a study, nor a solitary writer at a desk; he was, rather, always engaged in dialogue, working in teams and in the theatre, and always concerned with the practice of the theatre. This is a characteristic of his work from very early on, from the 1920s, when, alongside his trusted friend, the designer Caspar Neher, and others, he was first forming his vision. Many of the traces of that work in the theatre are already abundantly evident in the writings in the companion volume to this one, *Brecht on Theatre*, not to mention in the plays themselves and in the accompanying texts in the *Collected Plays* volumes in the Methuen Drama series. For example, the first full formulation of Brecht's ideas of epic theatre (with the famous tabular confrontation of the epic and the dramatic) comes in a set of, for the most part, eminently practical reflections on the creation and production of the opera *Rise and Fall of the City Mahagonny* in the years 1927 to 1930. The input of Neher and the composer Kurt Weill is explicit. Later, in exile from Nazi Germany, the idea of *Verfremdung* is elaborated in relation to Chinese acting, and then to the practical experience, again, of his own play, *Round Heads and Pointed Heads*, on the stage in Copenhagen. As the years progress, so the influence of other practical experiences and voices becomes ever more apparent, not just those of designers and composers, but also of directors (e.g. Max Gorelik) and actors (Mei Lan-fang, Charles Laughton, Brecht's own wife Helene Weigel, and others). Brecht himself was becoming an ever more experienced director and teacher of stagecraft and direction. His directorial work from 1947 onwards brought with it all sorts of practical reflections, also evidenced in the writings in *Brecht on Theatre*, on set design, make-up, rehearsal techniques, the speaking of verse and of dialogue, and so on. 'Performance' (used here in the sense of 'staging practices') is not a minor category in Brecht's work, but at the centre.

---

[1] For a detailed discussion of these terms and their translation, see the Introduction in *Brecht on Theatre*.

The present volume concentrates on the later years and contains just two parts. First is a new and full edition of one of Brecht's most fragmentary works, or perhaps not a 'work' at all, but a compilation of deliberations about the practice of the theatre (and much else besides) which remained unpublished in his own lifetime. Brecht gave it the somewhat enigmatic title, *Der Messingkauf* (explained in 'Setting the Scene', below). It has become known in English as the *Messingkauf* or *Messingkauf Dialogues*, but it translates literally as *Buying Brass*. Part Two attempts, through a series of excerpts and extracts, a representation of the several published *Modelbooks*, which Brecht and his team at the Berliner Ensemble produced towards the end of his career, alongside some related material from the same period. The *Modelbooks* are descriptions and documentations, in text and image, of his own productions of his plays, documents of practice therefore, and quite far from the sort of theory we tend to think of in relation to Brecht. *Messingkauf/Buying Brass* was largely written in 1939 to 1945 with sporadic further contributions right up until 1955. The idea of the *Modelbooks* dates back to the 1930s too, but nothing substantial was realized until after the Beverly Hills and New York productions of *Life of Galileo* in 1947 and 1948.

These two collections of Brecht's writings can stand alone, individually, but they will be more productive if considered in dialogue with each other, with other writings, and especially with *Brecht on Theatre*, to which this volume forms a companion. The two convolutes – *Buying Brass* and *Modelbooks* – do not exactly belong together. True, they are both about the theatre and performance, but then so are many of Brecht's other writings. We hope, however, that the juxtaposition will be a suggestive and compelling one. It would not be misguided to see *Buying Brass* and *Modelbooks* as both attempting an elucidation of epic theatre, but from opposite directions. The *Modelbooks* record and reflect on key moments and problems in the staging of a real production; performance, and the manner of a particular performance, is the starting point. Performance is written and assembled so that it may be read, rather than experienced. From a study of that record a more generalized understanding of a theatrical approach may be induced. *Buying Brass*, on the other hand, imagines a series of theoretical deliberations, and actively transports these, as dialogues or as performances, into the theatre. In form at least, much of *Buying Brass* purports to be theory written to be performed – or at least it is written as a conversation (sometimes a rather mannered and manipulative conversation) for the edification of the participants. Theory may thus be transformed and become experiential. It is hard to speak generally of what emerges from these processes – the whole point is that they are open and non-prescriptive experiments. One can hold fast to just three overarching insights. The first is the importance of all of the participants, and that includes emphatically the audience, in the realization of epic theatre. Just as the actors came to have such a central role in the realization, not just in the performance but in the whole educative process, of the *Lehrstücke*, so all the discussants in *Buying Brass* have their roles, and so Brechtian performance, more generally, seeks to help the participants, including the audience, to articulate problems themselves and actively invites input from both actors and spectators. Second, in the service of this articulation, Brecht's theatre is a theatre of showing – models of the theatre, and models of the world, which we are to perceive, not as immutable but, precisely the contrary, as transformable by our own intervention: this is a theatre we can change, this is a world we can change. Third, pointing the way to the possibilities of such change, is the centrality of performing difference and what one might call an aesthetics of interruption. Brechtian theatre loves to demonstrate contradictions and uses this relatively simple technique to jolt participants and audiences out of familiar ways of viewing characters and dramatic events and, beyond them, the world.

An edition of Brecht's 'non-literary writings' (and even that is not a category Brecht himself would ever have allowed) faces many pragmatic choices. In this Methuen edition we have four volumes. *Brecht on Film and Radio* (2000) gathers a thematically self-contained set of essays and notes – although several of these are about far more than merely film or radio (especially the commentaries of 'The *Threepenny* Lawsuit'). *Brecht on Theatre* (originally 1964, new edition 2014) was a classic collection, the integrity of which we wanted to maintain even as we revised and updated it. *Brecht on Art and Politics* (2003) was to some extent a response to the original *Brecht on Theatre* and sought to bring into the public domain a range of Brecht's most important writings which were less focused on the theatre. *Brecht on Performance* now extracts these two major works or sets of writings, both of which featured in little more than suggestive hints in the first *Brecht on Theatre*, and offers, simply, a far fuller account of them. We hope that readers will dip into these four volumes and read them in multifarious constellations, so that all the texts can rub shoulders, both with one another and above all with the more conventionally 'literary' works, the plays themselves. Brecht himself first collected his works in suggestive combinations in a series he called *Versuche* – 'Experiments': thin pamphlet volumes with the look of a scientific journal, each juxtaposing a play (or two), often some poems, perhaps a prose work, and some theoretical deliberations. So, for example, volume 11 of the *Versuche* contained Brecht's Berliner Ensemble adaptation of the *Sturm und Drang* classic *The Tutor* and a short radio play, *The Trial of Lucullus*, alongside some poems from the 1930s on classics of European literature, the essay on a 'New Technique of Acting', and the 'Practice Pieces' from the *Buying Brass* material; volume 14 had *Life of Galileo*, the 'Poems from *Buying Brass*', and another play *Horatians and Curiatians*; and volume 15 had a play, *The Days of the Commune*, an important late theoretical essay, 'Dialectics in the Theatre', some practical reflections on *Life of Galileo*, three speeches and two letters. The *Antigone Model* itself featured as *Versuche* 34. This is perhaps altogether the best way to read Brecht, alternating one genre and mode with another, never settling into the 'purely' literary, the merely practical, or the abstractly theoretical.

The editorial work on this volume has been undertaken largely by Tom Kuhn (*Modelbooks*) and Steve Giles (*Buying Brass*), and Marc Silberman has been closely involved at every stage of its development too. The editors have been supported by a team of translators and assistants to whom we are profoundly indebted: Charlotte Ryland, Romy Fursland and Birgit Mikus; and we have taken advice from other Brecht and theatre scholars scattered around the globe, in particular Meg Mumford (University of New South Wales), David Barnett (University of Sussex) and Simon Shepherd (Royal Central School of Speech and Drama, University of London). Di Trevis made a very important contribution by workshopping some of the material, bringing practice back into the theory, and helping us to form our views especially of *Buying Brass*; she then went on to write an essay, included at the back of this volume, about the usefulness of this material for the theatre and for theatre education today. We are grateful to John Willett's heirs for permission to use and modify his original work, as well as to Suhrkamp Verlag and the Brecht heirs for the encouragement to pursue the double project of this volume and the new *Brecht on Theatre*. The support of Bloomsbury Publishing and specifically of Mark Dudgeon in championing the project has been essential. We are much indebted to the Bertolt Brecht Archive in Berlin, and especially to its director Erdmut Wizisla and photo archivist Anett Schubotz. Finally, we acknowledge the financial assistance of the Arts and Humanities Research Council and of St Hugh's College of the University of Oxford, without which we would not have been able to complete our work so efficiently.

The Editors

Readers will note that editors' commentaries appear asterisked (*) after the relevant fragment of text in the *Buying Brass* section, Part One, and indented at the end of each Brecht text in Part Two. In addition, square brackets indicate editorial explanations or additions. Footnotes inserted originally by Brecht are numbered anew at the bottom of the relevant page, whereas editors' footnotes in the introductions are sequentially numbered.

Part One

Messingkauf, or *Buying Brass*

Introduction

The *Messingkauf* has long been regarded as Brecht's single most extensive and – together with the *Short Organon for the Theatre* (in *Brecht on Theatre*) – as his most significant exposition of his views on theatre. It was first published in German in 1963, in volume 5 of Brecht's *Schriften zum Theater/ Writings on Theatre*, edited by Werner Hecht, while John Willett's English translation *The Messingkauf Dialogues* appeared in 1965. Willett's version was based on Hecht's *Dialoge aus dem Messingkauf*, a re-edited and reduced version of the 'full' text that had been published in 1963. These seemingly minor differences in the work's title and content are symptomatic of a fundamental problem. During his lifetime, Brecht never completed or published a work called the *Messingkauf,* and the term *Messingkauf* – devised by Brecht – actually refers to a diverse and disparate corpus of texts produced by Brecht between 1939 and 1955, the year before he died. There has been much speculation as to why Brecht never finalized the *Messingkauf* – the disruption and confusion of the exile years, the systematic focus on his own practical theatre work when he returned to East Berlin – but no conclusive explanation has ever been provided.

Most of these texts were contained in four bundles of papers that Brecht had labelled *Der Messingkauf,* supplemented by various other texts also marked in this way. The contents of the bundles correspond to the three main phases in Brecht's work on the project: early 1939 to early 1941 in Scandinavia (two bundles), 1942–3 (one bundle) and 1945 (one bundle), both in the USA. The overwhelming majority of the *Messingkauf* texts are allocated to the Four Nights of discussion and debate that structure the intended work, while the remainder are not allocated to specific Nights. The first phase in the project was the most productive, in terms of the volume of material produced and implementing the Four Night structure. The second phase is notable for the significant amount of additional material produced for the First Night, the third for the high proportion of unallocated miscellaneous material, and the fourth phase (1948–55) for the paucity of new material.

The *Messingkauf* papers thus present the editor – and translator – with a seemingly intractable problem: how to produce a consistent, reliable and readable version of Brecht's 'work'? This problem is exacerbated by the fact that some 50 years after its initial publication, there are still scholarly disputes and disagreements as to which texts actually belong to the *Messingkauf* corpus. Prior to the publication of the revised German edition of the *Messingkauf* in the Berliner und Frankfurter Ausgabe (BFA) in 1993 (vol. 22, pp. 695–869), the most comprehensive compilation was contained in volume 5 of Brecht's *Writings on Theatre*, whereas *Dialoge aus dem Messingkauf* excluded the *Messingkauf* poems and several classic essays – for example 'The Street Scene' and '*Verfremdung* Effects in Chinese Acting' (both in *Brecht on Theatre*); and Willett's *Messingkauf Dialogues* also omitted the *Practice Pieces for Actors*. All three volumes were problematic, however, as they shared a contentious editorial approach when constructing their respective versions (the basic principles and rationale informing their approach are outlined in the 'Notes' to Willett's translation, pp. 106–11). Texts are switched between Nights; miscellaneous texts are allocated to specific Nights; separate texts are run together to constitute questionable wholes; in the Hecht and Willett *Dialogues* volumes, 'fragments' are distinguished from 'dialogues'; and headings are interspersed from Brecht's various and inconsistent plans for individual Nights. Hecht and Willett are quite open about what they have attempted to do, namely produce a readable version from an extensive and unwieldy corpus of materials, but their respective versions are neither consistent nor reliable.

Nevertheless, Willett's translation has been the canonical version of the *Messingkauf* in English for half a century, and Hecht's editions are still much better known in the German-speaking world than the radical new version published in BFA in 1993. The BFA version of the *Messingkauf* constitutes a drastic piece of re-editing. Whereas Hecht and Willett had presented the reader with a relatively coherent and eminently readable work, the BFA version does not provide us with a work at all. Instead, it presents some 200 texts in chronological sequence, following the *Messingkauf*'s key phases of composition: 1939–41, 1942–3, 1945, and 1948–55. Within those phases, the texts are allocated to the Nights Brecht had indicated; unattributed texts follow the four Nights. The BFA version is eminently reliable, in that the texts contained in it correspond sequentially to what Brecht had actually written between 1939 and 1955, and it is also rigorously consistent, by abjuring any attempt to reconstruct a definitive version of the 'work'. Whereas this may be fascinating for Brecht scholars, it poses considerable difficulties for the general reader, theatre directors or teachers and their students, who need a more user-friendly edition. Just one example suffices: in the BFA version, the famous opening scene does not appear until 78 pages into the text.

The version of the *Messingkauf* devised for this translation is based on the following principles (see also the table of Contents above): texts are sequenced by individual Night, not in order of composition; within each Night, texts are organized in terms of thematic clusters; miscellaneous texts not allocated to individual Nights are presented in a separate section, but here too organized thematically; the integrity of each separate individual text is retained – separate texts are not 'run together'; the date of composition of each text is indicated, and each text is identified by using its BFA reference number. In contrast to the Hecht and Willett versions, no distinction is made between 'dialogues' and 'fragments' – *Messingkauf* consists almost by definition of fragments – and 'headings' drawn from Brecht's various 'plans' are not used: all subheadings are the editor's, as are the headings Preamble, Miscellaneous Texts, and Plans and Appendices. Although this new edition aims to be significantly more accessible and readable than the BFA version, it also enables the reader to appreciate how Brecht's *Messingkauf* project developed over time, especially between 1939 and 1945; to identify and compare shifts of emphasis in Brecht's conception of individual Nights; and even to speculate as to where the Miscellaneous Texts might be allocated in a real or imaginary performance of this intractable 'work'.

What emerges is a quite different version of the *Messingkauf*, entitled *Buying Brass*, the literal English translation of the German title. But it is also a version that generates fundamental questions regarding how *Buying Brass* should be read, performed and interpreted. One key question concerns the genre it represents, in view of the variety of text types that it incorporates. There are dialogues varying in length from a few lines to several pages; speeches long and short; essays; poems; texts with and without titles or headings, some of them mere snippets, whose generic status is unclear; and more than twenty meta-texts, such as the various plans and outlines that Brecht produced between 1939 and 1948 or the four Appendices written in August 1940 when less than half of *Buying Brass* was in place.[1] There are also textual anomalies. In the Second Night, the Actor refers to 'the fourth wall we were talking about earlier' (B28, written 1939–41), but the initial reference to the fourth wall occurs at the beginning of the Third Night, when the Dramaturg asks the question 'What about the fourth wall?' (B135,

---

[1] BFA identifies meta-texts with the letter A, and all other texts with the letter B.

written c. 1945). Should both dialogues be included in the same night, even though Brecht allocates them to different nights; be switched between nights; or remain where they are, as a flashback or flash-forward? Similarly, in the 'Finale' in the Fourth Night, the Dramaturg refers to the Philosopher's earlier comment on the notion of ease (B87), but the Philosopher's only discussion of ease is contained in an unallocated text (B153, Miscellaneous Texts (iii)). Ultimately, we are confronted by the question as to whether *Buying Brass* can actually be construed as a 'work' at all, even in this readable version – or is it rather 'a loose baggy monster',[2] a Brechtian pot-pourri, to be used or appropriated in any way its readers choose?

In a *Journal* entry dated 19 August 1940, Brecht noted that whenever he opened *Buying Brass* it was as if a cloud of dust was being blown into his face, and he asked himself 'How can one imagine something like this ever making sense?' His initial idea of writing a theoretical work in dialogue form was already being superseded by his own practice, as exemplified in the variety of text types indicated above. By the time the *Buying Brass* papers were largely in place, the proportion of dialogue to other text types in each Night varied considerably, from 5:1 in the First Night to 1:2 in the Second, and 2:3 in the Miscellaneous Texts. The generic variety of *Buying Brass* presents the reader who wishes to establish Brecht's theoretical views as expressed in it with a fundamental problem. Even if we put to one side the interpretative issues raised by presenting theory in dialogue form, in the rest of *Buying Brass* only the meta-texts can be reliably attributed to 'Brecht'. Most of the speeches are attributed to specific characters, but some are not and so remain indeterminate; and several texts seem to be short essays, with no clear indication as to who the intended 'author' might be. Furthermore, all the Miscellaneous Texts are de-contextualized by virtue of not being allocated to a specific Night, so that we can do no more than speculate as to the interpretative nuances that follow from assigning them to one Night rather than another. If we add to this the fact that there are no clear or reliable indications regarding the linear structure of the individual Nights – the thematic complexes identified by the editor are suggestive, rather than definitive – then Brecht's question would seem to be unanswerable, and his interpretative dust clouds impossible to dispel.

Brecht himself, however, inadvertently offers two escape routes from this dilemma: by using the terms 'literarization' and 'montage' in his first plan for *Buying Brass* (see A2), and via a *Journal* entry on 18 August 1948 where he describes the *Short Organon for the Theatre* as a condensed version

---

[2] Henry James uses this term in the 1908 preface to his novel *The Tragic Muse* (1891) to refer pejoratively to blockbuster nineteenth-century novels.

of *Buying Brass* – a minor pendant to the magnum opus, as it were. There are of course significant thematic parallels between the *Short Organon* and *Buying Brass*, concerning the superannuated nature of illusionist theatre, the characteristics of a theatre for the scientific age, the relationship between art and science, Marxist social and cultural theory, and the need for a new kind of artistic realism. In other respects, however, the two are fundamentally different, and in one crucial sense not comparable at all in that the *Short Organon* is a finished product, published in Brecht's lifetime, whereas *Buying Brass* is anything but a stable and coherent work whose philological status is uncontroversial and unproblematic. Even more importantly, the *Short Organon* is a systematic, tightly structured, strategically calibrated piece of critical analysis, modelled stylistically on Francis Bacon's *The New Organon* (see *Brecht on Theatre*, Introduction to Section 3), whereas from a structural, rhetorical and stylistic point of view *Buying Brass* is its diametrical opposite. To use Roland Barthes's terminology, the relationship between the two is analogous to that between the Work and the Text, where *Buying Brass* displays classic features of Barthes's Text. It lacks a centred structure, does not encapsulate an identifiable determinate meaning, bombards its readers with fragmentary perceptions, is a network with multiple entry points lacking a unilinear dynamic, and produces its meanings in collaboration with its readers in a playful and pleasurable manner.[3]

Yet *Buying Brass* is also a quintessentially Brechtian text, with montage as its primary structural principle and the responses of its presumed reader or audience grounded in literarization, a term Brecht defines in the 'Titles and screens' section of the 'Notes to *The Threepenny Opera*' (see *Brecht on Theatre*). Literarization refers to the strategy of linking the theatre with other intellectual institutions by incorporating written text – for example scene titles – into the production, so as to provoke a different mode of reception on the part of the audience. By so doing, literarization rejects the notion that the action of the play, or even the dramatic work itself, could or should say everything that needs to be said about its own subject matter. Instead of the audience's responses being predetermined by the unilinear dynamic of dramatic theatre, they are encouraged to look up and down and from side to side, so that their visual space transcends that of the action on stage in a process termed complex seeing. This process is modelled in part on the way in which readers of a book consult footnotes, or flip between its pages in order to compare one situation with another. Moreover, complex seeing,

---

[3] See Roland Barthes, 'From Work to Text', *Image Music Text* (London: Fontana, 1979), pp. 155–64. On Brecht and post-structuralist theory, see Giles, *Bertolt Brecht and Critical Theory*, chapter 7.

complemented by 'thinking across the flow', is precisely the mode of reader or audience response embedded in *Buying Brass* and elicited by Brechtian montage. Its unfinished status notwithstanding, one notable feature of *Buying Brass* is the dispersal of key themes across individual Nights – a feature that tends to be obscured by the Hecht/Willett versions – as may be seen by tracing the thematic links between the editorial subheadings in this new version: Empathy in I and II; Science and social science in I, II and III; Emotion in III and IV; V-effect in II and III; Acting in II and III; Shakespeare in II and IV; the Augsburger in II, III and IV; Piscator in II and III. Thus a performance of *Buying Brass* could also reinforce complex seeing and thinking by using projections of episodes and texts taken from previous and later episodes, or recycled from the Miscellaneous Texts.

The performance dimension of *Buying Brass* just highlighted adds a further layer of complexity to the process of trying to make sense of it. In any performance text there is always a significant element of 'free-play' and even indeterminacy between the written script and the ways it might be rendered on stage. Dialogues and speeches that on the printed page might come across as self-evident, apodictic or even authorial might then display a further feature of Barthes's Text – which he compares to a post-serial music score demanding a practical collaboration from its reader or audience.

The Preamble to *Buying Brass*, together with the stage directions for the opening scene (B115, The First Night), establishes the theatrical conventions that inform it and foregrounds its performance dimension from the start. A discussion is to take place on stage, in a theatre after the evening show, between a Philosopher and a group of theatre people: an Actor and Actress, a Dramaturg, and a backstage worker, variously referred to as the Lighting Technician, the Stage Hand or the Worker. We, the audience, are welcomed by the Dramaturg, who exposes the stage mechanisms that are designed to deceive us, and as the discussion begins, we see the stage set being dismantled. We are confronted from the beginning with an anti-illusionist and self-reflexive piece of theatre reminiscent of Luigi Pirandello's *Six Characters in Search of an Author*, of which Brecht had a personal copy (published in 1925). *Buying Brass* and *Six Characters* are both grounded in the modernist crisis of representation that had also informed Brecht's early plays (see the section 'Brecht and Modernism: 1918–26' to the Introduction to Part One of *Brecht on Theatre*), but with a crucial difference. Pirandello's play presents a classic modernist critique of theatrical illusionism that also radically questions the coherence of the self and personal identity, the very possibility of linguistic communication and interpersonal understanding, and the nature of reality as such. In contrast, Brecht's critique of illusionism – typically designated as Naturalism and associated with the Russian theatre director Konstantin Stanislavsky – is the springboard for a revised and revitalized theory and practice of artistic realism. Similarly, Brecht rejects Pirandello's modernist preoccupation with metaphysical issues, and focuses instead on the theatre as a social institution that engages critically with political issues.

The thematic complexes that inform *Buying Brass* are presented dialectically, however, whether through sequences of dialogue or the montage of variegated text types described above.[4] The four main characters are identified by their differing views on the nature and function of theatre, and indeed of art in general (see A3, Characters in *Buying Brass*), but by the end of the Fourth Night of discussion and debate (see 'Finale') they have all modified their views to a greater or lesser degree. Not only have they developed their roles in relation to each other in true Brechtian fashion, *Buying Brass* itself could even be construed as a sophisticated variant on the *Lehrstück*. Nevertheless, ever since its first publication in 1963 (German) and 1965 (English), critics have sought to establish the definitive viewpoint of 'Bertolt Brecht' regarding the themes and issues discussed, typically by identifying him with the Philosopher. In one sense this is not surprising, as many of the questions that concern the Philosopher also preoccupied Brecht. He also uses Brechtian terminology – for example '*thaëter*' – to characterize his new type of theatre, orchestrates (some might say manipulates) many of the discussions, delivers seemingly authorial major speeches, and is of course the progenitor of the term *Buying Brass*. Nevertheless, it is also important to bear in mind not only the interpretative ramifications of the theatrical complexity of *Buying Brass*, but also that even in his more 'straightforward' theoretical writings Brecht can be elusive, playful, disingenuous and ironic, characteristics well exemplified in the *Short Organon* (see *Brecht on Theatre*, Introduction to Part 3).

Let us consider, for example, the Philosopher's disquisition on 'buying brass'. Towards the end of the opening scene (B115), the Philosopher enlarges on his pragmatic and utilitarian approach to theatre and the arts in general by comparing himself to a scrap-metal dealer watching a brass band. His only interest in the trumpeter's trumpet is its commercial value as metal, whereas its value for the trumpeter is of a fundamentally different order. Although the Philosopher's provocation puts in question non-material or ethereal values that might be associated with artistic pursuits, it could also be argued that his own position is that of a vulgar materialist: not just in terms of his appreciation of musical instruments, but also in relation to his crass comment in the Fourth Night towards the end of a serious discussion of the

---

[4]   An extensive and meticulous analysis of the main themes in *Buying Brass* may be found in J.J. White, *Bertolt Brecht's Dramatic Theory*, chapter 5.

nature of dramatic art, 'And now I propose that we take advantage of the fact that we've stood up to go and relieve ourselves' (B89). The Philosopher seems to be unable to grasp the Marxist distinction between the exchange value and use value of a commodity, and to be oblivious to Marx's view that aesthetic production is an intrinsic and defining feature of humanity. At the same time, his crassness, which he attempts to legitimize by referring to our basic drives, is redolent of Brecht's comment in his *Autobiographical Notes* in 1927, 'A year of screwing or a year of thinking!' (*Autobiographische Aufzeichnungen 1920–1954*, BFA 26, p. 289), while his utilitarian materialism is reminiscent of Brecht's approving remarks in 1929 on the Vandals burning wood carvings for fuel ('Conversation about Classics', *Brecht on Art and Politics*, p. 79). In the East Berlin theatre production of *Buying Brass* in 1963, the leading Brechtian actor Ekkehard Schall played the Philosopher as a pastiche of Brecht – but of Brecht as he was known in the 1950s.[5] Perhaps future productions might play the Philosopher as a pastiche of the 'Bert Brecht' of the late 1920s, with his iconic leather jacket and cropped hair.

The Philosopher's views on the function of art are also similar to ideas that Brecht articulates around 1930, rather than those developed by the mid-1930s in 'Theatre for Pleasure or Theatre for Instruction' (in *Brecht on Theatre*). Whereas in the latter essay Brecht emphasizes that learning and instruction should be fused with entertainment and pleasure, the Philosopher focuses on learning to the detriment of enjoyment, just as Brecht had in his explanatory notes to *The Flight of the Lindberghs* from 1930 – 'means of learning, not means of enjoyment' (*Collected Plays: Three*, Explanatory Notes, p. 319). In his later theoretical writings, and indeed at the end of the fourth Appendix to *Buying* Brass, Brecht resurrects the classical and early modern notion that poetry should involve *prodesse* and *delectare* – it should teach and delight. In so doing he rejects the post-Romantic and Modernist view that art should be expressive or an end in itself, a view associated with the Actor in *Buying Brass*. But the Philosopher's utilitarian perspective restricts the function of art to *prodesse* at a time when Brecht himself is moving towards the emphasis on *delectare* we find in the *Short Organon*. Rather intriguingly, however, by the beginning of the Fourth Night the Philosopher has modified his previous position, and now defines art as an intrinsically human capacity, able to create reproductions of social reality that produce a unique kind of emotional, intellectual and practical response in its audience (B99).

---

[5]   See David Barnett, 'Brechtian Theory as Practice: The Berliner Ensemble Stages *Der Messingkauf* in 1963', in *Theatre, Dance and Performance Training* (vol. 2 (1), 2011), pp. 4–17.

Nevertheless, the view that there is a fundamental commonality between Brecht and the Philosopher, whereby the Philosopher is a touchstone for readers and audiences seeking to establish the true message of *Buying Brass*, is one that still holds sway, particularly when it is construed as a written artefact rather than a performance text. There are, however, two further figures within the dramatic constellation of *Buying Brass* who undermine this assumption: the Dramaturg and the raisonneur. Midway through the First Night, the Dramaturg presents an incisive critique of the internal inconsistencies of Naturalism, deploying arguments reminiscent of Brecht's own, and he is also the primary expert on epic theatre as practised by both Erwin Piscator and Brecht from the mid-1920s to the late 1930s. Indeed, his expositions of Brecht's theatrical practices function as a counterpoint to the Philosopher's theoretical precepts (B132, end of subsection (i), Third Night), and he also mediates between the Philosopher and the Actor when they argumentatively take up opposing positions (B116, second scene in the First Night). In other words, the Dramaturg, committed to developing the new type of theatre but less dogmatic than the Philosopher, might also be construed as an avatar of Brecht. But it is the Actor, rather ironically, who ultimately undermines the argument that the Philosopher – or any other character – is the theoretical keystone of the fragile edifice that is *Buying Brass*. The Actor elaborates on the Dramaturg's critique of Naturalism in the First Night by exposing the inconsistencies and implausibilities in the role of the raisonneur – 'a character who voiced the playwright's own opinions', a role 'often filled by the hero', 'a fairly schematic figure' with whom as many spectators as possible should be able to identify (B111). The notion that any of the characters might be Brecht's raisonneur is perverse – for that to be the case, *Buying Brass* would have to be an antiquated and obsolete piece of theatrical Naturalism. It is of course no such thing, a tissue of voices rather than a monological text, comparable to the articulation – as Brecht so eloquently puts it in the *Short Organon* – of 'a man standing in a valley and making a speech in which he occasionally changes his opinion or simply utters sentences that contradict one another, so that the accompanying echo brings them into confrontation' (Section 39, see *Brecht on Theatre*).

Steve Giles

Preamble

A1
1939–41

BUYING BRASS

A philosopher has come to a large theatre after the performance has finished, to talk with the theatre people. He has been invited by an actress. The theatre people are dissatisfied. They have been involved in efforts to create a theatre of the scientific age. Science has not benefited much from this, however, while the theatre has suffered all kinds of losses.

A3
1939–41

CHARACTERS IN BUYING BRASS

The Philosopher wants to use the theatre ruthlessly for his own ends. It must provide accurate depictions of incidents between people, and facilitate a response from the spectator.

The Actor wants to express himself. He wants to be admired. Plot and characters serve his purpose.

The Actress wants a theatre with an educational social function. She is politically engaged.

The Dramaturg puts himself at the Philosopher's disposal, and promises to apply his knowledge and abilities to the conversion of the theatre into the *thaëter* envisaged by the Philosopher. He hopes for a new lease of life for the theatre.

The Lighting Technician represents the new audience. He is a worker and dissatisfied with the world.*

* Brecht uses different terms for this character in the various stages of *Buying Brass*. In the Third Night (B135, p. 63 below) he is referred to as the Worker, and in the opening scene of the First Night (B115, p. 13 below) and in the Fourth Night (B144, p. 95 below) as the Stage Hand.

B1
1939–41

DRAMATURG: Welcome to the houses of fabricated dreams! Here you can see both the old and the new machinery that we use to deceive you. Every age has contributed its own few tricks. Since the invention of powerful lamps we've been able to represent night-time on stage. The techniques of perspective, which are somewhat older, have helped a great deal. And recently we've started using projectors! Yes – all of this has led to a steady improvement in our ability to create illusions. During the performance, these bits of scenery that look so pathetic in the inadequate light of rehearsals become more magnificent than the real pillars in whose image they are made. We build our theatres without windows, as brewers do their cellars, but only so that we can more clearly illustrate daytime and night-time.

The First Night

(i) Setting the Scene

B115
1942–3

THE FIRST NIGHT

A stage on which a Stage Hand is slowly dismantling the set. An Actor, a Dramaturg and a Philosopher are sitting on chairs or props. The Dramaturg reaches for a small basket put there by the Stage Hand, takes out some bottles and uncorks them. The Actor pours the wine into glasses and hands it round to his friends.

THE ACTOR: You get thirsty sitting on a stage what with all the dust everywhere, so take a good swig!

THE DRAMATURG *glancing at the Stage Hand*: We might have to ask our friend here not to take the set down too quickly – it'll churn up too much dust otherwise.

THE STAGE HAND: I'll take my time. It's all got to be out of the way tonight though; they're rehearsing something new tomorrow.

THE DRAMATURG: I hope you're all right sitting here. We could have used my office but it's colder there, as I don't pay for a ticket like the beloved audience do. And it would mean I'd have to sit there with the countless scripts I'm supposed to have read staring me reproachfully in the face. Besides, you as a philosopher like to see behind the scenes, and you as an actor can play to the auditorium, even if there's no audience. We can talk about theatre and feel as if we were holding this conversation in front of an audience, as if we ourselves were performing a little play. And we'll also be able to stage one or two little experiments if necessary, to clarify what we're talking about. So let's make a start; and why not begin by asking our friend the philosopher what interests him about theatre in the first place?

THE PHILOSOPHER: What interests me about your theatre is the fact that you apply your art and your whole apparatus to imitating incidents that occur between people, making your spectators feel as though they're watching real life. Because I'm interested in the way people live together, I'm interested in your imitations of it too.

THE DRAMATURG: I see. You want to learn something about the world, and we show what goes on in the world.

THE PHILOSOPHER: I'm not sure you've fully understood me. I'm not sure because I would have expected you to show a little more uneasiness if you had.

THE DRAMATURG: What is there to be uneasy about? You say you're interested in our theatre because we show what goes on in the world – and that's exactly what we do.

THE PHILOSOPHER: I said you deal in imitations, and that these imitations interest me in so far as they correspond to what's being imitated, because that's the thing that interests me most: the way people live together. As I said it I was expecting you to look askance at me and wonder whether I could possibly be a good spectator, with an attitude like that.

THE DRAMATURG: Why should that stop you being a good spectator? We gave up putting gods, witches, animals and ghosts on stage a long time ago. *#In the last few decades the theatre has done all it could to reflect real life. It's made huge sacrifices in its efforts to help solve social problems. It has shown how wrong it is that women are used as mere playthings, that individuals' business conflicts have been carried into the home and turned marriages into battlefields, that the money for the educational refinement of rich people's children comes from other parents selling their children into vice, and much more. And it has paid for these services to society by forfeiting virtually all of its poetry. It hasn't managed to devise a single great plot fit to stand alongside those of the classics.

THE ACTOR: Or a single great character.

THE DRAMATURG: But we do show banks, hospitals, oilfields, battlefields, slums, millionaires' villas, cornfields, stock exchanges, the Vatican, arbours, mansions, factories, conference tables – in other words, the whole of reality as we know it. We show murders being committed, contracts being signed, adultery, heroic deeds being done, and wars being declared; we show people dying, breeding, buying, slandering and hustling. In short, the way people live together is presented from every possible angle. We embrace any kind of powerful effect, we don't shy away from any kind of innovation, and we jettisoned all aesthetic laws a long time ago. Our plays can have five acts or fifty, five different settings can be shown on stage at once, the ending can be happy or unhappy – we've even had some plays where the audience got to choose the ending themselves. What's more, our acting can be entirely naturalistic one night and stylized the next. Our actors can speak blank verse or the language of the gutter with equal fluency. Our musical comedies are frequently tragic, our tragedies include songs. One night the stage can show a house that replicates a real house to the last little detail, to the last stovepipe; the next night a wheat market can be suggested by a few coloured beams. Our clowns make the audience cry, our tragedies reduce it to helpless laughter. With us, in other words, anything is possible – I'm tempted to say, 'unfortunately'.

THE ACTOR: Your description sounds a bit desperate to me. You make it sound as if we weren't serious about our work any more. But we're not just frivolous buffoons, I can assure you. We're hardworking, highly disciplined people and we give our all – we have to, given that there's so much competition.

THE DRAMATURG: Our portrayals of real life were exemplary. We enabled audiences to study the subtlest inner moods and feelings. Our portraits of family life were meticulously drawn. Some ensembles would spend ten years or more growing attuned to each other, so that you would get representations of a landowner's family, for example, where every movement any of the actors made was authentic and you could almost smell the scent of the rose garden. I was often amazed at the way the playwrights managed, time and time again, to identify some new psychological state people might find themselves in – just when we thought we knew them all. No, no effort was spared, and we were never hampered by doubts or hesitation.

THE PHILOSOPHER: So what you're mainly concerned with is imitating incidents between people?#

THE DRAMATURG: Without imitating incidents between people we can't practise our art at all. The most you could accuse us of is producing bad imitations. In that case you'd be arguing that we're bad artists, because our art consists in giving our imitations the stamp of authenticity.

THE PHILOSOPHER: That's not what I'm arguing at all. I want to talk about your art where it's done well, not badly. And when it's done well, it certainly does give imitation the stamp of authenticity.

THE ACTOR: I don't think I'm being arrogant when I say that I could act out any action you can think of, even the most wildly improbable, in such a way that you'd believe it without question. I'll show you the Emperor Napoleon chewing hobnails if you like, and I bet you'll find it completely natural.

THE PHILOSOPHER: Very true.

THE DRAMATURG: Excuse me, but you're sidetracking us. You're getting off the point.

THE ACTOR: How am I sidetracking us? I'm talking about the art of acting.

THE PHILOSOPHER: I wouldn't say we were getting sidetracked either. An account of some well-known exercises for actors,[1] designed to encourage natural acting, includes a drill whereby the actor has to place a cap on the floor and then behave as if it were a rat. This is supposed to teach him the art of *make believe*.

THE ACTOR: An excellent exercise! Without mastering the art of *make believe*, how could we ever hope that a few scraps of canvas or even just a screen with some writing on it would make spectators believe they were watching the battle of Actium, or that a mask and a few old-fashioned articles of clothing would make them believe they were watching Prince Hamlet?** The greater our art, the fewer aids we need from reality in order to construct a slice of life. It's true that we imitate incidents from real life, but there's more to it than that. To hell with the incidents! What's important is our reason for imitating them.

THE PHILOSOPHER: Well, and what is the reason?

THE ACTOR: It's that we want to fill people with passions and emotions, to take them out of their everyday lives and everyday incidents. The incidents are the scaffolding, as it were, upon which we exercise our art; they are the springboard we take off from.

THE PHILOSOPHER: Exactly.

THE DRAMATURG: I don't like that 'exactly' of yours one bit. I can imagine you not being particularly keen on those emotions and passions you're meant to be filled with. You didn't say a word about that when you were explaining why you've come to our theatre.

THE PHILOSOPHER: That's true, I admit it. I apologize. To your good health!

THE DRAMATURG: I'd prefer to drink to yours, frankly. Because what we were actually meant to be talking about was how *you* could get satisfaction from the theatre, not how we could.

---

[1] Rapoport's account of the Stanislavsky School. [Brecht is referring to Josef M. Rapoport's essay 'The Work of the Actor', published in the first volume of *Theatre Workshop. Quarterly Journal for the Theatre and Film Arts*, October–December 1936.]

THE ACTOR: Surely he's not going to try and say he objects to us livening up his sluggish soul a bit? I know he's more interested in what we're imitating – the incidents – than he is in us; fair enough. But how are we supposed to imitate those incidents for him without calling on our emotions and passions? If we gave a cold performance even he would just get up and walk out. Anyway, there's no such thing as a cold performance. Every incident affects us emotionally, unless we're completely unfeeling.

THE PHILOSOPHER: Oh, I've got nothing against emotions. I agree that emotions are necessary if portrayals or imitations of incidents from people's lives together are to be possible, and that such imitations must excite emotions. The only thing I'm not sure about is whether your emotions, and especially your efforts to excite particular emotions, do your imitations any good. I still have to insist, you see, that it's the incidents from real life I'm particularly interested in. So I'd like to stress once more that I feel like an intruder and an outsider in this building with all its mysterious practical bits of apparatus – like someone who has not come here to feel at ease, and would in fact have no hesitation in generating unease, because he has a very special interest in coming here. The special nature of this interest cannot be emphasized enough, and it strikes me so powerfully that I can only compare myself to a man who, let's say, deals in scrap metal, and goes to see a brass band wanting to buy not a trumpet or any other instrument, but simply brass. The trumpeter's trumpet is made of brass, but he is hardly going to want to sell it as brass, according to its value as brass, as so-and-so many pounds of brass. But that is exactly how I am approaching you in my search for incidents between people – which you do imitate here in some way, even if your imitations serve a very different purpose from that of satisfying me. In a nutshell: I'm looking for a way of getting incidents between people imitated for particular purposes; I've heard that you manufacture such imitations; and now I'm hoping to find out whether they are the kind of imitations I can use.

THE DRAMATURG: To tell the truth, I am actually starting to feel a little of that uneasiness you were expecting to arouse. The imitations we manufacture – as you rather prosaically put it – are naturally of a particular type in so far as they are designed for a particular end. You'll find this point discussed in Aristotle's *Poetics*. He defines tragedy as an imitative portrayal of a morally serious, self-contained action of a given duration, in heightened language whose different varieties are employed separately, distributed among different parts; he also maintains that it is not narrated, but presented by people acting, and that by evoking pity and terror it brings about the cleansing of those same emotional states. In other words, it's a matter of imitating those real-life incidents of yours, and the imitations are supposed to have particular effects on the soul. Since Aristotle wrote these things, the theatre has undergone many transformations, but not on this particular point. We must assume that if it changed in this respect it would no longer be theatre.

THE PHILOSOPHER: So you don't think it's feasible to separate your imitations from your purpose in producing them?

THE DRAMATURG: It's impossible.

THE PHILOSOPHER: But I need imitations of incidents from real life for my purposes. What can we do about that?

THE DRAMATURG: The fact is, if the imitations were separated from their purpose then they just wouldn't be theatre any more.

THE PHILOSOPHER: That wouldn't necessarily bother me too much. We could give the result a different name: *thaëter*, for instance. *All laugh.* It would work like this: you'd just be artists I was hiring for a non-artistic job. Because I can't find anybody else who's skilled in the art of imitating human beings in action, I'd like to engage your services for my purposes.

THE DRAMATURG: What are these mysterious purposes?

THE PHILOSOPHER *laughing*: Oh, I hardly dare tell you. You'll probably think they're terribly mundane and prosaic. I thought we might use your imitations for very practical purposes: simply to find out the best way to behave. We could turn them into something similar to physics (which deals with mechanical bodies) and develop techniques from them.

THE DRAMATURG: So your purposes are scientific ones! That's got nothing to do with art, you know.

THE PHILOSOPHER *hastily*: Er … of course not. That's why I only called it *thaëter*.

THE DRAMATURG: All right, let's have your ideas then. There'll be something for us in them, too. It might be a roundabout way of picking up a few hints about how to 'manufacture' good imitations, which is absolutely what we're after; we know from experience that our portrayals are much more powerful when what we're portraying is plausible. Who's going to sympathize with a jealous wife, for instance, if we imply that her husband is cheating on her with her grandmother?

THE PHILOSOPHER: If I hire you, though, you'll need to make sure you pursue those benefits in such a way that they don't disadvantage me. I think the first thing for me to do is to carefully investigate how you're used to working, so that I can see what needs changing in your methods if I'm to get the kind of imitations I'm looking for.

THE DRAMATURG: Perhaps you'll even come to realize that our imitations are not so unsuitable for your purposes after all, even if we do 'manufacture' them in the old-fashioned way. In fact, I really don't see why people shouldn't be able to draw practical lessons from our theatre as well.

* An alternative version of this scene in Brecht's typescript (see Bertolt Brecht Archive, Mappe 126) transposes the material from pp. 14–15 (between the #s) to the end of the scene.
** The battle of Actium is depicted in Act III, Scenes 8–10 in William Shakespeare's *Antony and Cleopatra* (1606). Prince Hamlet is the central character in Shakespeare's *The Tragedy of Hamlet, Prince of Denmark* (1600–1).

B116
1942–3

THE PHILOSOPHER: You should know that I am consumed by an insatiable curiosity about people; I can't see or hear enough of them. The way they socialize, strike up friendships and enmities, sell onions, plan military campaigns, get married, make tweed suits, circulate forged banknotes, dig potatoes, observe the movement of the planets; the way they betray, favour, teach, interrogate, judge, maim and support each other; the way they hold meetings, form societies, concoct schemes. I always want to know how their undertakings come about and how they turn out, with the aim of identifying certain laws that might enable me to make predictions. Because I wonder about how I myself should behave if I want to succeed and be as happy as possible, and of course this depends on how other people behave, which makes me very interested in that too – and especially in the possibility of influencing them.

THE DRAMATURG: Well, let's hope you can get your pound of flesh from us.

THE PHILOSOPHER: Yes and no. I confess that's exactly what I wanted to talk to you about. I'm not entirely happy here.

THE DRAMATURG: Why's that? Is there more you want to see that we're not showing you?

THE PHILOSOPHER: No, I can see enough. That's not the issue.

THE DRAMATURG: Perhaps you see things that you don't feel are portrayed correctly?

THE PHILOSOPHER: I also see things that I do feel are portrayed correctly. I think the trouble is that I find it impossible to distinguish right from wrong with you. I haven't given you a full account of myself yet. I have another passion besides curiosity, you see: it's argumentativeness. I like to carefully examine everything I see and get my two bits in, as they say. I take great pleasure in doubting things. As poor people do their pennies, so I turn what people do and say over and over in the palm of my hand. And I don't think you people leave any room for my doubts, that's the issue.

THE ACTOR: Aha, a critic!

THE PHILOSOPHER: Hm. Have I touched a nerve?

THE DRAMATURG: We've got nothing against intelligent criticism. We don't get enough of it.

THE ACTOR: It's all right. I understand: we'll always have to reckon with criticism of some sort.

THE PHILOSOPHER: You don't seem particularly enamoured of my passions. But I can assure you I didn't mean to belittle your art just now. I was just trying to explain the sense of uneasiness that comes over me in your theatres and takes a lot of the enjoyment out of it for me.

THE ACTOR: I hope you'll look inside yourself for the cause of that uneasiness and not just blame us.

THE PHILOSOPHER: Of course. It's not all bad news. First of all I'd like to clear the air by saying I'm much less concerned with the way you portray things – whether or not you imitate them correctly, in other words – than with the actual things you're imitating. Suppose you give a good imitation of a murder. My passion for criticism will then compel me to subject the murder itself and all its details to tests of utility, elegance, originality and so on.

THE DRAMATURG: And you can't do that here?

THE PHILOSOPHER: No. You won't let me. It's to do with the way you arrange your imitations, even the best of them, and the way you present them to me. There was a time when I used to go to open-air performances and smoke during the play. As you know, a man who is smoking adopts an attitude highly conducive to observation. He leans back, thinks his own thoughts, relaxes in his seat, enjoys everything from a protected position, and is only half involved in what is going on.

THE DRAMATURG: Did it help you to see any better?

THE PHILOSOPHER: No, my cigar went out.

THE ACTOR: Bravo! A double bravo! One for the actor who managed to bring you under his spell, and one for yourself for not being a cold fish!

THE PHILOSOPHER: Stop! I must protest. It didn't work out the way I expected. The experiment was a failure.

THE ACTOR: Just as well, my dear man, just as well!

THE PHILOSOPHER: I wasn't satisfied.

THE ACTOR: Shall I tell you how you could have been satisfied? If the chaps on the stage had been terrible actors with no idea what they were doing.

THE PHILOSOPHER: I rather fear you're right.

THE DRAMATURG: What do you mean, you fear?

THE PHILOSOPHER: Well, isn't it a bit frightening to think that the better you act, the harder it is to satisfy me? It sounds like a hopeless situation.

THE DRAMATURG *to the Actor*: Stop tapping him patronizingly on his knee. I've seen people disagree with even the most reasonable arguments just for that.

THE PHILOSOPHER: It's true, you are quite a tyrannical person. I feel tyrannized by you constantly when you're on stage, too. I'm always supposed to do what you want. Without getting any time to think about whether I do want what you want.

THE DRAMATURG: You see – now he feels as though you're patronizing him even when you're up there on stage! What did I tell you?

THE PHILOSOPHER: Don't you think we're on to something important here? Think about it! A member of the audience says he feels like he's being patronized! Being seen through, being understood better than he understands himself, caught out in secret desires which are then satisfied! Isn't there something repugnant about that?

THE ACTOR: That's enough now. It's no good trying to discuss things when we're angry. I've already hidden my hands in my pockets.

THE PHILOSOPHER: Who says you want to have a discussion, angry or otherwise? You never discuss things on the stage, after all. You excite all sorts of passions, just not the passion for discussion. Even when it's there, in fact, you don't satisfy it.

THE DRAMATURG: Think before you reply. He's talking very much to the point.

THE ACTOR: As he always does. To his point.

B9
1939–41

THE DRAMATURG: You seem to think we perform barbaric war dances here in honour of obscure and obscene cults, mumbo-jumbo, enchantments, black masses?

THE ACTOR: Ibsen's Nora a black mass! The noble Antigone a barbaric war dance!* Hamlet, mumbo-jumbo! Priceless!

THE PHILOSOPHER: I must have misunderstood you. I admit it.

THE ACTOR: Very much so, my friend!

THE PHILOSOPHER: It must be because I took your discourse seriously and didn't realize the things you said about yourselves were just a joke.

THE DRAMATURG: Now what are you driving at? What things we said?

THE PHILOSOPHER: That you are 'servants of the *word*', that your art is a 'temple', that the audience is supposed to sit 'spellbound', that there is 'something divine' in your performances, etc., etc. I really believed you were trying to uphold some ancient cult.

THE DRAMATURG: They're only figures of speech! It just means we take it very seriously.

THE ACTOR: It sets us apart from the hubbub of the marketplace. From cheap entertainment and all that.

THE PHILOSOPHER: Of course. I wouldn't have been misled by it if I hadn't actually seen 'spellbound' spectators in your theatres. Take tonight, for instance! As your Lear* cursed his daughters, a bald-headed gentleman next to me started gasping in such an unnatural way that I wondered why, having lost himself completely in your wonderful portrayal of madness, he didn't start frothing at the mouth.

THE ACTRESS: He'd had better evenings!

* The plays referred to are Henrik Ibsen, *A Doll's House* (1879); Sophocles, *Antigone* (c. 441 BC); Shakespeare, *Hamlet* (1599-1602) and *King Lear* (1605-6).

B8
1939–41

THE ACTOR: We actors are completely dependent on the plays we are given. We don't just go out and witness a few of your *incidents* and then imitate them on the stage. We'd have to wait for new plays to come along, that means – plays that would allow for the sort of performance you want.

THE PHILOSOPHER: Then we might be waiting till kingdom come. I suggest we leave the composition of plays out of it – for the time being, anyway. Generally your playwrights take such incidents from real life as would arouse sufficient interest in real life, and tailor them in such a way as to make them effective on the stage. Even when they make things up, their inventions are such that – except in completely fantastical plays – it seems as though the incidents have been lifted from real life. All you ought to do is take the incidents themselves as seriously as possible, and the playwright's use of them as lightly as possible. You can partially ignore the playwright's interpretation, you can insert new elements; in short, you can use plays as raw material. I'm assuming from the start that you only pick plays whose incidents are of sufficient public interest.

THE ACTOR: What about the spirit of the work, the authors' sacred words; what about style, what about atmosphere?

THE PHILOSOPHER: Oh, I'd say the authors' intention is only of public interest in so far as it serves the public interest. Their words may be treated as sacred if they are the right answer to the question of the people, style will depend on your own taste anyway, and the atmosphere needs to be clear, whether the authors makes it so or not. If they respect these interests and the truth, follow them; if not, improve them!

THE DRAMATURG: I'm not sure you're talking like a person of taste.

THE PHILOSOPHER: But like a person, I hope. There are times when we have to choose between having good taste and being human. And why should we go along with that ugly custom of attributing good taste only to people who know how to wear beautiful clothes, and not to the people who make them?

THE DRAMATURG: I still think it's difficult to learn this new way of portraying things from Naturalist plays or from the older ones, which try to excite emotions using only a few indications – or reminiscences – of reality. Perhaps we could take real-life court cases from legal casebooks and rehearse them, or something like that. Or put well-known novels to new uses. Or portray historical incidents as everyday incidents, the way caricaturists do.

B119
1942–3

THE ACTOR *getting up*: He's no theatregoer.

THE ACTRESS: What do you mean?

THE ACTOR: He's got no feeling for art. He's out of place here. From an artistic point of view he's stunted, a poor wretch who was born lacking one specific sense: a sense of art. Of course, he may be a perfectly respectable person in other ways. When it comes to finding out whether it's raining or snowing, whether Mr Smith is a good person, whether Mr Jones is intelligent, etc., etc., then you can count on him – no reason why not. But he knows nothing about art, and what's more, he doesn't want art: it makes him sick, he'd like to see it abolished. I know his sort. He's the fat man in the stalls who's come to the theatre to meet a business associate. As I'm pouring my heart out on stage over whether to be or not to be, I catch his goggle-eyes fixed on my wig; as the wood comes towards me on Dunsinane Hill I can see him examining it to see what it's made of.* The highest plane he can haul himself up to is the circus, I'm sure of it. A two-headed calf: that's the kind of thing that fires his imagination. A leap from a height of fifteen feet: that's the epitome of art for him. There's a really difficult feat for you. Something you could never do yourself: that's what art is, isn't it?

THE PHILOSOPHER: As you are so very insistent, I have to admit that I do find a fifteen-foot leap interesting. Is that so wrong? But I'm interested in calves with just the one head, too.

THE ACTOR: Of course: as long it's the real thing, a genuine calf, not an imitated one, eh? The calf in the flesh, in the context of its environment and with particular reference to its nutrition. You've come to the wrong place, sir!

THE PHILOSOPHER: But I assure you I've seen you yourself perform the equivalents of such leaps, and watched them with great interest. You too can do things I can't do myself. I think I've got just as much feeling for art as most people: it's something I've often noted, sometimes with satisfaction and sometimes with concern.

THE ACTOR: You're just trying to talk your way out of it! Talk, talk, talk! I can tell you exactly what art means to you. It's the art of making copies, copies of what you call reality. Sir, art is a reality in itself! Art is so far above ordinary reality that we should really call reality a copy of art. And an incompetent copy at that!

THE ACTRESS: Aren't you and your art trying to leap rather too high?

* 'To be, or not to be' are the opening words of Hamlet's soliloquy in *Hamlet*, Act III, Scene 1; Birnam Wood comes *to* Dunsinane in Shakespeare's *Macbeth* (1606), Act V, Scene 6.

B112
1942–3

IMITATION AND OBJECT

ACTOR: Can't you see he's afraid we might mistake some deliberate affront for amiability? What do you think the painter Gauguin* would have said if someone had looked at his Tahitian pictures purely out of an interest in Tahiti, because of the rubber trade for example? He had the right to expect us to be interested in Gauguin, or at any rate in art in general.

PHILOSOPHER: And what if somebody did happen to be interested in Tahiti?

ACTOR: He could use material other than Gauguin's paintings.

PHILOSOPHER: What if there wasn't any other material? What if the interested person didn't want statistics or dry facts but a general impression, to get an idea of what it was like to live there for example? The rubber trade isn't enough to stimulate a really deep, many-sided interest in an island like Tahiti, and as I told you I have a real interest – deep and many-sided – in the object you are imitating.

DRAMATURG: Gauguin still wouldn't be the right reporter though. He doesn't have enough to offer for such purposes.

PHILOSOPHER: Possibly. They weren't what he'd had in mind. But could he give the right kind of report?

DRAMATURG: Maybe.

ACTOR: By sacrificing his artistic interests!

DRAMATURG: Oh, that wouldn't necessarily have to happen. There's actually no reason why, as an artist, he shouldn't be interested in the sort of task our friend would be setting him. I seem to remember Holbein** being recruited by Henry VIII to paint the portrait of a lady the king wanted to marry, but hadn't yet met.

ACTOR: I can see it now. Holbein at his easel. The courtiers standing around him. *He acts.* 'Master, Master! Do you not see that her Highness's lips are as soft and full as … etc.' – 'Suffer not such voluptuous painting of your Highness's lips, your Highness! Consider the foggy airs of England!' – 'And besides, they are thin, thin, thin. Be not so foolhardy as to deceive the king.' – 'It is the lady's nature that concerns his Majesty; he is a man of much experience. It matters not only whether the lady attracts him, but whether she will attract others.' – ''Tis bad the posterior should be hid from him.' – 'And far too lofty a brow.' – 'Remember, Maestro, that these are high politics. For France's sake, pray put more grey on your brush.'

ACTRESS: Does anyone know if the marriage came off?

PHILOSOPHER: There's nothing about it in the art history books, at any rate. The aesthetes who wrote them didn't understand that kind of art. But our friend here would have understood it, to judge from her question.

ACTRESS: Ah well, the lady's dead and her royal suitor's turned to dust as well. But Holbein's portrait hasn't lost its meaning, even now that marriage and politics are off the agenda.

DRAMATURG: Nevertheless, the picture might have taken on some special quality that we can still perceive today. It had so many important things to reveal about a woman, things that interest us even now.

PHILOSOPHER: We're getting off the point, my friends. All that matters to me is that this portrait became a work of art. I think we can all agree about that aspect of the matter at least.

ACTOR: For Holbein the commission simply gave him a reason to make art.

DRAMATURG: But the fact that he was an artist was the reason the king commissioned him to perform a service he needed.

* The French painter Paul Gauguin lived on Tahiti from 1891–3.
** Hans Holbein was court painter to King Henry VIII of England, and produced portraits of at least five candidates for the king's hand. Brecht was probably thinking about the story of the portrait of Anne of Cleves.

B117
1942–3

THE ACTOR: Quite frankly, I've started to wonder if he's really a philosopher.

THE DRAMATURG: Why? You can't say that without giving a reason.

THE ACTOR: A philosopher thinks about what exists. Art exists. So he thinks about it. It's like this or it's like that, and if he uses his loaf a bit he might be able to explain why. If so, then he's a philosopher.

THE PHILOSOPHER: You're absolutely right. There are philosophers like that. And there is art like that too.

THE ACTOR: What sort of art do you mean?

THE PHILOSOPHER: Art that's like this or like that, and that's all there is to it.

THE ACTOR: Oh – is there some other kind of art, then? Art that isn't like this or that, and so doesn't exist?

THE PHILOSOPHER: Take your time; I know you aren't used to taking your time, but just try.

THE ACTOR: All right: I shall think about it. *He strikes a pose.* Is that how you do it?

THE PHILOSOPHER *feeling the Actor's calf muscles*: No. You need to relax your muscles. Let's begin our thinking with a confession on my part. I'm a philosopher who didn't have enough loaf for the kind of philosophizing you were talking about.

THE ACTOR: Here, come and weep on my bosom!

THE PHILOSOPHER: I'd prefer the lady's, to be honest, and for laughing rather than crying. But to get back to the question of the philosopher and the loaf: a few centuries ago, when some philosophers were starting to make discoveries and inventions in the realm of nature, others were beginning to wonder whether they had the loaf to grasp and to refute certain claims being made by the ecclesiastical and other authorities. These claims were to the effect that everything is good and legitimate the way it is. They wore themselves out in a critique of reason. They really didn't have enough in the way of loaves or any other kind of nourishment to be able to take on such powerful institutions as the Church. So I in turn have been trying to think how the general supply of loaves can be increased.

THE ACTOR *laughing*: When I said 'uses his loaf' I meant for thinking, obviously, not for eating.

THE PHILOSOPHER: Oh, the two things are intimately connected. The more loaves there are, the more loaves there are.

B4
1939–41

DRAMATURG: Diderot*, who was a great revolutionary dramaturg, said the theatre should serve the purposes of entertainment and instruction. It seems to me that you want to abolish the first.

PHILOSOPHER: You've already abolished the second. There's nothing instructive about your entertainments any more. Let's see if there's anything entertaining about my instruction.

* Denis Diderot was a leading philosopher, novelist and dramatist in the French Enlightenment; his best-known work on dramatic theory is *On Dramatic Poetry* (1758). Brecht had several copies of his writings.

B3
1939–41

ACTOR: God, moralizing makes me sick! Holding a mirror up to the powerful – as if they didn't thoroughly admire their own reflections! And as if, as a seventeenth-century physicist once put it, murderers, thieves and profiteers murder, steal and profiteer only because they don't realize how ugly it is! And pleading with the oppressed to start feeling sorry for themselves at last for God's sake! That bitter draught of sweat and tears! The public conveniences are too small, the workhouses have smoking ovens, the ministers have shares in armaments firms and the clergymen have sexual organs! And I'm supposed to be taking a stand against all that.

ACTRESS: Fifty nights running I played a bank manager's wife whose husband treats her like a plaything.* I was championing the cause of women being allowed to have careers too, and take part in the great rat-race, as hunter or hunted or both. By the end I was having to drink myself silly just to be able to get the lines out.

ACTOR: There was another play where I got my chauffeur to lend me some trousers belonging to his unemployed brother, and I made compelling speeches to the proletariat. Not even in my kaftan as Nathan the Wise* had I cut such a noble figure as I did in those trousers. I pointed out that all the wheels would stop turning if the strong arm of the proletariat so willed it. This was at a time when there were several million workers going around without work. The wheels had stopped turning even though their strong arm had not willed it at all.**

* The plays in question are Ibsen, *A Doll's House* (see also B9 above), and G. E. Lessing, *Nathan the Wise* (1779).
** 'The wheels had stopped turning even though their strong arm had not willed it at all' refers to F. Freiligrath's 'Anthem for the General German Workers' Union' (1863), where the workers' arms do stop the wheels of industry from turning.

(ii) Naturalism, Realism, Empathy

B2
1939–41

NATURALISM

DRAMATURG: Stanislavsky's* most important works were those of his Naturalistic period, although he did also experiment a lot, and produced fantastical plays as well. You have to talk about works in his case because, as is customary in Russia, some of his productions have been running unaltered for more than thirty years, although they're now performed by entirely different casts of actors. His Naturalist works, then, consist of minutely detailed depictions of society. They're a bit like those soil samples dug up from deep underground that botanists bring into their laboratories to examine. The action in these plays is minimal, their entire duration is given over to illustrating conditions, and their concern is to investigate the inner life of various individuals, although there's something in them for social scientists too. When Stanislavsky was in his prime, the Revolution broke out. His theatre was treated with the greatest respect. Twenty years after the Revolution his theatre was like a museum where you could still study the way of life of social classes that in the meantime had vanished completely.

PHILOSOPHER: Why are you talking about social scientists? Were they the only ones who could learn something about the structure of society from his work? Couldn't all the spectators?

DRAMATURG: I'd like to think so. He wasn't a scientist but an artist; one of the greatest of his age.

PHILOSOPHER: I see.

DRAMATURG: What mattered to him was naturalness, and as a result everything in his theatre seemed far too natural for anyone to stop and examine it. You don't usually examine your own home or your own eating habits, do you? But his works still have historical value, let me tell you, even though he wasn't a historian; put that in your pipe and smoke it.

PHILOSOPHER: Yes; they have historical value for historians, it seems.

DRAMATURG: He doesn't seem to interest you.

PHILOSOPHER: Oh, he may serve various social interests, but hardly those of social research, even if he can be made to contribute to it. People can't demonstrate the law of gravity by dropping a stone, nor by merely giving an exact description of its fall. You might say that their assertions don't contradict the truth, but we need more than that – I do, at any rate. Like nature, they simply seem to be saying 'question me'. But, like nature, they will put immense obstacles in the questioner's way. And of course they won't be as good as nature itself. An image that is mechanically drawn and made to serve many purposes will inevitably be very imprecise. There are bound to be short-cuts at the most instructive points; everything about it is sure to have been superficially done. Such images are usually just as puzzling to the researcher as 'accurately' depicted flowers. Magnifying-glasses are no more help than any other scientific instrument in interpreting them. So much for their value as objects of research. And, I might add, the social researcher is more likely to get something useful from the opinions expressed about social conditions than from the conditions themselves. But the main issue for us is that this kind of art needs researchers in order to deliver the sort of results we are interested in.

DRAMATURG: All the same, some of the works associated with Naturalism did give rise to social impulses. The audience was made to feel that a great many intolerable conditions really were intolerable. The teaching in state schools, the way women were prevented from gaining their independence, hypocrisy in sexual matters – these things and many others were decried.

PHILOSOPHER: That sounds good. By acting in the public interest, the theatre must have aroused the interest of the public.

DRAMATURG: Oddly enough the theatre didn't gain much by its self-sacri- ficing attitude. Some of the abuses were remedied or else (more frequently) they were overshadowed by worse ones. The subject matter of the various plays was quickly exhausted, and their theatrical portrayal was often shown to be very superficial. And the theatre had sacrificed so much. All of its poetry, and much of its ease.** Its characters were as flat as its action was banal. It was as shallow from an artistic point of view as it was from a social one. Of Stanislavsky's works, those that were the least interventionist and the most descriptive were the ones that lasted the longest and came across as the most artistic and – to tell the truth – the most socially significant. But even they did not depict a single great character or a single plot worthy of comparison with those of the old plays.

---

* Konstantin Stanislavsky was one of the most important directors and theorists in the twentieth century. He was best known for his work at the Moscow Art Theatre, founded in 1898, particularly his productions of Anton Chekhov's plays. He continued to produce plays at the Moscow Art Theatre after the 1917 Russian Revolution.
** The notion of 'ease' is clarified in B145 and 153 in Miscellaneous Texts, pp. 111–13, below.

B21
1939–41

DRAMATURG: Naturalist performances created the *illusion* that you were in a real place.

ACTOR: The spectators looked into a room and felt they could smell the cherry orchards at the back of the house; they looked inside a ship and seemed to feel the pressure of the storm.*

DRAMATURG: That it was *no more than* illusion was made clearer by Naturalist plays than by Naturalist productions. The playwrights were of course as painstaking about the arrangement of their incidents as the non-Naturalist ones. They cut, combined, had characters meet in unlikely places, treated some incidents more broadly and others more subtly, and so on. They stopped short the moment there was any risk of breaking the illusion that this was reality.

ACTOR: So you're trying to say it's only a question of degree, of more or less realistic portrayals? But it's precisely the degree that's so important.

DRAMATURG: I'd say it's to do with the degree of the *illusion* one has of dealing with reality. And I think it's more productive to sacrifice that illusion if you can swap it for a portrayal that conveys more of reality as such.

ACTOR: You mean one that arranges, combines, cuts, and brings together without worrying about maintaining the illusion that we're dealing with reality?

PHILOSOPHER: Bacon says that 'Nature reveals herself more through the harassment of art than in her own proper freedom'.**

ACTOR: You do realize that what you're dealing with in that case is only the playwrights' views on nature, not nature itself?

DRAMATURG: And you realize that the same applied to Naturalist plays? The first Naturalist dramas (e.g. Hauptmann's, Ibsen's, Tolstoy's, Strindberg's) were rightly accused of being tendentious.

---

* The plays in question are Chekhov, *The Cherry Orchard* (1903), first produced by Stanislavsky at the Moscow Art Theatre in 1904, and – possibly – Reinhard Goering's Expressionist play *Battle at Sea* (1917).
** The quotation is from Brecht's personal copy of *Franz Baco's Neues Organon*, edited by J. H. Kirchmann (Berlin, Verlag L. Heimann, 1870), p. 64. The English translation is from Francis Bacon, *The New Organon*, edited by Lisa Jardine and Michael Silverthorne (Cambridge University Press, 2000), p. 21.

B110
1942–3

DRAMATURG: We had representations. The representations found in Naturalism led to a critique of the real world.

PHILOSOPHER: To a powerless critique.

DRAMATURG: How might we have created a powerful one?

PHILOSOPHER: Those Naturalist representations of yours were done badly. The point of view you chose for your portrayals did not facilitate any genuine criticism. People empathized with you and came to terms with the world. You were as you were, and the world stayed as it was.

B111
1942–3

NATURALISM – REALISM

DRAMATURG: Naturalism didn't manage to last very long. It was accused of being too shallow for the politicians and too boring for the artists, and it turned into *Realism*. Realism is less naturalistic than Naturalism, even if Naturalism is not considered to be any less realistic than Realism. Realism does not furnish entirely accurate depictions of reality; in other words, it avoids the full-length reproduction of the kind of dialogues you would hear in real life, and is less concerned about being mistaken for real life. On the other hand, it does try to go deeper into reality.

ACTOR: Between you and me, it's neither fish nor fowl. It's just unnatural Naturalism. Whenever anyone asks the critics for examples of Realist masterpieces, they always cite Naturalist works. If challenged, they point to a certain arbitrariness on the playwright's part, arrangements of 'reality', distortions in its 'reproduction' and so on. All that proves is that Naturalism never in fact created an exact reproduction; it only pretended to offer one. This was what it was like with the Naturalists: when you went to one of their performances you felt like you were entering a factory or a private garden. You saw (and also felt) just as much of reality as you saw (and felt) in the place itself, in other words very little. You felt nagging tensions or experienced sudden outbursts, etc.; in other words, you got nothing more than you would have got outside the theatre. For this reason many Naturalists decided to insert a so-called raisonneur, a character who voiced the playwright's own opinions. The raisonneur was Naturalism's version of a chorus: it was a chorus in disguise. This role was often filled by the hero. He saw and felt particularly 'deeply' – that is to say he was in on the dramatist's secret intentions. Those spectators who identified with him were able to feel they had 'mastered' situations. For the spectators to identify with him, he needed to be a fairly schematic figure with as few individual characteristics as possible, so that as many spectators as possible would be 'included'. So he had to be unrealistic. Plays with heroes like this were then labelled 'realist', because such heroes did communicate something about reality, but in a non-naturalistic way.

B118
1942–3

EMPATHY

The epic acting style helps the actors to answer the new questions that their spectators ask of people who take it upon themselves to show the way people live together. The questions asked in this century are different from the ones asked in previous centuries.

The last acting style in bourgeois theatre thus far to be underpinned by a coherent theoretical plan is the style associated with the Russian director and actor Stanislavsky. It employs techniques designed to guarantee the *truth* of a performance. The way the actors behave on stage is not supposed to differ in any way, not even in the tiniest detail, from the way people behave in real life. By way of a special psychological act of empathy with the characters they are playing, the actors produce minutely detailed imitations of the reactions of living human beings. This psychological act consists in a process of intense introspection, during which the actors 'immerse themselves' in the soul of the character and transform themselves completely into that character. If the act is performed properly, then the spectators will begin to engage in it, so that they too will completely immerse themselves in the character they are watching. Stanislavsky, credited with having studied this act with almost scientific precision and stipulated what is necessary to induce it, sees no need to defend himself from criticism of any kind; he does not anticipate any such criticism. For him, empathy is a phenomenon that is inextricably linked to art – so inextricably that it is impossible to classify something as art if it does not induce empathy. Those who wish to refute this idea – and I for one feel compelled to do so – find themselves initially in a difficult position, because they cannot deny that the phenomenon of empathy does indeed play a part in the way people experience art. Nevertheless, they must always keep the concepts of empathy and art separate in order to formulate their criticisms, and their observations become rather vague when they only talk about *how* empathy plays a part in art, where it is to be found etc. It would be easier for them – although it would mean leaving the realm of facts – if they could simply claim that empathy should be completely eradicated from art. And yet the phenomenon of empathy loses much of its significance once it is located within art (and not outside of it), in exactly the place where one new theory suggests it belongs.

The reason some people have, in recent years, abandoned all those techniques which induce complete empathy (and there are plenty of them – Stanislavsky's is just one among many) is that these styles of acting are unable to illustrate the whole truth about the way people live together (as shown in the theatre).

The Stanislavskian style of acting can undoubtedly be used to portray a simple process such as the development of jealousy in an individual, for example, in such a way that nothing happens on the stage which could not also happen in real life. Unnatural inflections can be completely avoided, and there is no risk of actors failing to strike the right note with their gestures or guises. It is plain to see, however, that this kind of truth does not automatically answer all the questions that might potentially be asked. It makes any incident between people on a real street corner 'true' and at the same time incomprehensible. What the spectator sees of such an incident is anger, and perhaps also its immediate cause, and it is the same with its reproduction in the theatre. But everybody knows, nowadays, that causes come in chains, in that every cause is itself caused by something. The incident on the street corner and its 'true' reproduction in the theatre both have very short causal chains, immediately comprehensible; the causal nexus is sparse and primitive, and in the theatre it is considerably more sparse than on the street corner. This is because a particularly suggestive reproduction will lead spectators to immerse themselves instantly in the acting character and thus fail to ask the questions which they might potentially have asked on the street corner. The spectators themselves succumb to anger or jealousy, and completely lose the ability to understand, as it were, why it is that people become angry or jealous. In this way they lose interest in the causal nexus of these 'natural' (i.e. self-evident) emotions which do not seem to call for any further examination.

It is always difficult to find an image which conveys unambiguously what you are trying to say. The following comparison seems to me to come closest to achieving it.

(iii) Tragedy; Learning, Science, Marxism

B12
1939–41

PHILOSOPHER: For the ancients, the object of tragedy was to inspire pity and terror. That could still be a desirable object nowadays, if pity were taken to mean pity for people, and terror to mean terror of people, and if serious theatre were thus to help eliminate those conditions in which people need to pity and fear one another. For humanity itself has become the fate of humanity.

B13
1939–41

PHILOSOPHER: The causes of a great many tragedies are outside the control of those who suffer them, or so it seems.

DRAMATURG: So it seems?

PHILOSOPHER: Of course it only seems so. That which is human cannot be outside of humanity's control, and the causes of these tragedies are human ones.

DRAMATURG: Even if that were true, it wouldn't make any difference to the theatre. In the old days opponents used to confront one another on the stage. How's that supposed to happen now? A man in Chicago can set in motion a mechanism that will destroy twelve people in Ireland, or twelve thousand.

THE PHILOSOPHER: Then obviously that mechanism must reach as far as Ireland. The opponents can confront each other on the stage. A lot of technical changes will be needed, of course. Many human characteristics and passions that used to be important have become irrelevant. On the other hand, others have taken their place. In any case, it's difficult to grasp very much without seeing beyond individuals to the major group conflicts.

B10
1939–41

FROM THE 'PHILOSOPHER'S SPEECH ON IGNORANCE'

PHILOSOPHER: It's because people know so little about themselves that their knowledge of nature is of so little use to them. They know why a stone falls this way and not that when someone throws it, but why the person throwing it acts this way and not that is another matter. This means that people can cope with earthquakes but not with their own kind. Every time I leave this island I'm afraid that the boat may go down in a storm. I'm not really afraid of the sea, though, but of the people who might fish me out.

B11
1939–41

PHILOSOPHER: Because people live in very large groups nowadays, upon which they are wholly dependent, and because they always live in several groups at a time, they have to go about everything in a very roundabout way if they want to achieve anything. It may look as if their own decisions no longer influence anything, but the reality is that decisions have just become more difficult.

B14
1939–41

THE PHILOSOPHER: We all have very unclear ideas about the impact of our actions; often we don't even know why we do the things we do. Science does little to combat people's prejudices on this point. People's actions are very often said to have such dubious motives as greed, ambition, anger, jealousy, cowardice and so on. If we look back at things that have happened, we think we can identify certain calculations we made, certain judgements about our situation at the time, plans we formed and obstacles we came across that were outside our sphere of influence. We never made these calculations, however; we just infer them from our own past actions. We only dimly realize how dependent we are in every way in all our decisions. It's all interconnected in some way, we can feel it, but we don't know how. That's why most people experience the price of bread, the declaration of war or the lack of jobs in the same way as they experience natural phenomena like earthquakes or floods. For a long time, natural phenomena like this seemed only to affect a certain number of the population, or to affect individuals only in a small proportion of their habits. It's not until much later that normal life is shown to have become abnormal, and that this applies to everybody. Something has been neglected, something has gone wrong. The interests of large social groups are threatened without these groups ever having banded together to protect the interests they have in common.

B15
1939–41

FROM THE 'VISITOR'S SPEECH ABOUT THE IGNORANCE OF THE
MANY' TO THE THEATRE PEOPLE

PHILOSOPHER: Permit me to inform you that those countless people who
are suffering and in danger are unaware of the causes of this suffering and
danger. There is a not insignificant minority, however, that is aware of those
causes. They in turn have taught a considerable number of people a great
deal about the tormentors' methods. But there are fewer people who can see
which methods might be used to remove the tormentors. They can only be
removed once enough people understand the causes of their own suffering
and the dangers they face, and know exactly what is going on and which
methods could be used to remove the tormentors. It's a question, therefore,
of communicating this knowledge to as many people as possible. It's not
easy, however you go about it. Today I would like to discuss with you theatre
people what you might be able to do to help.

B16
1939–41

PHILOSOPHER: The mere fact of an incident occurring is not enough to
teach the spectator something. The incident won't be understood simply by
dint of being observed.

DRAMATURG: So you want some kind of commentary on it?

PHILOSOPHER: Or something in its portrayal that will be equivalent to
commentary, yes.

DRAMATURG: And what about learning from experience? You don't just
see things in the theatre, you experience them. Is there any better way of
learning?

PHILOSOPHER: We'd need to look at how people learn from experience
when no elements of commentary have been incorporated in it. The first
thing to say is that there are many factors which prevent people from
learning (i.e. becoming wiser) through experience. For instance, when
certain changes in a situation come about too gradually – so gradually as to
be imperceptible. Or when people's attention is distracted by other incidents
happening at the same time. Or when people look for the causes of incidents
and identify the wrong ones. Or when the person undergoing the experience
has strong prejudices.

DRAMATURG: Can't people get rid of their prejudices by undergoing certain other experiences?

PHILOSOPHER: Probably not unless they've reflected on them. Which may well have brought them up against the obstacles I mentioned.

DRAMATURG: But don't people learn best by doing things themselves?

PHILOSOPHER: The kind of experience conveyed by the theatre is not the same as doing things yourself. And it's wrong to treat every experience as an experiment and to try to take from it all the benefits an experiment can yield. There's a huge difference between an experience and an experiment.

ACTOR: Do me a favour and don't give us a detailed explanation of the difference. I can work it out for myself.

DRAMATURG: What about the direct transfer of emotions? Like when horror is aroused by horrific actions, or when seeing other people's horror with your own eyes intensifies your own?

PHILOSOPHER: The fact that horror can be aroused by horrific incidents (simulated ones) does not concern us here, except where this horror is strongly and infectiously expressed by an individual, as happens on stage. In such cases there are some relevant lessons to be learned from modern physiology. Do you know about the physiologist Pavlov's experiments with dogs?*

ACTOR: Out with it then, at least it's something factual for once, by the sound of it.

PHILOSOPHER: Of course, this is only an example. People are not dogs, even if you treat them as such in the theatre, as you will see. Pavlov threw meat to dogs and rang a bell at the same time. He measured how much the dogs salivated when they saw the meat. Then he rang the bell without throwing any meat. His measurements showed that the dogs salivated just the same. They only needed their saliva to digest the meat, not to help them tolerate the ringing of the bell, but they salivated nonetheless.

DRAMATURG: And how is this relevant in practice?

THE PHILOSOPHER: Your spectators experience extremely rich, complex, many-sided incidents which could be compared to those of Pavlov's dogs: feeding plus bell-ringing. Potentially, the reactions you had aimed to provoke might then be provoked in real-life situations with only some of the features in the situations your spectators had experienced with you; the secondary features perhaps. In that case you'd have made them ill, just as Pavlov did his dogs. But of course this can also happen in real life. Even when experiencing real incidents people can go astray in this way; they learn the wrong lessons.

ACTRESS: Can our star have an example of that?

PHILOSOPHER: Many petty bourgeois react to revolutions as if the only thing that happened during a revolution was their own shop windows getting smashed.

DRAMATURG: There's some truth in that. I remember a play we did once about the Paris Commune. There was a popular uprising in it. At first, we realistically depicted a shop being smashed up in the course of this uprising. But then we decided to leave that bit out, because we didn't want to suggest that the Commune was hostile to small tradespeople. It made for a very unrealistic uprising.**

ACTOR: That's a badly chosen example! All you needed to do was to show the shopkeeper's indifference to this 'secondary circumstance'.

DRAMATURG: Nonsense. No real shopkeeper would have been able to empathize with him then.

PHILOSOPHER: I fear you're right. No: those kinds of realistic touches will need to be left out.

* Ivan Pavlov was a Russian physiologist and Nobel Prize winner best known for his work on conditioned reflexes.
** Brecht is probably referring to Nordahl Grieg's play *The Defeat* (1937), translated into German by Margarete Steffin and published in the Moscow periodical *Das Wort* in 1938. Brecht's play *The Days of the Commune* (1949) was based on Grieg's play. The Paris Commune governed Paris from 18 March to 28 May 1871 when it was under siege by the Prussian army.

B17
1939–41

PHILOSOPHER: Science searches in every domain to find opportunities for experiment or for the graphic representation of problems. Models are constructed to show the movements of the constellations; an ingenious apparatus is used to show how gases behave. Experiments are also carried out on people, although in this case the opportunities for demonstration are very limited. So my thinking was to use your art of imitating people for the purpose of such demonstrations. Incidents from the way people live together in society, which are in need of explanation, could be imitated in such a way that these graphic demonstrations might help people acquire practically applicable knowledge.

B18
1939–41

DRAMATURG: I take it that these demonstrations can't just be staged any old way. There needs to be some kind of direction, some kind of criteria for selecting the incidents, a presumption or two at least. How would that work?

PHILOSOPHER: There exists a science of the way people live together in society, which has devised a major theory of cause and effect in this area. It can provide our point of view.

THE DRAMATURG: You mean Marxist theory?

THE PHILOSOPHER: Yes. But I must point out one limitation of this theory. It deals primarily with the behaviour of large masses of people. The laws it postulated apply to the movement of large units of people, and although it has much to say about the position of the individual within these large units, even this is usually only in reference to the individual's relationship to these masses. But in our demonstrations we'd be more concerned with the way individuals behave towards one another. Even so, the main principles of this theory are a great help when it comes to judging the individual too. Take for instance the principle that people's consciousness is shaped by their social being, which takes it for granted that people's social being is continually developing, so that their consciousness is continually changing too.* A great many well-worn principles are taken out of circulation, such as 'money makes the world go round', and 'history is made by great men', and 'one equals one'. And there is no question of them being replaced by opposing principles that are equally well worn.

* The Philosopher is referring to Marx's 'Preface' to the *Critique of Political Economy* (1859).

B20
1939–41

THE PHILOSOPHER'S OBSERVATIONS ON MARXISM

PHILOSOPHER: It's important that you should understand the difference between Marxism, which advocates a particular way of looking at the world, and what is commonly known as a *Weltanschauung* ['world view']. Marxist theory posits certain methods of observation, certain criteria. These lead it to make certain judgements about phenomena, certain predictions and suggestions for practical action. It teaches a type of thinking that actively intervenes in reality, in so far as reality is subject to social intervention. It is a theory that criticizes human praxis and expects in turn to be criticized by it. A true *Weltanschauung*, however, is a picture of the world mediating supposed knowledge of how things happen, usually formed in accordance with an ideal of harmony. This distinction, which you could also learn about elsewhere, is important for you because you should definitely not be constructing your imitations of incidents to illustrate Marxist principles, of which there are many, as I've mentioned. You must investigate everything and prove everything. The only way to throw light on your incidents is by using other incidents.

DRAMATURG: Give us an example!

PHILOSOPHER: Let's take the play *Wallenstein* by the German author Schiller.* In it, a general betrays his sovereign. It is not proven by the sequence of events in this play that this betrayal must inevitably result in the moral and physical destruction of the traitor; it is assumed right from the start. The world cannot continue to exist on a foundation of treachery, thinks Schiller – but he does not prove it. Nor would he be able to prove such a thing, because then the world would no longer exist. But he does think it would be unpleasant to live in a world like that, where people betray each other. Not that he proves this either, of course.

DRAMATURG: What would a Marxist do?

PHILOSOPHER: A Marxist would represent this as a historical matter, with causes from that period and effects in that period.

DRAMATURG: And the moral question?

PHILOSOPHER: He would treat the moral question as a historical one too. He would consider the utility of a particular moral system within a particular social order, observe the way it functions, and arrange the sequence of incidents so as to explain how the moral system works.

DRAMATURG: So would he criticize the moral views of this Wallenstein?

PHILOSOPHER: Yes.

DRAMATURG: From which point of view?

PHILOSOPHER: Not from that of his own moral principles.

* Brecht is referring to Friedrich Schiller's *Wallenstein* trilogy, written 1798–9.

B19
1939–41

DRAMATURG: This is where we've got to: you want to deploy certain arts for particular purposes, and in such a way that things which have been seen as central to art until now will cease to apply. Our arts will be used as mere skills. How that's supposed to work I don't know – you haven't spoken about it yet, at any rate, and I think we'd do best to leave it to you. But there's one thing I would still like to ask. The purposes you mention are extremely serious ones. Yet theatre is a playful activity. Is it supposed to give up its playful aspect too?

B126
c. 1945

END OF THE 'FIRST NIGHT'

DRAMATURG: So, let's meet here again the day after tomorrow!

PHILOSOPHER: Yes, we need to stop for today. You can feel it getting cold now. The warmth supplied for the audience's benefit is already wearing off. We've been leeching off it long enough.

The Second Night

(i) Intoxication, Empathy, V-effect

B120
1942–3

WHAT IF PHILOSOPHERS TOOK OVER THE THEATRE?

The theatre has gone downhill in many ways. But, like insolvent aristocrats, it still observes the traditional forms. It refuses, for example, to address the audience directly. It refuses to be commonplace, however feeble-minded and corrupt it may have become. One can only associate with it in a roundabout way. The actors certainly don't seem to be acting for the people who are paying them to do so. They are acting, in the presence of onlookers, for a sort of deity somewhere beyond the set. Those Broadway theatres where girls show their bottoms to the audience after a few teasing hesitations have disqualified themselves – they no longer deserve to be called theatres and invite contempt, although their displays still have more art about them than the performances of their earnest competitors. *They* would never sink so low; their girls would only ever show their bottoms to their fellow actors, and it would be left to the audience's discretion to put themselves in the position of those fellow actors. Any form of direct address to the audience is frowned upon; only at the cabaret are songs brought right down into the audience.

The way we engage with the incidents we see on our stages is quite peculiar – it takes quite some thought to realize exactly how peculiar. These incidents are very simple, mindless even for the most part, and easy to take in at a glance; children could understand them, if their minds had been dulled to a certain extent by schooling, at any rate. But we treat these performances as highly mysterious, ritualistic exercises, only accessible to the subconscious mind. By way of a strenuous act of self-transformation we identify with these strangers up on stage, in order to share in their emotional life, see with their eyes, hear with their ears, even think with their brains. This involves considerable strain; successful enjoyment of art is indicated by a significant level of exhaustion. These excesses are no different in kind from those of the Central African tribes who dance themselves into a state of ecstasy, in a way we find unsettling to watch. [...]

B28
1939–41

ACTOR: What the hell have you got against intoxication? And if you're anti-intoxication, how can you be for art? Even the shabbiest wreck of a philistine becomes an artist of sorts when he's drunk. His imagination is aroused. The walls of his room or his local pub collapse, especially the fourth wall we were talking about earlier.* He attracts an audience and starts to perform. The porter throws off the loads he's been given to carry, and the subordinate defies his superior because he's an agitator. He finds the ten commandments comical, he pinches respectability's bottom. He philosophizes – cries, even. More often than not his sense of justice is heightened, he gets angry about things that don't affect him. He sees the funny side of the mechanisms that work against him. That's how he rises above them, as far as his legs will carry him. In other words, he becomes more human in every respect, and begins to produce.

* The fourth wall is 'first' referred to in the Third Night, B135, p. 63 below, in a dialogue written c. 1945.

B29
1939–41

PHILOSOPHER: As I'm just like you – cold behind me, strife before me, and never able to do what I am capable of – I frequent these drug dens too. They help me to forget and to take some sort of interest in life. Because at night I'm a mess, just like the city I live in.

B36
1939–41

THINKING

PHILOSOPHER: What kind of thinking are we talking about here? And is it thinking that's opposed to feeling, that mere struggle to keep sober? Such an appeal to sobriety – pleas like 'Let's not make any decisions in an intoxicated state!' or 'Better think it over!' – is by no means misplaced given the activities of our magicians on the stage, but it's only a first step. As we've already established, we need to do away with the conviction that art cannot be enjoyed unless you abandon sobriety and approach intoxication – we know that the whole range from sobriety to intoxication, and the opposition between sobriety and intoxication, are both present in artistic enjoyment.

B37
1939–41

Any effort to present scenes and characters in such a way that they could be coldly noted and weighed up would be quite unnecessary and even harmful for our purposes. All the suppositions, expectations and sympathies we bring to our dealings with people in real life can be called upon here too. The audience shouldn't see characters who are simply doers of their own particular deeds and thereby justify their presence on stage, but human beings: shifting raw material, not fully formed and not fully defined, capable of surprising us. Only when faced with these sorts of characters will the audience practise real thinking: thinking, in other words, that is conditioned by interests and initiated and accompanied by emotions, a kind of thinking that displays every stage of awareness, clarity and effectiveness.

B23
1939–41

DRAMATURG: So does that mean the spectators are no longer supposed to inhabit the stage in spirit? They're supposed to just sit down below and watch?

PHILOSOPHER: They do sit down below and watch, but in spirit they inhabit the world you're portraying.

B27
1939–41

PHILOSOPHER: The theatre presents the spectator not only with solved problems but with unsolved ones too. Being opposed to confusion in descriptions does not mean you have to rule out descriptions of confusion.

B38
1939–41

Empathy

ACTOR: I'm slightly afraid to bring the conversation back round to something which might well make you angry. I'm talking about empathy. You forbade us to practise it during the performance. For our work during rehearsals you included it, reluctantly, among the various methods used to construct characters and scenes. Now I'd like to know whether there's a permissible form of empathy for the spectator, too, during the performance.

B58
1939–41

ACTOR: Does the suppression of *empathy* amount to suppressing every emotional element?

PHILOSOPHER: No, no. The emotional attentiveness of the audience and the actors should not be hindered, and neither should the portrayal of emotions or the actor's use of emotions. Only one of the many possible sources of emotions needs to be left unused, or at least treated as a subsidiary source, and that is empathy.

B24
1939–41

DRAMATURG: But the link between the stage and the auditorium is being severed! The cord is cut when empathy is suspended! Or is there some other sort of connection we can make? We have to arouse interest on the stage somehow, after all.

PHILOSOPHER: This brings us to the V-effect.

B57
1939–41

PHILOSOPHER: Just as empathy turns a special event into something ordinary, so *Verfremdung* turns an ordinary one into something special. The most utterly generic incidents are stripped of their monotony when they are portrayed as special. The spectator is no longer taking refuge from the present in history; the present becomes history.

B49
1939–41

ACTOR: But isn't it necessary to elevate the theatre above the level of the street, and invest acting with a special character – as it doesn't in fact take place in the street or by coincidence, and isn't performed by laymen or prompted by some incident?

PHILOSOPHER: All the factors you mention elevate it as much as it needs, I'd say. All these differences between theatre and street should be highlighted with particular clarity. Nothing should be glossed over, certainly! But however much you differentiate the two kinds of demonstration, the theatrical one will inevitably retain something of the original function of the everyday one. And it's precisely by underlining the element of difference, professionalism, preparation and so on that you keep this function fresh.

(ii) Acting, Performance

B44
1939–41

DRAMATURG: The kind of portrayal that would suit your purposes best would probably be the kind that explorers give of the customs and habits of savage peoples. They describe the most frenzied war dances in the most dispassionate of tones. Although it does make a difference if the portrayal is to be a physical one. Aside from the fact that certain movements are very difficult to make without certain emotions, and that certain movements induce certain emotions, how is the actor supposed to portray those signs of passion that surely need to be reported too?

B40
1939–41

DRAMATURG: I know you feel we are lacking that which is particular, distinctive, striking. But we do provide that as well. We don't act as if *all* scientists would get angry at such an insinuation. We can portray different types.

PHILOSOPHER: And how do you do that?

ACTOR: If he's the type that gets angry, then I make him that way from the start. His outburst has to arise in a logical way, to fit in with his other remarks, to emerge from the overall course of things. Everyone will understand that it's *my* man who's getting angry.

PHILOSOPHER: So that then what happens, happens.

DRAMATURG: You've got a nasty way of saying that, as if we only supplied what there's demand for, and only said what people like to hear. But you should really say 'what must happen, happens'.

B41
1939–41

PHILOSOPHER: Let's suppose someone gets angry about some insinuation that he feels is an insult to his dignity. That a servant should betray
his master, for instance, or a scientist his science. To start with, the actor
will produce something general, such as an illustration of the gestus *What
do they take me for?* This is a gestus which almost anybody can understand;
almost anybody can imagine a situation in which we get angry as we ask
ourselves *What do they take me for?* Of course, the actor will modify the
basic gestus to fit the character, and give to the servant what is the servant's
and to the scientist what is the scientist's. There will be some indication of
period, at least by way of the costumes. And what will be revealed? That I
am outraged by such an insinuation and so are you; that the servant and the
scientist are outraged by it, that people always have been outraged by it, and
that they always will be.

ACTOR: Exactly. Because we are performing in the present, and from the
passions of the past we have to pick those which still exist; and we are
performing for both servants and scientists at the same time.

PHILOSOPHER: Yes, which means you have to be careful that your outburst
of anger doesn't meet with astonishment. What happens must be able to
happen in the sense that what goes on must be able to carry on.

B42
1939–41

PHILOSOPHER: It's also important that actors should demonstrate their
awareness of being observed, because that way the spectator can learn to
behave in everyday life like someone under observation. This is where the
actor is a model to be imitated. The individual benefits enormously from the
awareness of being observed, and society too can only benefit from it.

B43
1939–41

PHILOSOPHER: If we observe sorrow on the stage and feel it at the same
time, then the fact that we are observing it at the same time also forms part
of our observation. We are sorrowful, but at the same time we are people
observing sorrow – our own – almost as if it were detached from us, in other
words like people who know no sorrow – for who else could observe it in
such a detached way? This means we are not completely dissolved in sorrow:

there is still something solid in us. Sorrow is hostile to thought, it stifles it, and thought is hostile to sorrow.

THE ACTRESS: It can be a pleasure to cry.

THE PHILOSOPHER: Crying is not an expression of sorrow so much as one of relief. But lamenting – in sounds, or better still in words – is a great liberation, because it means the sufferer is beginning to produce something. He's already mixing his sorrow with an enumeration of the blows he has received, he's already making something out of something utterly devastating. Observation has set in.

B121
1942–3

The process whereby certain people coat their faces with make-up, perform movements they have been rehearsing for weeks and speak lines they have learned by heart to other people sitting in silent rows below them, and this for hours at a time, night after night, must first of all be recognized as a strange thing to do by the people who behave in this way. They may subsequently get over this sense of strangeness, but they should never lose it altogether. They should never make up their faces in such a way that they genuinely resemble other faces without make-up, never perform their movements so that they seem to arise from the whim of that particular instant, never speak their lines as if they were completely their own. They should be content not to do these things so that they remain in touch with reality, and they should make use of the strangeness to good effect. It is enough that they know about other people and have the ability to show how other people behave; they do not need to completely transform themselves so that they don't even seem to know themselves any more; that would amount to less, from people as well as from artists. And they should not try to draw us in too much either, but let us use our own powers of reason and experience our own emotions.

B129
c. 1945

ACTOR: *Am I not bound hand and foot by the playwright's text?*

PHILOSOPHER: You could treat the text as a report which is authentic but has several meanings. A vaguely defined Caesar, so you are told, finding himself surrounded by aristocratic assassins, murmured to a certain Brutus 'Et tu, Brute'.* A report like that, if it comes not from a line in a play but from some other source, does not tell its hearers very much, their knowledge of

the world is not significantly increased. Even if they are inclined to gener-
alize, they can do so in a whole number of false directions. Then you, the
actor, burst into this vague, nebulous conception and represent life itself. By
the time you've finished, your spectators should have seen more than even
an eyewitness of the original incident would have.

DRAMATURG: What about fantastical plays? Do they not just give reports
about the writer?

PHILOSOPHER: No, not just that. You should treat them as reports of
dreams or sketches where the playwrights are likewise manipulating reality.
Even if you have to try to establish what they might have seen, what the
intention behind their story might have been and so on, you'll still have a
lot of leeway.

---

* See Shakespeare, *The Tragedy of Julius Caesar* (1599), Act III, Scene 1.

(iii) Science, Social Class, Learning

B52
1939–41

SPEECH ON OUR TIMES

PHILOSOPHER: Bear in mind that we are living in dark times, when people's
behaviour towards one another is particularly abhorrent and the deadly
activities of certain groups of people are shrouded in an almost impen-
etrable darkness, so that a great deal of thought and organization is needed
in order to shed some light on people's social behaviour. *The monstrous
oppression and exploitation of human beings by other human beings, the
wartime slaughters and peacetime degradations of every sort taking place
across the planet have almost come to seem natural to us.* For many people,
the exploitation of human beings seems just as natural as our exploitation of
nature: human beings are treated like fields or cattle. *For countless numbers
of people, great wars are just like earthquakes, it's as if they were not caused by
humanity but by forces of nature against which the human race is powerless.*
Perhaps what seems most natural of all to us is the way we earn our living:
the way one person sells another a bar of soap, a loaf of bread, their physical
labour. That's just a free exchange of things, we think; but look closer and
you realize what the terrible experiences of our daily life also go to prove:
that this exchange doesn't just take place between people but is controlled by

specific people. *The more we have been able to wrest from nature by means of great inventions and discoveries and the organization of labour, the more uncertain our existence seems to have become. We don't control things, it seems – things control us. But that is only because some people use things to help them control other people. We will not be freed from the forces of nature until we are freed from human force. Our knowledge of nature must be supplemented with knowledge of human society, of the way people behave towards one another, if we want to use our knowledge of nature humanely.*

B45
1939–41

PHILOSOPHER: The physicists tell us that in the course of their investigations into the very smallest particles of matter, they suddenly started to suspect that the process of investigation alters what is being investigated. The movements they observe under the microscope are supplemented by movements caused by the microscope. At the same time, the instruments are probably being altered too, by the objects they are focused on. If that's what happens when instruments do the observing, what happens when it's human beings doing it?

B46
1939–41

PHILOSOPHER: We view our social environment, too, as if it were part of the natural world, almost as a landscape. We look at money that produces interest in the same way as we look at a pear tree that produces pears. We view wars, which have similar effects to earthquakes and appear equally unavoidable, as if they too were earthquakes. We look at something like marriage and we say: 'That's the natural way.' It amazes us to hear that in other parts of the world, or in our own at other times, different kinds of relationships between men and women have been seen as the natural ones.

B56
1939–41

(See *Kautsky*, NZ, XXIII, 137)

PHILOSOPHER: We perceive the elements controlling social development in what is ordinary and everyday, not in what is extraordinary; we perceive them in the social relationships between people, not within the individual.*

ACTOR: Well, ordinariness can only lead to one reality, and that's boredom.

PHILOSOPHER: Where your art is concerned, at any rate.

* The Philosopher quotes directly from Karl Kautsky's essay on 'Rebellions in Schiller's Dramas', published in *Die Neue Zeit* (XXIII, 1904/5), in commemoration of the 1905 centenary of Schiller's death. Karl Kautsky was a leading theorist in the German Social Democratic Party.

B31
1939–41

PHILOSOPHER: What's bad is not failing to see every link in the chain, but failing to see the chain at all. We were complaining about how difficult it is to bring adversaries together on one and the same stage. It's true that new techniques can do a good deal to overcome this, but the most important thing is not to let it seem as if there were no such adversaries at all. If they do not see or cannot make visible the adversary, dramaturgs will often try to bring out some other element which is 'more obvious' and provides some kind of justification for the incident: the hero's own character, impediments specific to his situation, and so on. And they then develop a seamless sequence of motivations for the hero, even though in reality – because the motivating causes are external ones – there inevitably ensue twists and turns that cannot be explained in terms of the material already provided.

B32
1939–41

PHILOSOPHER: On the other hand, when adversaries are brought together on stage we often get a misleading picture – when their antagonism is made to seem a natural necessity, for instance. There's a play called *The Weavers* (written by a playwright who later, as a decrepit old man, played an ignominious role under the house-painter),* and in this play the factory-owner was simply portrayed as a miser, giving the impression that the weavers' misery could only be remedied by dealing with this miserliness. The hostility between the man who had the capital and the people who did the work seemed natural, as natural as that between the lion and the lamb.

* The playwright in question is Gerhart Hauptmann, who published an article supportive of the National Socialist regime in the *Berliner Tageblatt* in November 1933. His play *The Weavers* (1892) deals with the Silesian weavers' uprising of 1844. 'The house-painter' is Brecht's nickname for Adolf Hitler, and alludes to his job as a house-painter in his years in Vienna (1908–13), when he was trying to make a living as an artist.

B33
1939–41

ACTOR: The wagging finger, in other words! There's nothing audiences hate more than that. It's like they're being sent back to school.

PHILOSOPHER: Your schools must have been pretty awful to inspire such loathing. But your bad schools are no concern of mine. Get rid of them!

DRAMATURG: Nobody objects to a play having a meaning. But it shouldn't be in your face all the time. The lesson needs to be unobtrusive.

PHILOSOPHER: Believe me: people who want unobtrusive lessons don't want lessons at all. As for the meaning not being in your face all the time, that's another matter.

B34
1939–41

ACTOR: If only the didactic attitude wasn't so repellent! Teachers inevitably regard their pupils as stupid because they see it as their job to make them cleverer. It's insulting! It's an arrogant presumption!

DRAMATURG: He's got nothing against educating people, you understand, but he abhors didacticism.

ACTOR: When I laugh, cry, hope or despair, I'm making art. When I show you why someone is crying, laughing, etc., I'm teaching.

B39
1939–41

ACTOR: Soon everything will be completely *practical*! The themes will be 'Deficient Gutters in Street Prone to Flooding', and 'No Listening to the Radio at Night with the Windows Open'. Anything that isn't 'relevant' will be out.

ACTRESS: And that will be instead of 'Young Man's World-weariness on Account of Sexual Frustration' or 'Mother Hears Only Son is a Forger!', with full details!

DRAMATURG: As far as I can see, our friend hasn't said anything so far to suggest that any one of the four themes you've mentioned couldn't occur in his *thaëter*. As for how important the themes are, society as represented by the spectators is entirely capable of deciding that. *All* interests are brought together within society.

PHILOSOPHER: I think what our actor friend objects to is the narrowness of our so-called pure practitioners. He's afraid we might adopt their smart-alec methods, their way of 'coming to grips' with all our problems, of solving everything in the blink of an eye and brushing aside anything that cannot be solved. But why should we do that?

DRAMATURG: You have to admit that we more or less waved goodbye to *art* once we began to use it as a mere instrument. And it's the nature of art to raise questions without knowing the answer, to express the sense of oppression without identifying the shackles, etc.

PHILOSOPHER: That's the nature of science too, my friends.

DRAMATURG: Possibly, but science is still a lot more practical. If it presents something it doesn't understand, it doesn't intentionally eschew an understanding of it. Art makes a cult out of incomprehensibility. It is intoxicated by the 'fact' that there are things which lie beyond reason, out of our control. It allies itself with fate.

PHILOSOPHER: Science used to do that too in the past, and in some fields it still does. Nature couldn't always be controlled just like that, humanity hasn't always just submitted willingly to its fate.

ACTOR: Theatre or *thaëter*, we're still dealing with human nature. That's what determines humanity's fate.

PHILOSOPHER: The same applies to this part of nature as applies to nature in general and as a whole. We've agreed that we'll speak as little as possible about art, its particular laws, limitations, advantages, obligations, etc. We've downgraded it to a mere instrument, trodden it underfoot, violated and enslaved it and deprived it of its rights. We no longer feel obliged to express vague premonitions, subconscious knowledge, overpowering feelings and so on. But our new task calls on us to present the whole spectrum of things that happen between people, in all its contradictoriness, as resolvable or irresolvable. Nothing is irrelevant to society. We have to present the clearly defined, controllable elements in relation to those that are unclear and beyond our control, so that these too have a place in our *thaëter*.

B55
1939–41

PHILOSOPHER: Only with great effort and with great artistry will we be able to break up these clumps of human relationships that people see as 'fateful', and untangle 'fate' into a mesh of types of behaviour occurring between one person and another.

(iv) Elizabethan Theatre, Shakespeare

B48
1939–41

DRAMATURG: A few years before the appearance of Shakespeare's first play, Marlowe introduced iambic blank verse and thus refined the popular plays of the time so much that even the connoisseurs came to favour them over the wooden Seneca imitations of conventional literature. The weaving together of two storylines, which Shakespeare did so brilliantly in *The Merchant of Venice*, was a technical novelty at the time – a time which was full of that kind of rapid, headlong and reckless progress.* Plays were beginning to be treated as commodities, but property relations were still chaotic. Neither thoughts nor images, incidents, ideas or inventions were protected by law, the theatre was just as much of a treasure trove as life was. Its great characters are sophisticated versions of its crude ones, its elevated language is its vulgar language refined. How much of that was a concession to the educated public in the boxes and how much a concession to the groundlings? The colleges kept an eye on the beer gardens and the beer gardens on the colleges.

* Shakespeare's first play was *King Henry VI* (1591–2) in three parts; *The Merchant of Venice* was written in 1596–7. Brecht adapted Christopher Marlowe's *Edward the Second* (1594) as *Life of Edward the Second of England* (1924). The Ancient Roman philosopher Seneca (AD 4–65) wrote versions of classical Greek tragedies that were particularly influential on European neo-classical drama in the seventeenth and eighteenth centuries.

B50
1939–41

DRAMATURG: Nothing gives us a better idea of the secular, sober and healthy nature of the Elizabethan theatre than perusing Shakespeare's contracts with companies of actors, which guaranteed him one-seventh of the shares and one-fourteenth of the income of two theatres, or checking the cuts he made in his own plays, amounting to between a quarter and a third of all the lines, and noting his instructions to his actors (in *Hamlet*) to act in a restrained and natural manner. If you are also aware that they performed (and also rehearsed, of course!) by daylight in the open air, mostly without

any attempt to indicate the location of the action and in close proximity to
the spectators, who sat all the way round the stage as well as on it, while quite
a few of them were standing up or walked around – then you begin to get a
good idea of how earthly, profane and unmagical it all was.

B51
1939–41

ACTOR: So *A Midsummer Night's Dream* was performed in daylight, and
it was daylight when the ghost appeared in *Hamlet*?* What about illusion?

DRAMATURG: People were expected to use their imaginations.

* *A Midsummer Night's Dream* was written in 1595; the ghost of Hamlet's father
appears at midnight in *Hamlet*, Act I, Scenes 1 and 4.

B53
1939–41

PHILOSOPHER: Anyone who has looked with astonishment at the eating
habits, the judicial processes and the love lives of savage peoples will also be
able to look at our own eating habits, judicial processes and love lives with
astonishment. Miserable philistines will always find the same driving forces
in history: their own. And these only in so far as they are aware of them,
which is not very far. The archetypal man drinks coffee in the afternoons,
is jealous of his wife, wants to get on in the world, and manages to only
more or less – more often less. 'People don't change,' he says, and even if
he is more unpleasant to his wife now than he was twenty years ago, well,
men have always been more unpleasant to their wives at forty-five than at
twenty-five. 'Love has always existed,' he says, not wanting to know what
was once understood by 'love' or what was once practised in its name. He
changes only as much as a pebble in a river bed changes as it is ground
down by other pebbles. And like a pebble he moves forward. As he is not
pursuing any particular goal, he could achieve anything really, 'given the
right circumstances'; he could potentially conquer the world, for instance,
like Caesar. Anything can happen to him, he's at home in any disaster. He's
been rewarded with ingratitude like Lear, he's raged like Richard III.* He's
given up just about everything for his wife, as Antony did for Cleopatra, and
hectored her more or less as Othello* did his. He is as hesitant as Hamlet
to right a wrong by shedding blood, and his friends are like Timon's.* He is
exactly like everybody, and everybody is like him. Differences don't matter
to him, to him it's all the same. In all the men he sees he can see only Man,

he who is simply the singular of the plural form. And thus his intellectual poverty infects everything with which he comes into intellectual contact.

* The plays in question are Shakespeare's *King Lear*, *The Tragedy of Richard III*, *Antony and Cleopatra*, *Othello*, *Hamlet* and *Timon of Athens*.

B54
1939–41

TRAGEDY IN SHAKESPEARE

DRAMATURG: What about tragedy in Shakespeare?

PHILOSOPHER: Shakespeare takes a tragic view of the decline of feudalism. There's Lear, caught up in his own patriarchal ideas; Richard III, the dislikeable man who becomes a terrible one; Macbeth, the ambitious man tricked by witches; Antony, the libertine who gambles with world domination; Othello, whose jealousy ultimately kills him – they are all living in a new world that smashes them to pieces.

ACTOR: To many people that explanation might make the plays seem rather trite.

PHILOSOPHER: But how could there be anything more multifaceted, fascinating and important than the decline of great ruling classes?

B59
1939–41

SHAKESPEARE (I)
(Schück)*

DRAMATURG: In a play manuscript from 1601 several variants are included, and in the margin there is a note from the author saying 'One or the other of these modifications: choose whichever seems best to you' and 'If this form of words is difficult to understand or unsuited to the audience, you can use the other.'

* *Schück* is an abbreviation for Levin Schücking, a literary scholar who produced annotated editions of Shakespeare's plays and the monograph *Character Problems in Shakespeare's Plays: A Guide to the Better Understanding of the Dramatist* (Leipzig, 1919; London, 1922).

B60
1939–41

DRAMATURG: There were already women in the audience, but the women's parts were still being played by boys. There were no backcloths, so the writer took on the job of portraying the landscape. The stage didn't depict a specific area, it could be an entire heath. In *Richard III* (V, 3), between the tents of Richard's and Richmond's camps, a ghost appears in both men's dreams, visible and audible to both of them and addressing itself to both. A theatre full of V-effects!

B61
1939–41

DRAMATURG: People smoked in these theatres too. Tobacco was sold in the auditorium. So you had snobs with pipes sitting on the stage and dreamily observing how the actor portrayed Macbeth's death.

B62
1939–41

PHILOSOPHER: Our critical attitude springs from the fact that we have developed great faith in humanity's powers of work and invention, and have grown suspicious of the idea that everything must remain as it is even if it's bad, as our state institutions are. There may once have been a time when force and oppression compelled people to produce great works, when the possibility of exploiting people set minds working on plans that were also of some use to the general public. Today this just paralyses everything. So from now on, you actors can portray your characters in such a way that people are able to imagine them behaving differently from the way they do, even when there are good grounds for them behaving in that particular way. You can portray your characters in much the same way as when a more experienced and more broad-minded engineer comes along and corrects his predecessor's drawings by superimposing new lines on top of the old ones, crossing out numbers and replacing them with different ones, and adding critical remarks and comments. You can present the famous opening scene in *Lear*, where he divides his kingdom between his daughters according to the measure of their love for him and gets the measure quite wrong, in such a way that the spectator says: 'He's going about it the wrong way. If only he hadn't said that, or had noticed this, or at any rate thought twice.'

(v) The Augsburger, Piscator

B30
1939–41

THE AUGSBURGER* [1]

DRAMATURG: He was a young man when the First World War ended. He was studying medicine in southern Germany. The main influences on him were two authors and a popular comedian. In those years the author *Büchner*, who had written around 1848, was performed for the first time, and the Augsburger saw the unfinished play *Wozzek*.** He also saw the writer *Wedekind* perform his own plays in a style that had been developed in cabaret.*** Wedekind had worked as a balladeer, and he accompanied himself on the lute. But the man he learned most from was the clown *Valentin*, who performed in a beer-hall. He did short sketches in which he played recalcitrant employees, orchestral musicians or photographers, who hated their employers and made them look ridiculous. The employer was played by his assistant, a popular comedienne who used to pad herself out and speak in a deep voice. When the Augsburger was producing his first play, which included a half-hour-long battle, he asked Valentin what he ought to do with the soldiers. 'What are soldiers like in battle?' Valentin answered without a second thought: [sic]****

---

* Brecht is referred to here as 'the Augsburger' – he had grown up in Augsburg; his other pseudonym in *Buying Brass* is 'the playwright'.

** Brecht's comment on Georg Büchner is misleading, as he lived from 1813 to 1837. *Woyzeck* was drafted in incomplete form in 1837 and not published until 40 years after Büchner's death as *Wozzeck* (1877). It had a major impact on modern German drama from Naturalism via Expressionism to Brecht, who in 1928 described it as 'technically almost perfect' ('Productive Obstacles'/'Die produktiven Hindernisse', BFA 21, p. 255).

*** The modernist German dramatist Frank Wedekind was a major influence during Brecht's early years as a writer (see 'Frank Wedekind', *Brecht on Theatre*, and Introduction to Part One. 1918–1933).

**** Brecht contributed to Karl Valentin's cabaret in 1920 and 1921 (see the picture of Brecht with Valentin, Plate 1 in *Brecht on Theatre*). The production Brecht refers to is his *Life of Edward the Second of England*, premiered at the Munich Kammerspiele on 18 March 1924. Valentin's reported response to Brecht's question was 'White. Scared.'

B35

1939–41

THE AUGSBURGER [2]

DRAMATURG: Before the Augsburger became involved with theatre, he studied natural sciences and medicine. For him the arts and the sciences were at opposite ends of the same spectrum. Both occupations had to make themselves useful. He didn't hold the utility of the arts in contempt, as many of his contemporaries did, and he allowed the sciences to disregard utility. For him, they were arts too.

B25

1939–41

DRAMATURG: I believe Piscator* was the first person to think it necessary to provide *evidence* in the theatre. He projected authentic documents on to large screens. Many people immediately accused him of breaking the rules of art. Art had to construct its own realm, they said.

* Erwin Piscator was the most prominent Marxist theatre director in the Weimar Republic. His first systematic use of documentary projections was in his 1925 production of *In Spite of Everything* – see Erwin Piscator, *The Political Theatre,* edited and translated by Hugh Rorrison (London, Methuen, 1980), pp. 85–98.

B127

c. 1945

PISCATOR

For some time Piscator's followers argued with the Augsburger's about which of the two had invented the epic style of representation. In fact they were both using it at the same time, in different cities – in Piscator's case more in relation to the stage (in the use of captions, choruses, films etc.), in the Augsburger's case more in relation to acting style. Both of them were in fact just acknowledging the medium of film in their theatre.

B128

c. 1945

FROM THE 'DESCRIPTION OF PISCATOR'S THEATRE' IN THE 'SECOND NIGHT'

THE DRAMATURG: In the period after the First World War, before the house-painter came on the scene, Piscator opened his theatre in Berlin.

Many consider him to be one of the greatest figures in theatre. He got the money from a brewer, who thought that a theatre – given how difficult it was to audit its income and expenditure – might help him fox the tax authorities.* His experiments cost over a million marks. For each new play he put on he would convert the entire theatre, not just the stage. The stage, however, was where he effected the greatest changes. He made the floor moveable by laying two broad belts over the top of it, which could be set in motion by a motor so that the actors could march up and down without needing to budge from where they were. In this way he was able to make a whole play flow. He showed a soldier marching to the front, through recruiting office, hospital and barracks, along country roads, through camps and cowsheds, and into battle. The play showed how the soldier was marched off by his superiors but kept thwarting their plans, seemingly carrying out all their orders but never actually reaching the battlefield. As a backdrop to the same play he used a cartoon film caricaturing those superiors. Indeed it was he who first introduced films into the theatre, thereby turning the stage set into an actor. For another play he constructed several different locations on two overlapping revolving stages, and had the actors perform in the different locations simultaneously.** Both stage and roof began to sag; never before had this or any other theatre had to support machines.

* Brecht is referring to Ludwig Katzenellenbogen, managing director of the Schultheiss and Patzenhofer breweries.
** The productions in question are *The Adventures of the Good Soldier Schweik* (Piscator Stage, 1928; Piscator, *The Political Theatre*, pp. 250–69) and *Rasputin, the Romanovs, the War and the People which Rose Against Them* (Piscator Stage, 1927; Piscator, *The Political Theatre*, pp. 228–49). Film had been a key component of Piscator's theatre since his production of Alfons Paquet's *Tidal Wave* in 1926 (*The Political Theatre*, pp. 107–12).

The Third Night

(i) The Fourth Wall, Emotion; V-effect, Acting

B135
c. 1945

THE DRAMATURG: What about the fourth wall?

THE PHILOSOPHER: What's that?

THE DRAMATURG: Plays are usually performed as if the stage had four walls and not three, the fourth wall being on the side where the audience is sitting. The impression created and maintained is that what happens on the stage is a genuine incident from real life, in which of course there is no audience. Acting with a fourth wall, in other words, means acting as if there wasn't an audience.

THE ACTOR: You get the idea? The audience sees very intimate episodes without itself being seen. It's just like somebody looking through a keyhole at a scene between people who have no idea they are not alone. In reality, of course, we arrange it all so that you get a good view of everything. We just hide the fact that it's been arranged.

THE PHILOSOPHER: I see – so the audience are tacitly assuming they're not in a theatre at all, as nobody seems to notice they're there. They have the illusion of watching something through a keyhole. So perhaps they shouldn't start applauding until they get to the cloakroom.

THE ACTOR: But it's their applause which confirms that the actors have managed to perform as if the audience weren't there.

THE PHILOSOPHER: Do you think we need this elaborate secret understanding between the actors and yourself?

THE WORKER: I don't need it. But perhaps the actors do?

THE ACTOR: For realistic acting it's considered essential.

THE WORKER: I'm in favour of realistic acting.

THE PHILOSOPHER: But it's also a reality that we are sitting in a theatre and not with our eye pressed to a keyhole. How can it be realistic to try and gloss over that fact? No, we need to demolish the fourth wall: the agreement is hereby terminated. Don't be afraid, in future, to show that you've arranged everything in the way best calculated to help us understand.

THE ACTOR: So you are now officially informing us that from now on we can look straight at you and even talk to you?

THE PHILOSOPHER: Of course. Whenever it serves the purposes of the demonstration.

THE ACTOR *muttering*: So it's back to asides, to 'Honoured ladies and gentlemen of the audience, I am King Herod', and to girls high-kicking to the officers in the boxes!

THE PHILOSOPHER *mutters*: There's no advance more difficult than the return to reason!

THE ACTOR *explodes*: Sir, we all know the theatre has gone downhill in many ways. But so far it has at least observed the forms. It never addressed the audience directly, for instance. However feeble-minded and corrupt it may have become, at least it refused to make itself common. You could only associate with it by going through the proper channels. Until now, sir, we've performed not for the sake of any Tom, Dick or Harry who could afford a ticket, but for the sake of art!

THE WORKER: Who does he mean by Tom, Dick or Harry?

THE PHILOSOPHER: Us.

THE ACTOR: Art, sir! And you are just people who happen to be there watching. Perhaps you might be better off trying the building next door – where there are establishments where the girls will show you their bottoms on demand.

THE PHILOSOPHER: And in yours the girls only show their bottoms to their fellow actors, and it's politely left to our discretion to put ourselves in those actors' shoes; is that it?

THE DRAMATURG: Please, gentlemen!

THE WORKER: *He's* the one that brought bottoms into it.

THE PHILOSOPHER: And at the most, all they are showing us is their souls!

THE ACTOR: And you think that can be done without shame? And what do you mean by 'at the most'?

THE DRAMATURG: It's not good that you always take the bait. You've reacted with philosophic anger – couldn't you now at least act with philosophic composure?

B64
1939–41

DRAMATURG: Why is it that the middle class always accused the brass merchant of lacking emotion and of being determined to eliminate the emotional in favour of the rational?

PHILOSOPHER: His rationality stirred no emotion in their souls. Indeed, their emotion rebelled against him and his reason. They found him far too critical. Yet he never appealed to their reason, but to that of their enemies. And for him, criticism was one of a number of practical ways to bring about change. He would collect complaints about the course of rivers and the taste of fruit as one half of an undertaking whose other half consisted in damming the rivers and improving the fruit trees. His criticism was practical – and necessarily emotional as well, therefore – whereas their idea of criticism was associated with ethics rather than practical matters, and was thus restricted to the emotional sphere. So their criticism was largely fruitless, and this led them to label any and every form of criticism fruitless, including that of the brass merchant.

DRAMATURG: I thought the misunderstanding had simply to do with the fact that his objections to empathy in art were mistaken for objections to emotions in art.

PHILOSOPHER: No, the misunderstanding went deeper than that. In his day the middle class was always claiming that the rebellious masses in their emotional confusion could not see how reasonable the existing order of society was, and it was always accusing the masses' leaders of relying solely on cold rationality rather than the emotional life of the people, developed over thousands of years – its religious, moral and family feelings.

B65
1939–41

DRAMATURG: There's no V-effect when the actors, in adopting somebody else's facial expression, completely erase their own. What they should do is show the two faces overlapping.

B66
1939–41

The Actress plays a man.
PHILOSOPHER: If a man had been playing this man, he wouldn't have brought out his masculinity so forcibly, and seeing him – or the incident, to be more precise – played by a woman made us perceive as typically masculine many characteristics that we usually consider to be general human ones. Where gender is concerned, therefore, an actor needs to show something of what an actress would bring to a male role, and an actress something of what an actor would bring to a female one.

ACTOR: I think it's fair to say that I've hardly ever seen such feminine women as at the front during the war, where women were played by men.

ACTRESS: And you ought to see children playing adults! It makes so much of adult behaviour seem strange and odd. In a school I once saw some children performing *Man Equals Man*.* In that play somebody sells an elephant. It's an incident which would be impossible among children, and in the play too it suddenly became tinged with something of this 'impossibility', or at least came to seem barely 'possible', only just conceivable, imaginable perhaps under certain transient conditions.

DRAMATURG: I saw another example of the V-effect in an American film. A very young actor who up to that point had always played proletarian youths (and probably was one himself, too) played the part of a bourgeois youth who is given a tuxedo for his first ball. He didn't come across as not being bourgeois, but actually made the youth quite specifically bourgeois. Many people in the audience probably just saw a particularly youthful youth. The fact is that the difference between young and old varies across the two classes. In some respects a proletarian youth is more mature than a bourgeois one, in others more child-like.

* Brecht may be referring to a performance of *Man Equals Man* at the Aufbau Grammar School, Berlin in 1930. See also Brecht's 'Notes on the Comedy *Man Equals Man*' and production photographs in *Brecht on Theatre*.

B77
1939–41

DRAMATURG: Each character is built up out of his or her relationship to the other characters, giving actors as much of an interest in their counterparts' performances as in their own.

ACTOR: That's nothing new. I never steal my counterpart's thunder.

ACTRESS: Not always.

DRAMATURG: That's not what this is about.

B68
1939–41

PHILOSOPHER: Suppose you've got a play where the first scene shows man A bringing man B to be executed, but in the last scene, after all kinds of incidents have been shown, the process is shown in reverse, with man B bringing man A to be executed. This means that within one and the same incident (somebody being brought to be executed) A and B have swapped roles (the roles of executioner and victim). In such a case you'd undoubtedly arrange the first scene in such a way as to lend the greatest possible impact to the final scene. You'd make sure that the last scene would immediately remind the audience of the first one, that they would be struck by the similarity between the two, and at the same time you would make sure that the differences between them could not be overlooked.

DRAMATURG: We do of course have such procedures. The main thing in such a case is to make sure the first scene is not played as a transition into the next, it must carry its own specific weight. Every movement in it must be designed in relation to the equivalent (or altered) movement in the final scene.

PHILOSOPHER: And if the actor knows that later on he's going to have to change places with his colleague, I think he's likely to act differently from the way he would if he didn't know. He'll portray the executioner differently, if he thinks he's going to have to portray the victim too.

DRAMATURG: Obviously.

PHILOSOPHER: The last scene estranges the first (just as the first estranges the last, which constitutes the real impact of the play). The actor adopts procedures that produce V-effects. So now all you have to do is apply this mode of representation to plays where this last scene is missing.

DRAMATURG: You mean play all the scenes with reference to other possible scenes?

PHILOSOPHER: Yes.

B69
1939–41

PHILOSOPHER: The more tangibly a case is presented to spectators, the easier it is for them to abstract from it ('Lear does things like that – do I do things like that?') One particular father can be the most universal of fathers. Particularity is a mark of universality. Particularity is to be found everywhere.

B75
1939–41

THE DRAMATURG: And note the difference between *strong* and *crude*, *relaxed* and *loose*, *quick* and *hurried*, *imaginative* and *digressive*, *thought out* and *elaborate*, *deeply felt* and *blissful*, *contradictory* and *nonsensical*, *clear* and *emphatic*, *useful* and *profitable*, *high-flown* and *loud-mouthed*, *ceremonious* and *pompous*, *delicate* and *feeble*, *passionate* and *uncontrolled*, *natural* and *accidental*.

B132
c. 1945

THE DRAMATURG: I've been turning your ideas over in my mind and they've come across a thing or two there. A few years back, when I was visiting Paris, I stumbled across a small theatre where a tiny group of German exiles were acting a few scenes from a play which depicted conditions in their homeland. I've never come across a group whose members were so diverse in terms of background, training and talent. There was a working man who can hardly ever have set foot on a stage before and spoke in dialect, and alongside him a great actress whose resources, gifts and theatrical training may well be unrivalled. But they had two things in common: the fact that they had all fled their country to escape the house-painter's hordes, and a particular style of acting. I'm sure this style has a lot in common with the sort of approach to theatre you have in mind.

THE PHILOSOPHER: Describe their acting.

THE DRAMATURG: The play they were performing was called *Fear and Misery of the Third Reich*.* I was told it consisted of twenty-seven little plays, of which they performed seven or eight. These playlets showed the behaviour of the people in your country under the house-painter's rod of iron. You saw people from all walks of life, and how they resisted or submitted to what was happening. You saw the fear of the oppressed and the fear of the oppressors. It was like an extensive collection of gestures, artistically observed: the quarry looking back over their shoulders (and the look of their pursuers); the sudden silences; the hand clapped to your own mouth when you are about to say too much, and the hand that falls on the suspect's shoulder; the extorted lie; the whispered truth; the lack of trust between lovers; and much more. But what was so remarkable about it was that the actors did not present these terrible events in such a way that the spectators were tempted to shout 'Stop!' The spectators didn't seem to share the horror of the people on stage at all, and as a result there was frequently laughter in the auditorium, which didn't detract from the profoundly serious character of the performance. For this laughter seemed to be directed at the stupidity that found itself obliged to use force, and to be intended for the helplessness that manifested itself as brutality. Violent people were seen as blunderers, criminals as people who made mistakes or allowed themselves to be taken in. The spectators' laughter had many different nuances. It was a happy laughter when the quarry outwitted their pursuers, a relieved laughter when a good, true word was spoken. That's how an inventor might laugh on finding the solution after seeking it for a long time: it was so simple, and it took him so long to see it!

THE ACTOR: How did they do it?

THE DRAMATURG: It's not easy to say, but I didn't get the impression that it was all that difficult. The main thing was that they acted in such a way as to keep the audience's interest focused on the ensuing development, the continuation: on the mechanics of the events, as it were. On the play of cause and effect.

---

* The production referred to is the Paris premiere of Brecht's *Fear and Misery of the Third Reich* on 21 May 1938, directed by Slatan Dudow. The 'great actress' is Helene Weigel.

(ii) The Augsburger, Piscator, Weigel

B63
1939–41

DRAMATURG: The Augsburger drew a very clear distinction between mistakes made as a result of ignoring his rules, and those made despite or even because of observing them. 'My rules,' he would say, 'can only be applied by people who possess independence of judgement, a contradictory spirit and social imagination, and who are in contact with the progressive elements in the audience and so are themselves progressive, alert, thinking people. That being so, it's not for me to muzzle the ox that's treading out the corn.* So my actors make a whole series of mistakes that don't represent any infringement of my rules, as there are elements of their behaviour that are not controlled by me. There were nights when even Weigel burst into tears at certain points, quite against her will and by no means to the advantage of the performance. She once played the part of a peasant woman in the Spanish Civil War, and had to curse her son and wish him dead because she thought he had taken up arms against the generals – in fact he had already been shot dead by the generals' troops, while he was fishing and doing no harm to anybody. The civil war was still being fought at the time of this perfor-mance.** Whether it was because the war had taken a turn for the worse for the oppressed that day, or because Weigel was feeling particularly sensitive for some other reason, the fact was that as she spoke her curse against the murdered man, the tears began to flow. She was weeping not as the peasant woman, but as an actress, and for the peasant woman. I see that as a mistake, but I don't see it as having broken any of my rules.'

ACTOR: But her weeping wasn't acted! It was a completely personal thing!

DRAMATURG: Indeed it was. But the Augsburger rejected the audience's demand that actors should be entirely absorbed in their acting. His actors were not waiters who were expected to serve up the meat and have their private, personal feelings called gross importunities. They were neither the writer's servants nor the audience's. His actors weren't functionaries of a political movement, and they weren't high priests of art. Their task as political individuals was to further their social cause using art or any other means. Furthermore, shattering the illusion was something the Augsburger judged leniently. He was against illusion. On his stage there were private jokes, improvisations and extemporizations that would have been unthinkable in the old theatre.

PHILOSOPHER: Perhaps he also saw that treating such accidental, sponta-neous, arbitrary behaviour on the part of his actors so leniently was a way of denouncing their authority? They weren't supposed to give their interpreta-tions an incontestable character, were they, if I've understood correctly?

DRAMATURG: On no account.

* The Dramaturg is quoting Deuteronomy 25.4.
** The production referred to is the premiere of *Señora Carrar's Rifles* in Paris, 16 October 1937. See also the illustrations in *Brecht on Theatre*.

B78
1939–41

DRAMATURG: As we've seen, the Augsburger cuts his plays up into small independent playlets, so that the action progresses in jumps. He doesn't like scenes to slide imperceptibly into one another. So how does he cut, then, and from which points of view? He does it in such a way that each individual scene can be given a *title* of a historical or socio-political or socio-moral character.

THE ACTRESS: Give us an example!

DRAMATURG: 'Mother Courage goes to war as a tradeswoman', or 'Mother Courage is in a hurry because she's afraid the war may end suddenly', or 'While she is entertaining the recruiting sergeant, one of his men takes her son away'.*

THE ACTOR: What's historical or socio-political or socio-moral about that last title?

DRAMATURG: The play shows that it is typical of the age that kind-hearted actions cost you dear.

THE ACTOR: It's typical of our own age too – was there ever a time when it wasn't?

DRAMATURG: We can imagine one.

* See the *Mother Courage Modelbook* text and illustrations below.

B74
1939–41

ACTOR: This idea of continual self-analysis and drawing on personal experience might easily lead to someone wanting to alter the text. Where do you stand on that?

PHILOSOPHER: What does the playwright* say?

DRAMATURG: Actors are usually very selfish in their alterations. They see only their own parts. The result is that they not only answer questions, but also alter questions in such a way that the answers are no longer correct. If alterations are made collectively, and with no less interest and talent than has gone into the actual writing of the play, then it will be to the play's advantage. We mustn't forget that it's not the play but the performance which is the real goal of all our efforts. Altering things requires a great deal of artistry, that's all.

PHILOSOPHER: Actually I think that last sentence lays down the boundaries well enough. I'd also like to point out that being too keen to make alterations may result in a careless study of the text; but the possibility of alteration, and the knowledge that it may be essential, can provide deeper insights.

DRAMATURG: What's important if you're going to make alterations is having the courage and the skill to alter things enough. I remember seeing a production of Schiller's *The Robbers* at Piscator's theatre. The company felt that Schiller had been unfair in making one of the robbers, the extremist Spiegelberg, so unsympathetic from the audience's point of view. As a result he was played sympathetically, and the play literally fell apart. For neither action nor dialogue provided any point of reference that might allow for Spiegelberg's behaviour to appear sympathetic. The play came across as reactionary (which it isn't, historically speaking), and Spiegelberg's tirades failed to come across as revolutionary. It would have taken extensive alterations, made with considerable artistry as well as a sense of history, to have even the slightest chance of showing Spiegelberg's outlook – which is more radical than that of the main character – as the more progressive.**

* The 'playwright' is Brecht's alternative pseudonym in *Buying Brass*; see also B30 above (p. 59).

** The Dramaturg is referring to Piscator's production of Friedrich Schiller's first play *The Robbers* (1778) at the Staatliches Schauspielhaus in Berlin on 11 September 1926. Piscator radically cut and rewrote *The Robbers*, and the ensuing controversy is the subject of Brecht's 'Conversation about Classics' (*Brecht on Art and Politics*, pp. 76–83). The Dramaturg's comments are slightly odd, in that the transformation of Spiegelberg into a proletarian revolutionary – he wore a Leon Trotsky face mask – was well received by left-wing critics, but castigated by the right-wing press. See also Piscator, *The Political Theatre*, pp. 124–34.

B130
c. 1945

'WEIGEL'S DESCENT INTO FAME'
FROM THE 'THIRD NIGHT' OF *BUYING BRASS*

This is not a report of how she perfected her art until she was able to make the spectators not only laugh when she laughed and cry when she cried, but also cry when she laughed and laugh when she cried. No; it's a report of what happened next. Once she had mastered her art and wanted to bring it before the largest audience, the people, and apply it to the most important themes, those that concerned the people – by taking this step she lost her standing and her descent began. The very first time she performed one of her new creations, an old working-class woman – in such a way that in everything she did you could clearly see what she did to her advantage and what to her detriment – it provoked unrest in the audience, which was not made up of workers.* From then on the finer, better appointed theatrical establishments closed their doors to her, and when she performed in venues in the suburbs, the few connoisseurs of art who followed her there may not have denied her great artistry, but did feel that her art was being applied to inferior subject matter. And so word went round: she leaves people cold. The workers, who came to see her in droves, gave her a warm reception and thought she was excellent, but they didn't make much of a fuss about it because they were more preoccupied with the subject matter. Having expended so much effort in learning how to direct the spectators' interest towards major themes, namely the struggles of the oppressed against their oppressors, it was not without difficulty that she learned to accept the transferral of this interest from herself – the performer – to what was being performed – the subject matter. Yet it was this that represented her greatest achievement. Many artists succeed in getting their spectators, when faced with such artistry, to stop seeing and hearing the world: Weigel's achievement was to get them to see and hear more than just her. For she demonstrated not just one art, but many. She showed, for example, that goodness and wisdom are arts that can and must be learned. She never set out to display her own greatness, however, but the greatness of the characters she portrayed. She was embarrassed when somebody told her once, as a compliment: 'You didn't play that old woman of the people – you were her.' 'No,' she replied quickly, 'I did play her, and she must have been the one who impressed you, not me.' And indeed, when she was playing a fisherman's wife, for example, who loses her son in the civil war and then rises up herself to fight the generals, she made every moment a historical moment, every utterance the famous utterance of a historical figure.** And at the same time it was all done with the utmost naturalness and simplicity. This naturalness and simplicity was, in fact, what set these new historical figures apart from the old ones. Asked how it was that she managed to portray oppressed characters who rise up and fight as so noble, she replied: 'By imitating them in every detail.' She knew how to get people not only to feel but also to think, and this thinking process that she provoked in them was entirely pleasurable – sometimes a powerful source of enjoyment and sometimes a gentle one. But now I am talking about the workers who came to see her perform. The art connoisseurs stopped coming, and in their place came the police. The truths to which she lent her voice and her clarity summoned representatives of the law, which exists to combat justice. After the performances she frequently ended up in a police cell. It was at around this time that the house-painter came to power, and she was forced to flee the country. The only language she knew was the one nobody else knew the way she did. And so she performed only a few times for other refugees, with small troupes that were made up of workers and had little opportunity to rehearse. The rest of the time she spent doing housework and bringing up her children, in a little fisherman's house a long way from any theatre.*** Her endeavour to perform for large numbers of people had put her in a position where she was only able to perform for a very few. When she did act, it was only ever in plays that depicted the horrors of the age and the causes of those horrors. She may have made those persecuted people who listened to her forget their misery, but never the causes of that misery. And they always went away from her performances with renewed strength for the fight. This was because Weigel showed them their own wisdom and their own goodness. She continued to perfect her art, and she took ever more significant art to ever deeper depths. And so, once she had completely surrendered and lost her former fame, her second period of fame began: a lowly one, existing in the minds of a few persecuted people, at a time when many people were being persecuted. She was quite content, because it was her goal to be famous among the less fortunate – among as many of them as possible, but even among just these few, if nothing else was possible.

* The 'old working-class woman' is Pelagea Vlassova, the central character in Brecht's play *The Mother* (1932). Brecht discusses its premiere at the Komödienhaus am Schiffbauerdamm on 17 January 1932, and Weigel's performance, in his 1933 'Notes on *The Mother*', *Brecht on Theatre*.

** The fisherman's wife is Theresa Carrar in *Señora Carrar's Rifles*.

*** The exile performances for refugees were *Señora Carrar's Rifles* (Paris, 1937) and *Fear and Misery of the Third Reich* (Paris, 1938) – see B132 above (p. 68). The fisherman's house was the Brecht family residence in Svendborg, Denmark.

B131

c. 1945

FROM: 'WEIGEL'S DESCENT INTO FAME'

Here she gave an exemplary presentation of a true proletarian, in that she portrayed the proletariat as famous and did not sacrifice the ideal to realism, nor realism to the ideal, as so often happens. She showed the ruled as capable of ruling, the abused as capable of creating. The aspects of these people that had withered away were shown to be withered, but anybody could see what it was that had withered away: something flourishing and vibrant. It was as if somebody were drawing a picture of a tree, its growth stunted by its environment – the dry soil, the walls of the buildings, ill-treatment of all kinds – and at the same time were drawing a picture of the tree using a distinctly different pen stroke, depicting the way it would have grown had it not been for all these obstacles, making the difference quite clear.* But this simile is inadequate, because it doesn't illustrate the way she showed her proletarian woman's struggle to change the adverse conditions. She conveyed nobility by portraying the struggle to achieve what is noble, and goodness by portraying the struggle to make the world better. And all these difficult struggles were conveyed with the same ease with which the master describes the struggles of his apprenticeship: as successful in the end, after much perseverance. She did not call on the oppressors to have pity on the oppressed, but called on the oppressed to have confidence in themselves.

* The motif of the stunted tree also occurs in Brecht's 1939 poem *Bad Time for Poetry*, in Bertolt Brecht, *Poems 1913-1956* (London, Methuen, 1987), pp. 330-1.

(iii) Social Science and Art

B122
1942-3

What about those who deny that it is meaningful to talk about the eternal, and those who contend that things which last a long time do so because they are able to accommodate to change?

We are faced by a vested interest in letting the eternally human triumph over the temporal conditions among which it is forced to manifest itself. A few 'simple' drives are supposed to appear in all sorts of different guises. When love gets in the way of business, as is the case with the military operations in *Antony and Cleopatra*; in *Coriolanus* when the son's political plans are thrown into disarray by the intervention of his mother; in *King Lear* when the dying man, cursing those around him, asks 'Pray you, undo this button; thank you, sir'; and in *Antigone* when the sister breaks the law and buries her brother – then the human element, that which is private and personal, is triumphant, sending shivers down our spine. The creature emerges, resisting the order it has itself created, the natural rebels against the artificial, it is a revolutionary act. But in reality all that happens is that a split becomes apparent, a conflict of interest between the individual and society, a historical fact; after all, what is natural is also social, that is to say artificial and historical. In the case of the bourgeoisie, for instance, the family is a more natural form of union than the state, and the sexual relationship is felt to be more fundamental than any other kind, yet in the latter case we can see particularly clearly the extent to which it too is associated with the ownership complex artificially, historically, and as a result of transient conditions. If the ownership complex is removed from the list of drive complexes that are said to be eternal, because private ownership has ceased to be a motor of production and become a brake, then even the sexual drive loses its dominant position, at least until it binds itself in a new way. But above all, its potential to be represented depends upon its opposition to other interests. It's not the case in every social formation that the sexual drive leads to complications.

B71
1939–41

PHILOSOPHER: You can judge the completeness of a law by the extent of its limitations. You shouldn't seek law-like regularities in unduly compliant and 'fitting' types, but preferably in those who (within reason) dig in their heels. The types you select must have something approximate about them. If, for instance, you think that a peasant will act in a particular way in a given set of circumstances, then use a specific peasant who has not simply been selected or fabricated for his propensity to act in precisely that way. It's better still if you can show the law applying to different peasants in different ways. Laws only provide you with very broad outlines, averages, summaries. The concept of 'class', for example, is a concept which embraces a great many individuals and thereby deprives them of their individuality. There are certain laws that apply to class. They apply to individuals only in so far as those individuals coincide with their class, i.e. not absolutely; for the concept of class was only arrived at by ignoring certain idiosyncrasies of the individual. You are not portraying principles but human beings.

B72
1939–41

DRAMATURG: The difference between a scientific portrayal of a rhinoceros – a drawing in a book about natural history, for instance – and an artistic one lies in the fact that the latter suggests something of the artist's relationship to the animal. The artist's drawing contains stories, even if it only depicts the animal and nothing more. The animal will look lazy or angry or greedy or cunning. The artist will have incorporated a number of characteristics into the drawing that are not needed if all you want to do is study the rhino's anatomy.

B133
c. 1945

DRAMATURG: It seems to me that your liking for folk images has diverted us somewhat from the topic of the spectators' desire for knowledge, which is what you want to base your approach to theatre upon. These images are designed to fill people with horror. The horror of earthquakes, fires, atrocities, blows of fate.

THE PHILOSOPHER: We haven't been diverted, we've just gone back. The essence of this folk art is uncertainty. The earth quakes and fissures. The roof suddenly goes up in flames. Kings are subject to the vagaries of fortune. And uncertainty is also at the root of the desire for knowledge. The signals for rescue and redress may be more or less plentiful according to humanity's ability to help itself.

THE DRAMATURG: So it's possible to take pleasure in uncertainty?

THE PHILOSOPHER: Remember the English saying: 'It's an ill wind that blows no good.' People want to be made just as uncertain as they really are.

THE DRAMATURG: You don't want to get rid of this element of uncertainty in art, then?

THE PHILOSOPHER: Definitely not. Absolutely not.

THE ACTOR: So it's back to pity and terror after all?

THE PHILOSOPHER: Not so fast! Talking about this reminds me of a photograph used by an American steel company in a newspaper advertisement. It showed Yokohama just after it had been destroyed by an earthquake. There was a big pile of rubble – houses that had collapsed in the quake. Between them, however, there still towered one or two fairly tall buildings of reinforced concrete. The caption was 'Steel stood'.

THE ACTOR: That's lovely.

THE DRAMATURG *to the Worker*: Why are you laughing?

THE WORKER: Because it's lovely.

THE PHILOSOPHER: That photograph gave an unmistakeable hint to art.

(iv) 'Extreme Situations'

B67
1939–41

PHILOSOPHER: Take the death of the villain! The destruction of the anti-social figure in order to save lives. The necessity of this destruction must also be contested in some way. It's society's last resort – but might not other measures have been overlooked? The right to life, which society enforces so crudely that it cannot enforce it without denying it, is the basic right upon which all other rights depend. In the fight for life – a raw gasping for breath independent of any social enlargement or enhancement, a struggle simply to keep the heart beating, to cling on to a meagre existence – we have to stand by the dying man. We have to respect his humanity, even when it is reduced to this – he doesn't want to die, he doesn't want to cease being human – because it's his humanity that we share with him, even as we share in his inhumanity by killing him or wanting him dead. Oh, there's a lot that we share, even now. Something of the helplessness we feel towards him, he once felt too. If lives are worth anything, it is for society and because of it.

B73
1939–41

DRAMATURG: Take the scene where Lear dies! That line 'Pray you, undo this button: thank you, Sir.' A wish fights its way through his curses, life has become unbearable, and on top of that his clothes are too tight; it was a king who lived, a man who dies, he is very polite ('thank you, Sir'). The subject is fully dealt with, both broadly and in detail. A disappointed man is dying: dying and disappointment are shown, but don't quite coincide. No forgiveness is granted, but kindnesses are accepted. The man has gone too far, the dramatist does not. Lear's destruction is complete, there is a startling last demonstration of death as a special horror, Lear really does die.

B76
1939–41

THE PHILOSOPHER: When the married man comes home to find 'the beast with two backs' in his bed, he will experience and demonstrate a variety of sensations, both consistent and inconsistent.* The triumph of discovery ('Got here in the nick of time'); the reluctance to discover something he doesn't want to know ('Could my eyes be deceiving me?'); the disgust at sexual appetite ('Like animals!'); the gloomy understanding of basic human needs ('She's got to have it'); the feeling of contemptuous renunciation ('I haven't lost much if this is the kind of woman she is!'); the thirst for revenge ('She'll pay for this' and so on and so forth).

---

* The phrase 'the beast with two backs' is taken from Shakespeare, *Othello*, Act I, Scene 1, ll.116–17.

B70
1939–41

PHILOSOPHER: The wish to demonstrate certain incidents to society in a way that will enable it to resolve certain discrepancies should not lead us to neglect what lies outside its sphere of influence. But neither should we just be asking people riddles, solvable and unsolvable. The unknown can only develop from the known.

The Fourth Night

(i) The Nature of Art

B79
1939–41

PHILOSOPHER: From an *artistic* point of view we can say that our progress has been as follows: we have taken those imitations of reality that trigger all kinds of passions and emotions and we have tried to improve the imitations without bothering about the passions and emotions. We did this by structuring the imitations in such a way that they enable anyone who sees them to actively master the reality being imitated. We have found that more accurate imitations trigger emotions and passions, and indeed that emotions and passions can contribute to the mastering of reality.

B80
1939–41

DRAMATURG: It's no longer surprising, really, that when art was asked to perform a new task – that of destroying people's preconceptions about how they live together in society – at first it was almost ruined. We can see now that this happened because art took on this new task without abandoning one of its own preconceptions about itself. Its entire apparatus was designed for the task of getting people to accept their fate. It ruined this apparatus when in its productions, human beings suddenly emerged as humanity's fate. In short, it wanted to perform the new task but still be the old art. It did everything, therefore, in a hesitant, half-hearted, selfish way, and with a guilty conscience. But there is nothing worse suited to art than this. It was only by abandoning itself that it became itself again.

ACTOR: I see. What seemed unartistic was simply what didn't suit the old art, not what didn't suit art per se.

PHILOSOPHER: That's why some people, on seeing the new art seemingly so weak, or rather weakened – weakened by its new tasks, but not able to cope with them satisfactorily – regretfully turned their backs on it and decided it was better to give up on the new tasks.

B99
1939–41

DEFINITION OF ART

PHILOSOPHER: We've talked enough about how art can be used, how it can be produced and what its production depends upon, and we have also produced art during these four nights; so we can now risk a few cautious statements of an abstract nature on the subject of this intrinsically human capacity, in the hope that they will not be applied in a completely abstract way, independently of and unconnected to anything else. We might say, then, that art is the skill of creating reproductions of the way people live together, so as to generate a particular kind of feeling, thought and action in people that would not be generated in the same way or to the same extent by seeing or experiencing the reality represented. Out of their own seeing and experiencing of reality, artists have forged a representation that reproduces their thoughts and feelings for us to see and experience.

DRAMATURG: There's a good expression for that in German: 'der Künstler produziert sich'. It means 'the artist produces himself'.

PHILOSOPHER: It's excellent, if you take it to mean that in the artist humanity is producing itself: that art comes about when humanity produces itself.

B142
c. 1945

People who know nothing about either science or art believe that they are two vastly different things, neither of which they understand at all. They think they're doing science a favour by allowing it to be unimaginative, and they think they're promoting art if they stop people expecting it to be intelligent. People might be especially talented in one particular area, but they do not become more talented in that area the less talented they are in all others. Knowledge is as much a part of humanity as art is, even if, in our current rotten polity, humanity often had to get along without either for long periods of time. Nobody is entirely without knowledge, just as nobody is entirely without art.

B91
1939–41

Art is thus an inherent and fundamental human capacity: not just veiled morality or beautified knowledge, but an independent discipline that represents the various other disciplines in a contradictory way.

B92
1939–41

It's too passive and too much of a generalization to describe art as the realm of the beautiful. For a start, artists cultivate skill. What makes artificial things beautiful is the fact that they have been skilfully made. When people object that mere skill cannot give rise to artistic artefacts, they are referring – by using the word 'mere' – to a hollow, one-sided kind of skill based in a single 'domain' and absent from all others: i.e. a skill that is unskilful in moral or scientific terms. Beauty in nature is a quality that gives the human senses the opportunity to be skilful. The eye produces itself. This is not an independent process, which simply 'stops there'. It has been prepared by other processes, social processes, processes involving other types of production. Where would the mountain's vast sweep be without the narrowness of the valley, or the formless form of the wilderness without the formal formlessness of the city? Nobody's eye can be sated if they are not sated themselves. People who are exhausted or have 'ended up' in a place by chance will, even in the most 'magnificent' of locations, find that all it does is depress them in so far as there is no possibility of making any use of it; it is the impossibility of any such possibility that is depressing.

B93
1939–41

Untrained people often feel beauty's impact when contrasts grow sharper: when the blue water becomes bluer, the golden corn more golden, the red sunset redder.

B97
1939–41

ACTOR: But surely that's not all art can do – it wouldn't be enough. What about the dreams dreamt by dreamers, beauty with an admixture of terror, life in all its different registers?

DRAMATURG: Yes, it's about time we talked about enjoyment. You, for whom the goal of all philosophy lies in making life more enjoyable, seem to want art, of all things, not to involve enjoyment. Eating a good meal you estimate highly; those who serve potatoes to the people you condemn. But art shouldn't have anything in common with eating or drinking or love.

(ii) Emotion, Critique, Representation

B82
1939–41

ACTOR: It's understandable that people enjoy sharing in the characters' emotions and participating in their actions in spirit. But how are they supposed to enjoy criticizing those emotions and actions?

PHILOSOPHER: I've often found participating in your heroes' actions to be frustrating, and sharing in their emotions to be genuinely repugnant. But I do like playing around with your heroes; that is to say, it entertains me to imagine different ways of behaving and to compare your heroes' actions with the ones I imagine – which are equally possible.

DRAMATURG: But how else can they behave, being what they are, and being designed for what they are designed for? How can you imagine them behaving differently?

PHILOSOPHER: I can do it. And then I can compare them with myself, too.

B83
1939–41

PHILOSOPHER: Everything that glosses over things, that is innocuous, that removes contradictions, is alien to an art which makes use of V-effects.

B84
1939–41

DRAMATURG: So using your critical faculties is not a purely intellectual process?

PHILOSOPHER: Of course not. You can't possibly confine criticism to the intellect. Emotions are also involved in criticism, and maybe what you actually need to do is organize criticism by way of emotions. Remember that criticism arises from crises and intensifies them.

B85
1939–41

DRAMATURG: I agree we need to know as much as possible in order to stage even the smallest scene. Then what?

PHILOSOPHER: Degrees of knowledge vary widely. There's knowledge in your dreams and premonitions, in your hopes and fears, in sympathy and in suspicion. But more than anything, knowledge manifests itself in knowing better, i.e. in contradiction. All of this is your domain.

B89
1939–41

ACTOR: I hate all that stuff about art being the handmaiden of society. Society sits there all high and mighty, and art isn't a part of society; it just belongs to it, it's just society's barmaid. Do we all have to be servants? Can't we all be masters? Can't art be one too? Let's get rid of servitude – in art just as much as anywhere else!

THE PHILOSOPHER: Bravo!

DRAMATURG: What do you mean, bravo? You've ruined everything you've said with that piece of spontaneous applause. People only have to tell you they're oppressed, and straightaway you're on their side.

THE PHILOSOPHER: I hope I am. I see what he's getting at now. He's worried we're going to turn him into a state official or a master of ceremonies or a moralizer working 'through the medium of art'. Don't worry; that's not the idea. Dramatic art can only be treated as a fundamental form of human expression which contains its purpose within itself. That's where it differs from the art of war, whose purpose is external to itself. Dramatic art is one of society's fundamental forces; it is founded on a basic social faculty, on a desire felt by human beings within society; it's like language itself, it's a language of its own. I propose that we all stand, to make this tribute stick in our memory.

All stand.

And now I propose that we take advantage of the fact that we've stood up to go and relieve ourselves.

THE ACTOR: Oh God, you've wrecked the whole thing. I protest.

THE PHILOSOPHER: Why? Here too I'm obeying a basic drive, giving in to it, respecting it. And at the same time I'm making sure that the ceremony comes to a suitably banal conclusion.

There is a pause.

B95
1939–41

DRAMATURG: The theatre is where everything that goes on in people's lives is reported; it's in the business of gossip and historiography. It's built on people's curiosity about other people. It's part of the constant observation of everyone by everyone.

ACTOR: But at one time theatre was associated with religious cults, so it was different then.

PHILOSOPHER: It was and it wasn't. In the struggle to survive people were more dependent on nature back then than they are now. They saw nature as their fate. In order to be able to speak to nature, to negotiate with her, they anthropomorphized the forces of nature by creating the gods.

B96
1939–41

ACTOR: But there are so many different things people do. They rejoice; sigh; stretch when they are weary; hope; yawn; feel afraid. Your spectators are only supposed to learn. You're constricting art too much, my friend! The goings-on between Achilles and Patroclus,* Don Quixote's battle with the windmills, Lear's wailing on the heath: did that show the spectators and listeners what they must do? And nothing else? Didn't it also make them feel?

* The homoerotic friendship between Achilles and Patroclus is a major theme in Shakespeare, *Troilus and Cressida* (1602).

B86
1939–41

DRAMATURG: Can we depict the characters in a *parable* along the following lines: a peasant on the stage is not *the* quintessential peasant, the embodiment of all peasants, a schematic, average figure; he is *a* peasant, one particular peasant with his own personal character traits and his own special fate. In relation to an industrial worker or a public servant, however, he is *the* peasant. In that case he represents the specific point of view of the peasant class.

PHILOSOPHER: Yes, that takes account of the differences between individual peasants and the differences between peasants and other classes.

Of course, class itself is not a schematic thing either. This great organism displays individual characteristics too, and changes, and behaves 'illogically' – in other words it subjects our logic to constant criticism.

B136
c. 1945

PHILOSOPHER: I once saw a Russian play in which some workers gave a gun to a robber so he could protect them against robbers while they worked. The audience simultaneously laughed and cried at this.

B137
c. 1945

In the old theatre the hero used to be contrasted with a stock character. Caricature is the means by which the empathetic kind of representation expresses criticism. The actor is criticizing life, and the spectator empathizes with that criticism.

Epic theatre is probably only capable of staging such caricatures if it wants to show the process of caricaturing. The caricatures then make their appearance like masked dancers at the masked ball depicted on stage.

B138
c. 1945

The gliding, fast-moving, transitory (but not transporting) kind of portrayal is also necessary because every character's every expression is made striking, meaning that the course, connection and development of all these expressions needs to be made striking too. Genuine understanding and genuine criticism are only possible if the part and the whole, and the prevailing relationship between the part and the whole, can be understood and criticized. People's expressions are necessarily contradictory, so it is necessary to take in the whole contradiction.

B139
c. 1945

Actors don't need to present fully finished characters. They wouldn't be able to, and they don't have to. They're presenting not only criticism of an issue but also – and most importantly – the issue itself. They don't need to have fully worked-out opinions about everything they present. They draw on a pool of things seen and experienced.

(iii) The Augsburger

B98
1939–41

THE AUGSBURGER'S THEATRE

The Augsburger's theatre was very small. It produced only a few plays and trained only a few actors.

The principal actresses were Weigel, Neher and Lenya. The principal actors were Homolka, Lorre and Lingen. The singer Busch also belonged to this theatre, but he only rarely appeared on stage. The chief set designer was Casper Neher, no relation to the actress. The musicians were Weill and Eisler.*

Audiences in the Weimar Republic were not in a position to bestow any real fame on actors. So the Augsburger tried to give all his actors as much fame as possible in their own eyes. There is a little didactic poem, for instance, in which he advises Neher on how she should wash in the mornings: like a famous person, and in such a way that an artist could make a picture out of it.** They were all reasonably famous, but came on stage before the audience as if they were a lot more famous – modestly, in other words.

* The various artists Brecht refers to are those he worked with in Berlin between 1928 and 1932; see his 'Notes' on *The Threepenny Opera*, *Man Equals Man* and *The Mother*, in *Brecht on Theatre*, and the Introduction to Section 1: 1918–1933.
** See *Advice to the Actress C.N.* (i.e. Carola Neher), in Brecht, *Poems 1913–1956*, pp. 179–80.

B90
1939–41

ACTOR: Did the Augsburger say anything about his spectator?

PHILOSOPHER: Yes. He said this:

The other day I met my spectator.
On a dusty street
He was gripping a pneumatic drill.
For a second
He looked up. So I quickly set up my theatre
Between the buildings. He
Looked expectantly.
In the pub
I met him again. He was standing at the bar.

Dripping with sweat he was drinking, in his fist
A hunk of bread. I quickly set up my theatre. He
Looked in astonishment.
Today
I managed it again. Outside the station
I saw him, swept along by rifle butts
And drum rolls, being herded off to war.
In the middle of the crowd
I set up my theatre. Over his shoulder
He looked back at me:
He nodded.

(iv) Shakespeare

B81
1939–41

SHAKESPEARE [2]

THE DRAMATURG: Shakespeare's plays are extraordinarily full of life. They
seem to have been printed from the prompt books, along with the revisions
made during rehearsals and the actors' improvisations. The way the blank
verse is set down suggests that it must often have been done by ear. I have
always been particularly interested in *Hamlet* for the following reasons. We
know it was adapted from an earlier play by a certain Thomas Kyd, which
had been very successful a few years previously.* It was about the cleaning
out of an Augean stable. The hero, Hamlet, cleaned up his family. He seems
to have done so quite without inhibition, everything seems to be leading to
the final act. The star of Shakespeare's Globe Theatre, however, was a stout
man and short of breath, and so for a while all the Shakespearean heroes
had to be stout and short of breath; this went for Macbeth as well as Lear.
So the storyline was deepened for this actor, and probably by him, too.
Cascades and rapids were worked in. This made the play much more interesting. It looks just as though they modelled and adapted it on the stage as
far as Act IV, then found themselves with a problem: how were they to get
as far as the frenzied bloodbath at the end, which had been the highlight of
the original play, with this hesitating Hamlet? In Act IV there are a number
of scenes, each of which represents a solution to this problem. Perhaps the
actor needed to resort to all of them, or perhaps he only needed one, and the
rest were nevertheless included in the book. They all seem like bright ideas
somebody was struck by.

THE ACTOR: Maybe plays were made the same way films are made now.

THE DRAMATURG: Possibly. It must have been a really gifted writer who finalized them in the published version, though.

THE ACTOR: From your description it sounds like Shakespeare was adding a new scene pretty much every day.

THE DRAMATURG: Exactly. I think they were experimenting. They were experimenting, just like Galileo in Florence at that time and Bacon in London. And that is why it's right to produce the plays experimentally.

THE ACTOR: That will be seen as sacrilege.

THE DRAMATURG: The plays owe their existence to sacrilege.

THE ACTOR: But as soon as you alter them in any way, you lay yourself open to the charge of treating them as less than perfect.

THE DRAMATURG: That's just a mistaken idea of perfection, nothing more.

* Thomàs Kyd, *The Spanish Tragedy* (c. 1587).

B88
1939–41

HAMLET, EXPERIMENT

PHILOSOPHER: Both the Globe Theatre's experiments and Galileo's, which treated the globe itself in a new way, reflected certain transformations of the globe itself. The bourgeoisie was taking its first hesitant steps. Shakespeare could never have tailored the part of Hamlet to that short-winded character actor of his if the feudal family hadn't just fallen apart. Hamlet's new bourgeois way of thinking is one of his ailments. His experiments lead him straight into disaster.

DRAMATURG: Not straight, circuitously.

PHILOSOPHER: All right, circuitously. In a sense the play has the permanence of something makeshift, and that will need to be resolved if we are to preserve it, I quite agree.

B141
c. 1945

DRAMATURG: Have we got to scrap all those wonderful old plays, then?

THE PHILOSOPHER: No, you don't need to do that.

THE ACTOR: What about *King Lear*?

THE PHILOSOPHER: That play contains an account of the way people lived together long ago; you just need to complete it.

THE DRAMATURG: Many people think such plays should be produced just as they are, and say it's barbaric to make any changes to them at all.

THE PHILOSOPHER: But it's a barbaric play. Of course, you need to go about things very carefully so as not to spoil its beauty. If you're going to perform it in accordance with the new rules, so that the spectators don't empathize completely with the king, then you can stage nearly the whole play with only minor additions to keep the spectators using their reason. What you can't have is the spectators, even those who happen to be servants themselves, taking Lear's side to such an extent that they cheer when a servant is beaten for carrying out his mistress's orders, as happens in the fourth scene of Act I.

THE ACTOR: How can we stop that from happening?

THE DRAMATURG: He could still get beaten, but he could be badly injured by the beating and crawl out showing every sign of being in great pain. That would change the mood.

THE ACTOR: Then you'd have people turning against Lear for a reason that dates from very recent times.

THE DRAMATURG: Not if you're consistent about it. You could show the little band of servants attending the king everybody has rejected, and how they can't get a square meal anywhere any more and pursue Lear with silent reproaches. The sight of them would surely torment him, and that would provide a good justification for his rage. You just need to depict the feudal conditions.

THE ACTOR: In that case you could also take his division of his kingdom seriously and have him tear up a map in the first scene. Lear could toss the pieces to his daughters in the hope of securing their love that way. And if he took the third piece, the one meant for Cordelia, and tore it in half again to give to the other two daughters, that would be a particularly good way of making the spectators stop and think.

THE DRAMATURG: But you'd be destroying the play, because you'd be introducing something that doesn't lead anywhere.

THE PHILOSOPHER: Perhaps it would lead somewhere; we'd have to examine the play. In any case, it wouldn't do any harm if there were some abnormal episodes of this sort – if people were confronted with a few such hotbeds of inconsistency. The old chronicles are full of such things. It's impossible to perform these medieval plays anyway to spectators who have no sense of history. It would be a stupid thing to do. But Shakespeare is a great realist, and I think he would stand the test. He always shovelled a lot of raw material on to the stage, unvarnished representations of things he had seen. And there are those valuable fault-lines in his works where what was new in his age collided with what was old. We too are the parents of a new age, but the children of an old one; we understand a lot about the remote past, and we are still able to share emotions that were once overwhelming and were aroused on a grand scale. And the society we live in is just as complex, too. The human essence is, as the classics put it, the ensemble of all societal relations of all times.* All the same, there is much in these works that is dead, distorted and empty. It can stay in the books, because we can't tell whether it's really dead or only seems to be, and because it may help explain other phenomena of that bygone age. I'd almost prefer to draw your attention to the wealth of living elements to be found in these works at seemingly dead points. A tiny addition and they spring to life, now of all times, and for the first time. The most important thing is to perform these old works historically, which means setting them in stark contrast to our own time. For it is only against the background of our time that their form emerges as an old form, and without this background I doubt that they would have any form at all.

---

* The Philosopher is referring to Marx's *Theses on Feuerbach*, no. 6. Brecht typically uses the term 'the classics' to refer to the works of Marx, Engels and other key Marxist theorists.

(v) Finale

B87
1939–41

DRAMATURG: Well, we've studied as best we could your various directives for making the art of theatre just as instructive as science. You'd invited us to come and work in your *thaëter*, which was supposed to be a scientific institute. Making art was not supposed to be our goal. To achieve what you want, however, we've actually had to call on all of our artistic powers. Quite frankly, if we act in the way you want, with the aims you want, then we will be making art anyway.

PHILOSOPHER: I'd noticed that too.

DRAMATURG: You've discarded so much of what's generally considered to be essential for practising art, yet there was one thing you retained and that, it seems to me now, was enough.

PHILOSOPHER: What?

THE DRAMATURG: What you referred to as the ease of this activity. The knowledge that this process of pretending, of concocting something for the audience, can only be carried out in a cheerful, good-tempered frame of mind, by being willing to have a bit of fun and a joke. You really put your finger on how we should think of art when you pointed out the difference between the work of a man who's responsible for pushing five buttons on a machine, and a man who's juggling five balls. And you linked this ease with the great seriousness of social responsibility.

ACTOR: The thing that put me off most at the beginning was your insistence on working exclusively with the intellect. Thinking is such a flimsy thing, you see – it's fundamentally inhuman. Even if you were to argue that thinking is the very thing that makes us human, I'd say you were wrong, because you'd be forgetting our animal side.

PHILOSOPHER: And what do you think now?

ACTOR: Oh, I've come to see thinking as not such a flimsy thing after all. It certainly doesn't stand in contradiction to feeling. And what I arouse in the spectators are not just thoughts, but feelings too. I now see thinking simply as a type of behaviour, and a social behaviour at that. It's something that the whole body takes part in, with all its senses.

B94
1939–41

ACTOR: All the same, our theatre is still a serious obstacle to your _thaëter_, my friend. Your use of our abilities – which were developed in the theatre, for the theatre – is going to be adversely affected by the fact that on top of the abilities you can use, we have other abilities which are of no real use to you at all. It's just as much of a handicap that our abilities should in some ways exceed your requirements as that they should fall short.

PHILOSOPHER: In what ways do they exceed them?

ACTOR: You explained to us very clearly the difference between someone who _sees_ and someone who _looks closely_. You gave us to understand that the former must be replaced by the latter. Down with guessing, hurrah for knowing! Down with suspicion, hurrah for conviction! Down with feeling, hurrah for reasoning! Down with dreams, hurrah for plans! Down with yearning, hurrah for decisiveness!

The Actress claps.

ACTOR: Why aren't you clapping?

PHILOSOPHER: I've hardly made such definitive statements about the tasks of art in general. True, I was against all the slogans to the contrary: down with knowing, hurrah for guessing, and so on. I was against the idea of art remaining a strictly marginal thing. Slogans like these have no validity in the works of volatile times and progressive classes. But look at our own age! Look how much more artistically we perform works that embody the slogans I'm opposed to! Guessing is portrayed much more artistically than knowing! Even where works do contain clear ideas, what is artistic about them is found elsewhere: it lies in what is unclear. I don't just mean that people look for it there, but that they find it there too.

DRAMATURG: So you don't think there's any artistic form for knowledge?

PHILOSOPHER: I fear there isn't. Why would I want to shut down the whole realm of guessing, dreaming and feeling? People do tackle social problems in these ways as well. Guessing and knowing aren't opposites. Guessing gives rise to knowing, knowing to guessing. Dreams give rise to plans, plans turn into dreams. I yearn for something and I set out to get it, and I still yearn on the way. Thoughts are thought and feelings are felt. But there are also wrong turns and short circuits. There are phases in which dreams don't turn into plans, guessing doesn't turn into knowing, yearning doesn't get up and go. Those are bad periods for art; art itself becomes bad. The tension between guessing and knowing, which is what constitutes art, breaks down. The field loses its charge, as it were. Right now I'm less interested in what happens to artists who succumb to mysticism than in those who turn away impatiently from planless dreaming to move on to a dreamless planning, which is equally empty.

DRAMATURG: I see. We more than anyone – because we are trying to be of service to the society we belong to – should be fully covering *every* sphere of human striving.

ACTOR: So we don't only show what we know?

ACTRESS: But also what we guess.

PHILOSOPHER: And bear in mind that there are various things you don't know that the spectators may recognize!

B144
c. 1945

THE PHILOSOPHER: I can't keep this a secret from you any longer; I've got to come clean now. I've got no resources, no building, no theatre, not a single costume, not even a pot of make-up. I'm backed by *nobody* and *nothing*. Your efforts will have to be greater than any you've ever made before, but there won't be any money to pay you for them; and we can't even ask you to do it for the glory. Because we can't make you famous either. No newspapers have ever helped make our collaborators famous.

Pause.

THE ACTOR: So you would in fact be asking us to work for work's sake.

THE STAGE HAND: That's a terrible thing to ask. I'd never ask anybody to do that because I hear it all too often myself. 'Don't you enjoy the work itself?', they say disappointedly when I put in for my wages. 'Don't you do the work for its own sake?' No, we would definitely pay. Not much, because we haven't got much, but not nothing, because work has to be paid for.

THE DRAMATURG: I think you'd have a better chance of getting artists to work for nothing than for a pittance. At least if they act for nothing they get the satisfaction of giving something.

THE ACTOR: So you'd still pay a pittance would you? Well I'd accept it. Definitely. It regulates our relationship and makes it into an ordinary, workaday one. And you wouldn't look a gift horse in the mouth, if possible, and at the end of the day this is supposed to be an art whose mouth you can look into. I've understood that much: here's a horse who really wants his mouth to be looked into. That's the financial side sorted out, basically.

THE DRAMATURG: The carelessness of artists works in your favour there, it would seem. It's completely slipped his mind that he'd also have to give up transforming himself into a king every evening.

THE ACTOR: But in this new theatre it looks as though I'll be free to transform my spectators into kings. And not just pretend ones, but the real thing. And into statesmen, thinkers and engineers. What an audience I'll have! I'll hold up what goes on in the world for their judgement. And what a noble, useful and celebrated place my theatre will be, once it's become a laboratory for all these working people. I too will act according to the classic principle: change the world, it needs it!

THE STAGE HAND: It sounds a bit pompous. But why shouldn't it, if a great cause is behind it?

Miscellaneous Texts

(i) Illusionism, Realism, Naturalism; Social Function of Theatre; Empathy

B100
1939–41

ILLUSION AND HYPOTHESIS

PHILOSOPHER: The illusion of a particular location arises when the elements of that location are copied seamlessly with visual (and acoustic) accuracy, and the elements of the theatre are concealed. However, illusion can also be produced when the actors show very convincing reactions to things which are not present on stage.

ACTOR: True. When I'm playing Macbeth on the heath – i.e. the empty stage – then if I show enough dread, glance wildly from side to side, and spin round as if I thought there was something behind me, you'll clearly be able to see a heath.

B124
1942–3

THE PHILOSOPHER: But even when the spectators can empathize with such heroes or share their mental perspective, that still doesn't mean they will be able to master reality. Just because I can immerse myself in Napoleon doesn't mean I become him!

THE ACTOR: No, but you feel as though you're him.

DRAMATURG: Realism's for the scrap-heap too, I see.

PHILOSOPHER: That's not what we were talking about though, is it? It's just that what you labelled 'realism' doesn't seem to have been realism at all. People simply attached the label 'realistic' to things that were nothing more than photographic reproductions of reality. By this definition Naturalism was more realistic than so-called realism. Then a new element was introduced: mastering reality. This element led to the disintegration of Naturalism, which had been the only basis for people's talk of realism.

DRAMATURG: What went wrong?

THE PHILOSOPHER: You can't give a realistic portrayal of the characters you are making available for empathy (e.g. the hero) without making it impossible for the spectator to empathize with them. A realistic portrayal would mean that they have to change with events, which would make them too erratic to empathize with, and they must also be given a very limited viewpoint, which would inevitably mean that the spectator who shared it would lack an overall perspective.

DRAMATURG: So realism in the theatre is completely impossible!

PHILOSOPHER: That's not what I'm saying. The problem is that making reality recognizable in the theatre is just one of the tasks of true realism. You still need to be able to see through this reality, though. The laws that determine how the processes of life develop must be made visible. These laws aren't visible in photographs.* Nor are they visible if the spectators simply borrow the eyes or hearts of the characters involved in these processes.

---

* The Philosopher is referring to Brecht's critique of photographic realism in *The Threepenny Lawsuit*, in *Brecht on Film and Radio*, pp. 164–5. See also Giles, *Bertolt Brecht and Critical Theory*, chapters 6 and 7.

B125
1942–3

Tragic impact no longer arises (i.e. a noticeable lack of tragic impact becomes apparent) once the great round-up has lost its fatalistic character and come within range of society. Rose Bernd's tragedy doesn't work any more in the old way, now that the ban on abortion is being disputed and the divine law 'Thou shalt not kill' conflicts with a potential human recommendation: 'Thou shalt not subject thy child to an environment that will kill it.'*

---

* On Brecht's sociological critique of tragedy in relation to Naturalism see also 'Key Points in Korsch', *Brecht on Art and Politics*, pp. 109–11. Brecht's review of Gerhart Hauptmann's *Rose Bernd* (1903) at the Augsburger Stadttheater appeared in *Der Volkswille* on 1 October 1920 (see BFA 21, p. 75).

B168
c. 1945

ACTOR: It's one of the greatest achievements of the arts, however, that their representations are not made according to the requirements of utility, conforming to the moral demands of the age or endorsing its dominant attitudes.

DRAMATURG: Wait a minute! Even if these representations don't endorse the dominant attitudes – if they ignore the attitudes of those in positions of dominance, in other words – they can still follow the requirements of utility. It might even make it easier for them to do so.

ACTOR: The arts go further, though, or less far, if you like. They're able to make something enjoyable from the power, beauty and majesty of the torrential river that can flood whole villages. They find enjoyment in observing asocial individuals, in showing the murderer's vitality, the fraudster's cunning, the Harpies' beauty.

PHILOSOPHER: That's fine; such disorder is in order – as long as the flooded villages are not concealed, the murderer's victims are not blamed, the fraud is not condoned and the Harpy's claw is not portrayed as just an ingenious tool, then it's all fine.

ACTOR: I can't play the butcher *and* the sheep.

DRAMATURG: You're not the only person in the company, you know.

PHILOSOPHER: You can't portray both butcher and sheep simultaneously, but you can portray the butcher of the sheep, I fancy.

ACTOR: I'll either be appealing to the mutton-eater in my spectator or to the person who's in debt to the bank.

PHILOSOPHER: Mutton-eaters can be debtors too.

ACTOR: True, but you can't appeal to both qualities at once. No, I'm addressing the individual solely as a member of the whole of humanity. Humanity as a whole is interested in vitality in and of itself, irrespective of what its effects may be.

(The arts free of moral obligations)

B148
c. 1945

Are the magicians not great? Do they not cast their spell over everyone? They do not allow anybody to feel differently from how they feel, they infect everybody with their own thoughts. Isn't that great art? The hypnotism is skilfully done, certainly – perhaps even artistically – and perhaps we can still class it as art when the magicians put themselves into a trance; the experience they create, however, is an inferior one, and it enfeebles and degrades people.

See, with marvellous movements
The magician pulls a rabbit from the hat
But the rabbit breeder too
Could make marvellous movements.

Take a stick on to the stage and hit them on the calves with it while they're conjuring, and all their power will be gone. For their muscles are tensed to the point of cramp: that's how difficult it is to make us believe the unbelievable, to pass off stupidity as intelligence, baseness as superiority, and window dressing as real beauty.

B160
c. 1945

At a time when the playwrights were constructing long, tranquil, soulful acts and you could get good opera-glasses from the opticians, there was a huge rise in the use of facial expressions on stage. There was a lot going on in the actors' faces now, they had become mirrors for the soul and thus had to be held as still as possible, which meant that gestures fell by the wayside. Feelings were what mattered – the body was simply a container for the soul. Actors' facial expressions changed from one night to the next, they could not be guaranteed, and were influenced by a whole host of things. But even less organization was evident in the gestures, which seemed to matter almost as little as those of the musicians in the orchestra, who also execute a wide variety of gestures as they play. The actors improvised, or at least tried to give that impression. The Russian school designed exercises of its own, which were supposed to enable the actors to keep this spirit of improvisation alive throughout the whole run of a play. But still people memorized particular tones which had worked for them on a particular occasion, by 'justifying' these tones or expressions – in other words by analysing them, giving reasons for them and finding adjectives for them.

B161
c. 1945

THE ACTOR: Surely you're not telling me I'm supposed to imitate a character without first having put myself in that character's shoes?

THE PHILOSOPHER: A number of operations are needed to construct a character. Most of the time you're not imitating people you've seen, but individuals that you have to imagine before you can imitate them. You start with whatever you can infer from the lines you've been given, the actions and reactions laid down for you, and the situations in which your character is supposed to develop. You'll probably have to put yourself in your characters' shoes over and over again, to imagine yourself into their situation and physicality and way of thinking. It's one of the operations involved in constructing the character. It's entirely consistent with our purposes, just as long as you know how to take yourself back out of the character again. There's a big difference between having an idea of something, which requires imagination, and having an illusion of something, which requires ignorance. For our purposes we need imagination; we don't want to create illusions, but to give our spectators too an idea of an event.

THE ACTOR: I reckon you've got an exaggerated view – almost an illusion – of how deeply we actors of the old theatre empathize with the characters we play. I can assure you that when we're playing King Lear we're thinking about all kinds of things Lear is very unlikely to have thought about.

THE PHILOSOPHER: I don't doubt that – that you think about how you can create this effect and avoid that one, etc. And whether this or that prop has been put in the right place and whether or not the comedian is suddenly going to start waggling his ears again in the middle of your big speech. But all these thoughts are devoted to making sure the audience doesn't awake from its illusion. They may interfere with your empathy, but they only deepen the audience's. And it matters far more to me that the latter should be prevented than that yours should not be interfered with.

THE ACTOR: You mean we should only be trying to get inside our characters at rehearsals and not during the performance?

THE PHILOSOPHER: That's rather an awkward question to answer. I could just say you shouldn't try and get inside your character during the performance. I'd certainly be entitled to. Firstly because I made a distinction between empathizing with and getting inside a character, secondly because I really do believe that empathy is completely unnecessary, but most of all because I'd be afraid that any other answer, whatever it was, might open up the very can of worms I've just sealed shut. I'm still reluctant to say it, though. I can imagine borderline cases in which empathy could occur without any harm being done. There are a series of precautions you could take in order to prevent harmful results. The empathy would have to be discontinuous and only occur at specific junctures, or else be very, very weak and mixed with other more forceful operations. I have actually seen acting of that sort before. It was at the last in a long run of rehearsals, everyone was tired, the aim was simply to memorize lines and positions, the actors moved mechanically and spoke their lines quietly. I was pleased with the resulting effect, but couldn't be completely sure whether the actors were empathizing or not. I have to say, though, that the actors would never have dared to act like that in front of an audience, in such an unaccentuated way and with so little attention to the effect they were producing (because they were concentrating so much on 'externals'), so it's likely that the empathy, if there was any, only failed to jar because the acting lacked vitality. In other words: if I could be sure that you'd still be able to perceive the enormous difference between the new kind of acting and the old kind, which is based on complete empathy, as no less enormous if I were to concede the possibility of a quite small degree of empathy, then I would do so. But I'd still judge your mastery according to how little empathy you can get by with, and not (as is usually the case) according to how much you can generate.

THE DRAMATURG: So we might perhaps say that just as people who can't generate empathy are labelled amateurs nowadays, there may come a time when people will be labelled amateurs if they can't do without empathy? You don't need to worry. You haven't made your method of acting seem any less strange to us by your judicious admission.

(ii) Acting

B154
c. 1945

'THE ACTOR'S SPEECH ABOUT HOW TO PORTRAY A LITTLE NAZI'.
FROM *BUYING BRASS*

In accordance with our rules of thumb, I didn't try to make the character unfathomable in order to make him interesting; I tried instead to generate interest in his fathomability. My job was to depict this man in a way that would make it easier for our theatre's audience (which represents society) to deal with him, so naturally I had to portray him as a basically alterable personality. To this end the new type of dramatic art we've been discussing came in very useful. I had to generate insights into the character that would make visible as many as possible of the influences society had had on him at various times. I also had to give some idea of the extent to which he would be alterable under given circumstances, because society is not always in a position to mobilize its forces to alter each of its members in such a way that they immediately become useful; sometimes it has to make do with rendering one of its members harmless. At any rate, I certainly couldn't contemplate creating anything like a 'born Nazi'. What I had in front of me was something contradictory, a kind of atom of the people who were the enemy of the people: the little Nazi, acting as part of the masses against the interests of the masses, a brute perhaps when among Nazis, or a bigger brute when among the Nazis, yet at the same time a normal person – a human being, in other words.[1] Being part of the masses gave him a certain anonymity, let him share the characteristics of a group together with his own quite individual traits. It's a family like any other, and at the same time it's not a family like any other. I had to make every step he took an explicable one, and at the same time I had to suggest a different step he could take, one which would also be explicable. People should not be treated as if they could only behave 'this' way; they can always behave differently. The houses have fallen down, but they could still be standing.

B155
c. 1945

THE PHILOSOPHER: The main reason why actors must be clearly distanced from the characters they portray is this: in order to show spectators how to approach a character, or to show people who resemble the character (or are in a similar situation to the one the character is in) how best to solve their problems, actors need to adopt a standpoint which lies not only outside the sphere of their character but also at a more advanced stage of its evolution. The classics say that apes can be best understood by looking at human beings, their successors in the evolutionary chain.*

* The Philosopher is referring to Engels' essay 'The Part Played by Labour in the Transition from Ape to Man'/'Anteil der Arbeit an der Menschwerdung des Affen', first published in *Die Neue Zeit* (XIV, 1895–6).

B156
c. 1945

THE ACTOR: So what we should be trying to show is things like *this-far-and-no-further* or *no-further-but-this-far*. That's a bit different from the old sort of ranting which knows no bounds and always ends in ruin. There's an element of *relativity* there which you want us always to take into account. And of course it cannot have as powerful an effect as what is absolute. If I depict a man as relatively ambitious, people are hardly likely to be grabbed

---

[1] The whole thing is brutal, but the whole is more than the sum of its parts. The older ones were in it for what they could get, but there may well have been a kind of half-stifled social idealism in the younger ones.

by it in the same way as if I showed him to be completely consumed by ambition.

THE PHILOSOPHER: But in real life it's more common for people to be relatively ambitious than completely consumed by ambition, isn't it?

THE ACTOR: Maybe. But what about the impact we want to make?

THE PHILOSOPHER: You have to achieve it using something that's more likely to happen in real life. That's up to you to sort out.

THE ACTOR: A fine Macbeth that would make: ambitious one minute, unambitious the next, and only relatively more ambitious than Duncan.* And your Hamlet: very hesitant, but also very prone to impetuous actions, eh? And Clytemnestra: quite vindictive.** Romeo: fairly in love!

THE DRAMATURG: Yes, more or less. You needn't laugh. In Shakespeare, Romeo's in love before he's even seen Juliet. After that he's more in love.

THE ACTOR: Ha, a bursting scrotum! As if other people apart from Romeo didn't have that problem, and they're no Romeos.

THE PHILOSOPHER: All the same, Romeo does have one. It's a great feat of realism on Shakespeare's part to have noticed that.

THE ACTOR: And the fascination of Richard III: how can I illustrate that except by completely filling the character with it?

THE DRAMATURG: You mean, in the scene where he so fascinates the widow of the man he's murdered that she ends up falling for him?*** I can see two solutions. You either show that she's doing it out of sheer terror, or else you make her ugly. But however you show this fascination, it won't do you any good unless you can show how it fails him later in the play. So you need to show a relative power of fascination.

THE GUEST: Oh, you show that already. But in the same way that a trumpeter shows brass or an apple tree in winter shows snow. You're confusing two things: showing something, and having people come across it.

* Macbeth murders Duncan, King of Scotland in Act II of *Macbeth*.
** Clytemnestra murders her husband Agamemnon in *Agamemnon*, the first part of Aeschylus' trilogy *The Oresteia* (458 BC).
*** See *Richard III*, Act I, Scene 2.

B146
c. 1945

The Augsburger filmed Weigel putting on her make-up. He cut the film, and each individual frame showed a complete facial expression, self-contained and with its own meaning. 'You can see what kind of an actress she is,' he said admiringly. 'Every gesture can be broken up into any number of other gestures, all of which are complete in themselves. Everything is there both for its own sake and for the sake of something else. The jump is beautiful but so is the run-up.' What seemed to matter most to him, however, was that every movement of her muscles as she put on her make-up produced a complete expression of a psychological state. The people he showed these snapshots to, asking them what the various expressions meant, guessed such things as anger, gaiety, envy, compassion. He showed them to Weigel too, telling her that she only needed to know her own expressions in order to be able to express these emotional states without always having to experience them.

B149
c. 1945

ACTORS DESCRIBE WHAT DRAMATIC ART IS FOR

– it's to defend nature. But of course there's more to it than that.
– it's to affect nature. Nature is alterable. But that's not all.
– it's to show how people *really* are, what *really* happens to them. At least that's part of it.
– it's to contradict; to confirm, to copy, to change; to show oneself, to hide away; to clarify, to conceal, to simplify, to complete; and many other goals besides.

B167
c. 1945

ON ACTORS READING ALOUD

When actors read aloud, the most important gestus for them to produce is the *Reading-aloud-from-a-book* gestus. They need to construct the reader's relationship to the book, to every book and to this one in particular and so on and so forth, depending on the circumstances. And then the everyday, artless process of reading aloud needs to be used as a basis: somebody finds something in a book (or maybe a newspaper, or a letter) and wants others to enjoy it. Such a person will be in full control of their subject matter, according to what interests him or her, racing through the introductory or connecting text and emphasizing what seems important by virtue of its form or content. This person will not create a *Gesamtkunstwerk,** and will almost certainly not want to generate illusion where there is only reportage.

> * Compare Brecht's criticism of the Wagnerian *Gesamtkunstwerk* in the *Short Organon for the Theatre*, section 74: 'So let us invite all the sister arts of dramatic art to join us here, not in order to produce a *Gesamtkunstwerk* in which they all offer themselves up and disappear, but instead, together with dramatic art, to further the common task in their different ways, and their dealings with one another consist in the fact that they mutually estrange one another' (in *Brecht on Theatre*).

B170*
1948–55

THE DRAMATURG'S SPEECH
(FROM *BUYING BRASS*)

Parts are allotted wrongly and thoughtlessly. As though all cooks were fat, all peasants phlegmatic, all statesmen stately. As though all who love and all who are loved were beautiful. As though all good orators had fine voices!

Of course, there are many things to consider. This Mephisto and this Gretchen will go well with this particular Faust. Some actors are difficult to imagine as princes; there are many different types of prince, but they have at the very least all been brought up to command; and Hamlet is a prince among thousands.

And actors also need to be able to develop. Here we have a young man who will make a better Troilus once he has played Clerk Mitteldorf.** There we have an actress who doesn't have the lasciviousness needed for the Gretchen of the final act: will she be able to acquire it by playing Cressida, whose situations demand it – or Grusha, whose situations rule it out completely?

It's a fact that any actor will be better suited to some parts than to others. And yet it is dangerous for an actor only ever to play one particular character type. Only the most talented actors are capable of portraying different characters who closely resemble one another – twins, so to speak, recognizable as such and yet easily distinguishable.

It's very foolish to allot parts according to physical characteristics. 'He has a kingly figure!' What does that mean? Do all kings have to look like Edward VII? 'But he lacks a commanding presence!' How many ways of commanding are there, one might ask? 'She looks too genteel for Mother Courage.' Take a look at the fishwives!

Can you go by disposition? No, you can't. That too would be taking the easy way out.

It's true that there are gentle people and there are irascible, violent ones. But it's also true that every person possesses every sort of disposition. And the more of an actor the person happens to be, the truer that statement is. And the dispositions the person is suppressing, once they are drawn out, will often prove to have a particularly powerful impact. Moreover, parts conceived on a large scale (even the smaller ones among them) not only display strongly marked features, but also have room for additions; they resemble maps with blank patches. Actors need to cultivate all the dispositions they possess, because their characters come to life only by dint of their own contradictoriness. It is very dangerous to cast a major part on the strength of a single characteristic.

* B170 also includes 'The Playwright's Speech about the Theatre of the Set Designer Caspar Neher', pp. 116–18 below.
**Clerk Mitteldorf is a character in Gerhart Hauptmann's *Der Biberpelz* (1893).

(iii) *Thaëter*, Piscator, Neher

B103
1939–41

THE *THAËTER*

PHILOSOPHER: As we've seen, our *thaëter* is going to be vastly different from the ubiquitous, tried-and-tested, illustrious and indispensable institution that is the theatre. One important difference, it may reassure you to learn, is the fact that the *thaëter* is not going to stay open for all eternity. It is meant only as a remedy for the ills of the time, of our own time in particular – which is, undeniably, a pretty bleak one.

B115*
c. 1945

THE PHILOSOPHER: Let's look into it! In principle I'd very much like to stick with a theatre, because people are used to it and would reap significant benefits from my performances. Only out of extreme necessity would I establish a *thaëter*.

* BFA locates this text incorrectly at the end of the opening scene of *Buying Brass* (BFA 22, p. 80); see Bertolt Brecht Archive, Mappe 127, sheet 52.

B104
1939–41

ACTOR: This whole notion of practicable definitions strikes me as a bit cool and austere. All we'll be offering people is solved problems.

DRAMATURG: And unsolved ones as well!

ACTOR: Yes, but only so that they too can be solved! That isn't life any more. Some may choose to see life as a web of solved – or unsolved – problems, but there's a lot more to life than problems. Life has its unproblematic side too, not to mention all the problems out there that *can't* be solved! I want to do more than play charades.

DRAMATURG: I can understand him. He wants to 'dig deep'. He wants a mixture of the expected and the unexpected, the comprehensible and the incomprehensible. He wants to mix applause with terror, gaiety with sorrow. In short, he wants to make art.

B105
1939–41

THE PHILOSOPHER: The opponents of the proletariat are not a uniform, reactionary mass. Nor are the individual members of the opposing classes a uniform, cut-and-dried or entirely hostile body. The class struggle has got inside them. They are torn apart by their interests. Living among the masses they are bound to share the interests of the masses, however isolated they are. At the Soviet film *Battleship Potemkin* there were even some bourgeois who joined in with the workers' applause when the sailors threw their oppressors, the officers, overboard.* Although this middle class had been protected from the social revolution by its officer caste, it had never managed to assimilate this caste. It lived in fear of and constantly experienced 'incursions' – against itself. On occasion, the bourgeois joined the proletarians in voting against feudalism. And when they did, these bourgeois came into genuine and thrilling contact with the progressive elements in human society, the prole-tarian elements; they felt themselves to be part of humanity as a whole, as it solved certain problems on a grand and gigantic scale. This shows that art can create a certain unity in its audience, which in our age is divided into classes.

---

* The Philosopher is referring to Sergei Eisenstein's film *Battleship Potemkin* (1925), set in the 1905 Russian Revolution, and first shown in Germany in 1926.

B147

c. 1945

Many people assume that a human being is the finished article, looking like this in one light and like that in another, saying this in one situation and that in another; and so right from the start they attempt to grasp this figure and to become it completely. But it's better to see a human being as an unfinished article, one who should be allowed to develop gradually, from utterance to utterance and action to action. You may well ask yourselves, as you study your parts, what kind of a person says this and that in such and such a situation, but you also need to be aware of, and build upon, the fact that the specific human being will only have developed and come into view when all of his or her utterances and actions, in logical sequence, are portrayed in an expressive and a believable way.

> By saying yes, by saying no
> By hitting, by being hit
> By consorting with these people and consorting with those people
> That's how human beings are formed, by changing
> And that's how their image develops within us
> By resembling us and by not resembling us.

Does that mean, you ask, that we shouldn't portray a person who always stays the same by way of behaving differently in different situations? But then shouldn't it be a specific person who changes, in a specific way, differently from the way someone else changes? The answer is that you will end up with a specific person, as long as you do everything in the right order and keep thinking back to people you yourselves have observed. So many things are possible; a specific person may change in a specific way and remain as that specific person for a long time, and then one day turn into a different specific person, that sort of thing can happen. But what you really mustn't do is aim for one single incarnation in which everything is present right from the start and which simply plays its cards as occasion demands. Just deal with everything in the right order, study everything, be surprised by everything, make everything easy and probable, and you'll end up with a human being – you're human beings yourselves, after all.

B164

c. 1945

THE DRAMATURG: You assign a very important role to reason. It's as if you don't want to accept anything that hasn't passed through the filter of the brain. I don't think artists have less reasoning power than other people (as some believe), but they have more to work with than just their reason. If you're only going to let through things they've registered in their brains and assigned an entry permit to, then not much is going to make it on to the stage.

THE PHILOSOPHER: There's some truth in that. People do a lot of things that are reasonable without having reasoned them through first. It's more or less inevitable. You have to take instinct into account, and those behaviours which consist of an intractable tangle of highly varied and contradictory motives and efforts. I don't see any danger in pouring them on to the stage in ladlefuls. The important thing is to present them in such a way that they are open to examination – an examination which may well also have something instinctive and complex about it. There are other ways of positioning things, as you know.

THE DRAMATURG: Perhaps we could talk a little bit about the moral aspect, whereby things are labelled 'good' or 'bad'. Does everything need to carry those labels?

THE PHILOSOPHER: What a terrible idea! That would be the height of folly. Artists are naturally bound to feel some kind of love for human beings. Because they delight in humanity, artists can reach a point where even wicked impulses delight them – that is to say those impulses which, rightly or wrongly, are deemed harmful to society. I think it is enough for you to represent the point of view of society in its broadest possible sense, i.e. not just that of some particular transient social form. You don't have to persecute the individual human being, who is so often persecuted. You must keep the whole in mind, and make sure the spectator does as well.

B163
c. 1945

DRAMATURG: Doesn't the *Surrealist* movement in painting also use *Verfremdung* techniques?

PHILOSOPHER: Absolutely. These complex and sophisticated painters are the primitives, so to speak, of a new art form. They try to shock their observers by hampering, confusing and disappointing their associations – by attaching eyes instead of fingers to a woman's hand, for instance. Whether this has to do with symbolism (a woman seeing with her hands) or whether it's just a matter of her extremities not conforming to expectations, a certain degree of shock is produced, and both hand and eye are estranged. The very fact that the hand is no longer a hand gives rise to a concept of *hand* which has more to do with the everyday function of this instrument than that aesthetic decoration we've seen on ten thousand canvases. Admittedly, such pictures are often just reacting against the incomplete lack of functionality of people and things in this day and age; in other words, they are evidence of a serious functional breakdown. Further evidence of this functional breakdown is the way people complain about everything having to have a function – everything being a means and not an end, in other words.

DRAMATURG: And why do you say this is a primitive use of the V-effect?

PHILOSOPHER: Because the function of this art is also inhibited in societal terms, so that art too simply ceases to function here. What you end up with in terms of artistic effect is amusement brought about by the aforementioned shock.

B145
c. 1945

EASE

Once you have finished your work, it should have a quality of ease. This ease should bring to mind effort: it is effort overcome, or victorious effort. As soon as you begin work you should adopt the attitude that will help you achieve this quality of ease. You shouldn't skip over difficulties but collect them and, through your work, make light of them. Because only the ease that arises from victorious effort is of any value.

> See the ease
> With which the mighty river
> Rips through the dams!
> The earthquake
> Shakes the earth with unconcerned hand.
> The terrible fire
> Reaches gracefully for the city with its many buildings
> And consumes it comfortably
> A practised eater.

There is an attitude of beginning which may help you in your pursuit of ease. It can be learned. You know that mastery means having learned how to learn. When you want to exert all your strength, you must use it sparingly. You must not do what you are not capable of doing, nor do yet what you are not yet capable of. You need to split up your tasks in such a way that the various parts can be dealt with easily, for you will never attain ease through overexertion.

Oh, the joy of beginning! Oh early morning!
First grass, when green seems
Forgotten! Oh astonishing first page of the book
That was expected! Read
Slowly: all too quickly
The pages not yet turned will dwindle! And the first splash of water
On the sweating face! The fresh,
Cool shirt! Oh, the beginning of love! The wandering gaze!
Oh, the beginning of work! Filling the cold machine
With oil! First grip of the handle, first purr
Of the motor starting! And first drag
Of smoke, filling the lungs! And you
New thought!

B153
c. 1945

ON THE SUBJECT OF EASE

THE PHILOSOPHER: However much we may wish to relinquish what's considered essential to the art of theatre in order to further our new aims, there's one thing I think we must preserve at all costs, and that is theatre's quality of ease. It can't do us any harm, whereas if we relinquished it we would be forced to overstretch and spoil our resources. Theatre has, by its very nature, the quality of ease. This business of putting on make-up and adopting rehearsed positions, this reproduction of the world with so few points of reference, this giving an idea of life, these punch-lines and abbreviations – all this must retain its natural gaiety if it is not to become silly. Such ease makes any amount of seriousness achievable; without ease, none at all is possible. And so we need to put all our problems into a form which allows them to be performed and discussed, in a playful way. It's a delicate balance we're dealing with here – we have to make measured, elegant movements, oblivious to the ground burning beneath our feet. It may seem almost offensive that we are sitting here, at a time when bloody wars are being fought, and discussing – but not for the purposes of escapism – the kind of theatrical issues that seem to owe their existence to our need for distraction. Tomorrow we might all be blown to bits! But we are focusing on the theatre precisely because we want to turn it into another instrument to help us conduct our business. The urgency of our situation must not lead us to destroy the instrument we want to make use of. It's a case of more haste, less speed. The surgeon who carries a heavy burden of responsibility needs to hold the small scalpel effortlessly in his hand. The world is out of joint, certainly, and it will take powerful movements to set it right again. But among the various instruments that could be used for this purpose, one of them may be slight and delicate, and needs to be handled effortlessly.

B106
1939–41

THE AUGSBURGER'S RELATIONSHIP TO PISCATOR

Piscator was making political theatre before the Augsburger. He had taken part in the war, whereas the Augsburger hadn't. The revolution of 1918, which both of them had been involved in, had caused the Augsburger to become disillusioned and turned Piscator into a politician.* It was only later that the Augsburger came to politics through study. When they first started working together, they each had a theatre: Piscator had one of his own on Nollendorfplatz, and the Augsburger had one on the Schiffbauerdamm, where he trained his actors. The Augsburger reworked most of Piscator's major plays for him, and he also wrote scenes for them – on one occasion a whole act. *Schweik* was entirely his doing. Piscator, in turn, supported the Augsburger and came to his rehearsals. Both preferred to work collectively. They had collaborators in common, such as the musician Eisler and the graphic artist Grosz.** They both brought great artists to work with amateur actors and produced revues for the workers. Although Piscator never wrote a play himself – he hardly ever wrote so much as a scene – the Augsburger still deemed him the only competent dramatist there was, apart from him. Hasn't Piscator proved, he said, that it is also possible to produce plays by putting together a montage of scenes and sketches by other writers, drawing inspiration from them and furnishing them with documents and scenic extravaganzas? It is the Augsburger who must be credited with formulating the actual theory of non-Aristotelian theatre and with developing the V-effect, but Piscator utilized a lot of this too, and in a completely independent and original way. Above all, the theatre's conversion to politics was Piscator's achievement, and without this conversion the Augsburger's theatre would scarcely be conceivable.

* Piscator was a radio operator on the Western Front in the First World War, Brecht a medical orderly in Augsburg. Brecht's second play *Drums in the Night* (1922) thematized the German Revolution of November 1918 to January 1919; for Brecht's subsequent views on *Drums in the Night* see the 'Prologue to *Drums*' (written 1926), *Brecht on Theatre*.
** Some of the claims made in this account of the Augsburger's relationship to Piscator are misleading. Brecht did not rework most of Piscator's major plays for him, nor was *Schweik* entirely his doing. Hašek's *Schweik* was produced by Piscator in an adaptation by Max Brod and Hans Reimann in 1928; although Brecht worked on it, he was never

credited with the play. Brecht was also involved in Piscator's productions of *Rasputin* (1927) and Leo Lania's *Boom* (1928). George Grosz never designed a Brecht play or production, but he did illustrate his poem *The Three Soldiers* (1931).

B152
c. 1945

'PISCATOR'S THEATRE'
FROM *BUYING BRASS*

THE DRAMATURG: Piscator's theatre was funded by a brewer and the owner of a cinema – one had an actress girlfriend, the other was just socially ambitious – and it was frequented almost exclusively by the upper middle class, proletarians and intellectuals. The stalls were very expensive and the gallery very cheap; some of the proletarian spectators bought season tickets. This section of the audience placed a heavy financial burden on the theatre, because the sets were hugely expensive due to all the machinery they incorporated. It was an up-to-date theatre, not only when dealing with topical questions but also when engaging with problems of epochal significance. A collective of playwrights used to conduct a sort of non-stop discussion on the stage, and this discussion continued throughout that great city in the newspapers, salons, cafés and pubs. There was no theatrical censorship, and social antagonisms were stark – and becoming ever more so. The upper middle class feared the Junkers,* who still held the highest offices in the army and the state administration, and the workers were fighting petty-bourgeois tendencies within their own parties. Piscator's theatre provided them with object-lessons. It illustrated how the 1918 revolution had failed, how competition for markets and raw materials had started wars, how reluctant peoples had been used to fight these wars, and how successful revolutions had been achieved. The theatre itself, as an artistic institution, altered drastically with each new task it undertook; at times it didn't have much to do with art at all. The insertion of all kinds of illustrative material tore apart the plot and character development, and everyday language alternated jarringly with declamation, theatre with film, acting with lecturing. The backdrop, which had once been a stationary extra – and in neighbouring theatres still was – became the star of the theatre, hogging the limelight. It consisted of a cinema screen. Shots of current events, taken from cinema newsreels, were cut together into meaningful arrangements to provide the documentary material. Even the stage floor was set in motion. Two moving belts powered by motors made it possible to stage street scenes. There were speaking and singing choruses on the stage. The plans for a production were just as important as the finished article, or rather the half-finished one, as nobody ever saw anything that was completely finished. I've got a couple of examples. For a play illustrating the cruelty of the abortion law,** a certain building in a slum district was to be reproduced on the stage in such precise detail as to show every single burst pipe. In the intervals the audience was to come on stage and inspect it closely. For a play about the Chinese revolution*** the plan was to have several large banners mounted on poles and painted with short captions about the situation ('The textile workers go on strike'; 'Revolutionary meetings among the small farmers'; 'Shopkeepers buying weapons', etc.). They were supposed to have inscriptions on the back as well, so that they could be turned round to show other slogans as a background to the incidents on the stage ('Strike collapses'; 'Small farmers forming armed squads', etc.), indicating the new situation. This was a way of getting people to recognize the continually changing nature of situations, of showing how one circumstance may persist even after another has already changed, and so on.[1]

Piscator was one of the greatest theatre people of all time. He electrified the theatre, and rendered it capable of tackling major themes. He didn't have as little interest in acting as his enemies claimed, but he did have less than he himself made out. Perhaps he didn't share their interests because they didn't share his. At any rate, he didn't provide them with a new style, even if he himself wasn't all that bad an actor, especially in minor, sharply etched roles. He permitted several different acting styles on his stage at the same time, and didn't appear to have a particular preference for any of them. He found it easier to tackle major themes critically using ingenious and grandiose scenic extravaganzas than by using the art of acting. He only demonstrated his love of machinery, for which he was criticized by many and thought a little too highly of by some, when it allowed him to use his scenic imagination. He had a real feeling for simplicity – which also led him to describe the Augsburger's acting style as the one that came closest to fulfilling his own intentions – as simplicity was consistent with his goal: to lay bare the workings of the world

---

[1] When it came to the performance, this system of moveable captions was not put into practice. The paper flags did have writing on both sides, but only so that they could be swapped over between scenes and be used twice. During the first performance Piscator and the Augsburger walked around outside, as is usual on first nights, and talked about what had been achieved at rehearsal and what hadn't worked – they were more or less ignorant of what was going on in the theatre, as much had been changed at the last minute and was now having to be improvised. In the course of this conversation they discovered the principle of the system of moveable captions, its possibilities for dramatic art and its significance for acting. So these experiments often produced results that the audience never got to see, due to lack of time and money, but they nevertheless made subsequent work easier and did at least change the views of the experimenters themselves.

on a grand scale and to reproduce them in such a way that they could be more easily manipulated.

* The Junkers were aristocratic landowners who tended to have reactionary political views.
** Carl Credé, *§281. Women in Distress*, performed at the Wallner Theatre, Berlin, 1930; see Piscator, *The Political Theatre*, p. 341.
*** Friedrich Wolf, *Tai Yang Awakes*, performed at the Wallner Theatre, Berlin, 1931; see Piscator, *The Political Theatre*, pp. 343–4.

B170
1948–55

THE PLAYWRIGHT'S SPEECH ABOUT THE THEATRE OF THE SET
DESIGNER CASPAR NEHER
(FROM: *BUYING BRASS*)

Sometimes we start rehearsing without knowing anything about what the set is going to look like, and our friend simply produces for us little sketches of the incidents to be portrayed (for instance, six people grouped around a working-class woman who is upbraiding them).* We may then find that in the text there are only actually five people altogether, because our friend is not a pedant, but he shows us what really matters, and this sort of sketch is always a delicate little work of art. Whereabouts on the stage the woman, her son, and her visitors should sit is something we find out for ourselves, and our friend then seats them in those positions when he comes to construct the set. Sometimes we get his designs beforehand, and then he helps us with the blocking and the gestures, and quite often with characterization too, including the way the characters speak. His set is imbued with the spirit of the play, and fires the actor's ambition to be part of it.

He reads plays in a masterly fashion. Take just one example. In Act I, Scene 6 of *Macbeth*, Duncan and his general Banquo, invited by Macbeth to his castle, praise it in the famous lines:

… This guest of summer,
The temple-haunting martlet, does approve
By his lov'd mansionry, that the heaven's breath
Smells wooingly here …

Neher insisted on a half-ruined grey castle of striking poverty. The guests' words of praise were merely courtesies. He saw the Macbeths as petty Scottish nobility, and pathologically ambitious!**

His sets are meaningful statements about reality. He takes a bold sweep, not letting inessential detail or decoration distract from the statement, which is an artistic and an intellectual one. At the same time everything is beautiful, and the essential detail is lovingly crafted.

How carefully he selects a chair, and how thoughtfully he positions it! And it all benefits the performance. You'll get a chair with short legs, and the height of the table it stands at will have been carefully calculated, so that whoever eats at it has to adopt a specific position, and the conversation of these people, forced to bend over more than usual as they eat, acquires a special character, one which makes the incident clearer. And the sheer number of effects he can achieve using his doors of quite different heights!

This is a master of all crafts, who makes sure that the furniture is artistically made, even the shabbiest pieces, for the emblems of poverty and cheapness must be crafted with artistry. Thus materials like iron, wood and canvas are expertly handled and correctly combined, economically or lavishly, as the play demands. He goes to the blacksmith's shop to get the bent swords forged, and to the nurseryman's to get tin wreaths cut and woven. Many of the props are museum pieces.

These small objects he puts in the actors' hands – the weapons, instruments, purses, cutlery, etc. – are always authentic, and will pass the closest inspection; but when it comes to architecture (when this master constructs interiors or outdoor spaces, in other words) he is content to give indications, artistic and poetic portrayals of a hut or a locality which do as much credit to his powers of observation as they do to his imagination. They display a lovely mixture of his own handwriting and that of the playwright. And there is not one of his buildings, yards, workshops or gardens that does not also bear the fingerprints, so to speak, of the people who built it or who lived there. He makes visible the technical skills and knowledge of the builders, and the way of life of the inhabitants.

In his designs our friend always starts from 'people themselves' and 'what is happening to or through them'. He provides no 'sets', no frames or backgrounds, but constructs the space within which 'people' experience something. Almost all of what usually constitutes the set designer's trade – the aesthetic and stylistic aspects – he can do standing on his head. Of course Shakespeare's Rome was different from Racine's. He builds the dramatists' stage and it sparkles.[1] He can, if he chooses, achieve a richer effect with a varying structure of different greys and whites than many other artists can manage using the whole palette. He is a great painter. But more than anything he is an ingenious storyteller. He knows better than

---

[1]   The poverty of our lighting arrangements means, unfortunately, that the brilliance of Neher's sets cannot be reproduced photographically.

anyone that anything that doesn't contribute to a story is harmful to it. He is always content, therefore, to limit himself to hints when dealing with anything that 'doesn't play a part'. But these hints are stimulating. They activate the spectator's imagination, which would be paralysed by a 'perfect' reproduction.

He often makes use of a device that has since become common property internationally and been largely robbed of its significance. It is the division of the stage into two sections, within which arrangement a room, courtyard or workplace is constructed at half-height downstage while another environment is projected or painted behind it, changing with every scene or remaining in place throughout the play. This second milieu may consist of documentary material or a picture or tapestry. Such an arrangement naturally enriches the narrative and at the same time acts as a constant reminder to the spectators that the set designer has built a set: he sees things differently from the way they are outside the theatre.

This method, for all its flexibility, is of course just one of the many that he uses; his sets differ from one another as much as the plays themselves do. The basic impression is of very lightly constructed, beautiful pieces of scaffolding that can be changed quickly, all of which helps to tell the evening's story in an eloquent manner. Add to this the verve with which he works, the contempt he shows for anything cute or innocuous, and the gaiety of his constructions, and you will perhaps get some idea of the methods of the greatest set designer of our time.

* The reference is to Scene 2 of Brecht's *The Mother*.
** Neher designed the set for a production of *Macbeth* at the Zurich Schauspielhaus in 1946.

Plans and Appendices

(i) Plans

A2

1939–41

BUYING BRASS

First Night: The Philosopher is welcomed to the theatre / business is brisk / escape from reality into the theatre / there's old and there's new / competition from film / film, a test of gestic representation / literarization* / montage / reality / capitalism, poker-faced man / reality in the theatre / the Philosopher's requirements / the appeal / commitment

Second Night: Aristotle's *Poetics* / the emotion racket / the new subject matter / the hero / M type and P type** / Fascist theatricality / science / foundation of the *thaëter*

Third Night: The street scene / the V-effect / the smokers' theatre / exercises / *Fear and Misery* / variations on Shakespeare

Fourth Night: Reconversion to a theatre / Chaplin / comedy / fairground chronicle / Chinese acting / gay critique*** / the teachers
He can't pay

---

* Brecht defines the term literarization in the section on 'Titles and Screens' in his 'Notes to *The Threepenny Opera*' (*Brecht on Theatre*). The projection of scene titles and other textual material enables the spectators to reflect intellectually on what they are seeing on stage.

** M type and P type refer to two distinct types of theatre, merry-go-round and planetarium, one based on the spectator's empathetic involvement, the other on critical observation. See also *Short Organon for the Theatre*, section 28 (*Brecht on Theatre*).

*** 'Gay critique' is an amalgam of key philosophical notions in Nietzsche and Marx: Marx characterizes several of his works as critiques, and 'gay' alludes to Nietzsche's *The Gay Science* (1886). Both Brecht and Nietzsche use the term 'fröhlich', which can mean cheerful or blithe.

A4

1939–41

BUYING BRASS

First Night: The Philosopher is welcomed to the theatre / the theatre's business is good / the Philosopher's business is not so good / escape from reality into the theatre / the playground of the idle / the Philosopher's interests and expectations / reality in the theatre / Naturalism / empathy / buying brass

Second Night: The emotion racket (poem) / M type and P type / the V-effect / the social classes / Breughel / science / ease / foundation of the *thaëter*

Third Night: Experiments / the street scene / the smokers' theatre / the Bible scene* / variations on Shakespeare / *Fear and Misery*

Fourth Night: Reconversion of the *thaëter* to a theatre / comedy / fairground chronicle / the V-effect in Chinese acting**/ gay critique / the teachers / the Philosopher's empty hands / Weigel's descent into fame / the auditorium of statesmen

* Brecht may be referring to the Bible scene in *The Mother* (scene 11).
** Brecht's essay on the V-effect in Chinese acting was not included in *Buying Brass*: see 'Verfremdung Effects in Chinese Acting' (1936), *Brecht on Theatre*.

A20
c. 1945

1) Development towards *mimus*.* Realism, social criticism, reformism, science, psychology, Naturalism.
2) Practicable depictions of reality
3) Crisis and critique of empathy
4) The V-effect
   a) in everyday life (grammar, Socratic dialogue)
   b) in science (the commodity)
   c) in logic (discontinuity of processes and identity of opposites)
   d) in painting (Breughel), panorama
   e) Chinese theatre
5) V-effect and practicable depictions of reality

* The term *mimus* refers to the theatrical tradition of crude and obscene farce that originated in classical Greece and reached its peak in ancient Rome.

A22
1948–55

The *tragic* domain is curtailed when society bumps up against the limits of its potency.

When it has to sacrifice society's values in order to keep the entire value system going.

Critical, combative attitude of realism.

Correction of ideas.

Correction of relations.*

Cathartic effects: recognition of interests of society (as a whole).

* Brecht uses the German term 'Verhältnisse' in its Marxist sense of property relations or relations of production.

(ii) Appendices

A6

1939–41

[FIRST APPENDIX TO *BUYING BRASS* THEORY]

Skimmed through *Buying Brass*. The theory is relatively simple. It deals with the interaction between the stage and the auditorium, the way in which the spectator is to grasp the incidents on the stage. The theatrical experience comes about, as is established in Aristotle's *Poetics*, by way of an act of empathy. The elements that make up the theatrical experience, if it is brought about in this way, cannot include criticism; and the better the empathy works, the truer this becomes. Criticism is only generated in relation to the way empathy is generated, not in relation to the incidents the spectator sees reproduced on the stage. In fact you can't really talk about 'incidents that the spectator sees represented on the stage' in connection with Aristotelian theatre. Its plots and performances are not actually intended to depict incidents from real life, but to generate the strictly defined theatrical experience (complete with certain cathartic effects). This does, admittedly, call for actions that evoke real life, and these actions need to have a certain element of plausibility in order to create the illusion without which empathy cannot be generated. It is not necessary at all, however, to bring out the causal interconnections of the incidents; it is quite sufficient that no questions need to be asked about this.[1] Only somebody who is primarily concerned with the real-life incidents alluded to in theatres will be in a position to view the incidents on stage as depictions of reality and to criticize them as such. In doing so, this person steps outside the domain of art, for art does not see its primary task as being simply to produce depictions of reality. As I have mentioned, it is only concerned with specific depictions, i.e.

[1] In principle, it is possible to bring about a complete theatrical experience through an entirely misleading portrayal of an incident from real life.

depictions with specific effects. The act of empathy produced by these effects would simply be disrupted if the spectator adopted a critical approach to the incidents themselves. So the question is whether it is at all possible to make the representation of real-life incidents the task of art, and thereby to make the spectator's critical attitude towards those real-life incidents compatible with art. When you ponder this question, it becomes clear that so great a transformation could only be brought about by changing the nature of the interaction between stage and auditorium. This new method of practising art would cause empathy to forfeit its dominant role. Instead, the *Verfremdung* effect (V-effect) is produced, which is also an artistic effect and leads to a theatrical experience. It consists in representing real-life incidents on the stage in such a way that their causal interconnection is highlighted and engages the spectator. This type of art also generates emotions; indeed, it is the mastering of reality made possible by such performances that produces emotion in the spectator. The V-effect is an old artistic technique familiar from comedy, certain branches of folk art and Asiatic theatrical practice.

A7
1939–41

SECOND APPENDIX TO *BUYING BRASS* THEORY

A few points will serve to illustrate the part that the materialist dialectic plays in the theory:

1) The *self-evident* – i.e. the particular shape that our consciousness has given to experience – dissolves when it is negated by the *V-effect* and transformed into a new form of the *evident*. A process of schematization is thus destroyed. The individual's own experiences correct or confirm what he or she has absorbed from the totality. The original act of discovery is repeated.

2) The contradiction between empathy and detachment is intensified and becomes an element of the performance.

3) *Historicizing* involves viewing a particular social system from the point of view of another social system. The viewpoints in question result from the development of society.

Not finished.

Note: Aristotelian dramaturgy does not give any consideration – i.e. does not permit any consideration to be given – to the objective contradictions in any process. They ought to be turned into subjective ones (located within the hero).

A8
1939–41

THIRD APPENDIX TO *BUYING BRASS* THEORY

The need spectators have nowadays to be distracted from the battleground of daily life is continually reproduced by that daily battleground, but is just as continually in conflict with their need to be able to control their own fate. The division of needs into two categories – being entertained and sustained* – is an artificial one. Entertainment (of a distracting kind) is a continual threat to their ability to sustain themselves, because the spectators are led not into the void, not into an alien world, but into a distorted world – and they pay in real life for their excesses, which they regard as mere excursions. They do not emerge unscathed from having empathized with their enemies. It makes them enemies of themselves. Surrogates satisfy the need and poison the body. The spectators want to be diverted and converted at the same time – and they have to want both – to escape from the daily battleground.

The new theatre is simply a theatre of people who have begun to help themselves. Three hundred years of technology and organization have transformed them. The theatre has been very slow to complete the transformation. Characters in Shakespeare are helplessly handed over to their fate – to their passions, in other words. Society does not reach out a helping hand to them. The magnificence and vitality of any given character type then operates within a strictly defined radius.

The reason the new theatre is so applicable to social human beings is that humanity has helped itself socially in technological, scientific and political terms. Individual types and their ways of behaving are laid bare in such a way as to make visible their social mechanisms; only once these have been mastered can the individual types be properly grasped. Individuals remain individual, but become a social phenomenon: their passions become social issues as do their fates. The individual's position in society loses its 'natural' quality and becomes the main focus of attention. The V-effect is a social measure.

* Brecht also uses the word-play of 'entertain' and 'sustain' – 'Unterhaltung' and 'Unterhalt' – in the *Short Organon for the Theatre*: see for example section 77 (*Brecht on Theatre*).

A9
1939–41

APPENDIX TO *BUYING BRASS* THEORY

1) Aristotelian dramatic composition and the acting style that goes with it (the two concepts are ultimately interchangeable) deceive the spectator

as to the way in which the incidents shown on stage actually come about and take place in real life, and this deception is aided by the fact that the plot is presented as an indivisible whole. Its details cannot be compared individually with their equivalents in real life. Nothing must be 'taken out of context' – in order to put it into the context of reality, for instance. The remedy for this is a performance style which makes use of *Verfremdung*. The plot development here is discontinuous, and the unified whole is made up of independent parts, each of which can – and indeed must – be immediately confronted with the corresponding partial incidents from real life. This performance style draws all its force from constant comparisons with reality; in other words, it constantly draws attention to the causal interconnections of the incidents being represented.

2) In order to achieve the V-effect, actors must give up on being *completely transformed* into whatever character it is they are playing. They are *showing* the character, they are *citing* the script, they are *repeating* a real-life incident. The spectators are not completely 'mesmerized', not synchronized* psychologically, not led to adopt a fatalistic state of mind towards the fate being portrayed. (They can feel anger where the character on stage feels joy, etc. They are allowed, and sometimes even encouraged, to imagine a different course of events or to look for one, etc.) The incidents are *historicized* and *socially milieurized*. (The former, of course, occurs mainly in the case of present-day incidents: what is has not always been, and will not always be. The latter constantly calls the current social order into question and holds it up for discussion.) Achieving the V-effect is a technique that has to be taught from first principles.

3) In order to establish laws you need to perceive natural incidents with astonishment, as it were; you have to stop treating them as 'self-evident', in other words, if you want to gain an understanding of them. To discover the law acting upon an object that has been hurled, you have to imagine different possibilities for it; among these imagined possibilities the actual, natural possibility will then be the right one, and the imagined alternatives will turn out to be impossibilities. The theatre is able to induce this astonished, inventive and critical attitude in its spectators by means of its V-effect, and while it is true that this same attitude also needs to be adopted in the sciences, that doesn't make the theatre a scientific institution. It is merely a theatre of the scientific age. It takes the attitude adopted by its spectators in real life and applies it to the theatrical experience. Or to put it another way: empathy is not the only source of emotions that art has at its disposal.

4) Within the conceptual environment of Aristotelian theatre, the type of performance we have described would be merely a stylistic issue. It is much more than that. But it certainly won't cause the theatre to shed its

old functions of *entertainment* and *instruction*; instead, these functions will in fact be renewed. The performance will become completely natural once more. It can display a wide variety of styles. The engagement with reality sets the imagination off on the right track – a pleasurable one. Gaiety** and seriousness find a new lease of life in criticism, which is of a creative kind. All in all what we're looking at is a secularization of the old ritualistic institution.

* Brecht uses the National Socialist term 'gleichgeschaltet', a euphemism devised by the National Socialist regime to designate the process whereby it imposed totalitarian control on political, economic and social institutions in Germany from 1933 onwards. 'Gleichschaltung' is also sometimes translated as alignment or coordination.
** 'Gaiety' renders the German term 'Heiterkeit' here; see also note*** to Plan A2 above (p. 119).

Practice Pieces for Actors

(i) Parallel Scenes

The following adaptations, which transpose the murder scene from *Macbeth* and the argument between the queens in *Maria Stuart* into a prosaic setting, are designed to lend an element of *Verfremdung* to the classical scenes. In our theatres these scenes have long been played in a way which emphasizes not the incidents themselves but the fits of temperament the incidents make possible. The adaptations restore interest in the incidents, and also renew the actors' interest in the stylization and the verse form of the originals, helping them to see these features as something special, something additional.

THE MURDER IN THE PORTER'S LODGE
(Parallel Scene to Shakespeare's Macbeth, *Act 2, Scene 2)*

A porter's lodge. The porter, his wife and a sleeping beggar. A chauffeur has brought in a large parcel.

THE CHAUFFEUR: Careful. This thing's fragile.
THE WIFE *taking it*: What is it?
THE CHAUFFEUR: A Chinese good luck god, apparently.
THE WIFE: Did she buy it for him?
THE CHAUFFEUR: Yes, for his birthday. The maids will come and pick it up from you, Mrs Fersen – make sure you tell them to be extra careful with it. It's worth more than this entire lodge. *Exit.*
THE WIFE: What do they need a good luck god for, I'd like to know? They've got money coming out of their ears! We're the ones who could do with it.
THE PORTER: Stop complaining all the time – just be glad we've got jobs. That's luck in itself. Go and put it in the bedroom.
THE WIFE *taking the parcel to the door and calling back over her shoulder*: It's an outrage. They can afford to buy good luck gods that are worth more than a whole house, and we're lucky if we have a roof over our heads, and even then we have to work all the livelong day for the privilege. It's enough to make your blood boil.
She stumbles as she tries to open the door, and the parcel slips out of her hands.
THE PORTER: Careful!

THE WIFE: It's broken!

THE PORTER: Damn it! Why can't you be careful!

THE WIFE: This is terrible – they'll throw us out when they see this. The head's come off. I'll kill myself.

THE PORTER: They'll never give us a reference after this. We might as well just hit the road *(points to the beggar, who has woken up)* with him. You won't be able to explain this away.

THE WIFE: I'll kill myself.

THE PORTER: That won't put it back together again.

THE WIFE: What on earth shall we say?

THE BEGGAR *still half asleep*: Something wrong?

THE PORTER: Shut up. *(To his wife)*: There's nothing *to* say. It was given to us for safekeeping and now it's broken. What exactly do you plan to say? Better just start packing.

THE WIFE: Maybe there is something we can say. Anything. We could say it was already broken.

THE PORTER: He's been with them ten years. They're not going to take our word over his.

THE WIFE: There's two of us. Two witnesses against one.

THE PORTER: Rubbish. My testimony doesn't count – I'm your husband. I know the mistress. She'll auction the clothes off our backs just to get her revenge.

THE WIFE: We've got to think of something.

The doorbell rings.

THE PORTER: They're coming.

THE WIFE: I'll hide it. *(She runs into the bedroom with the parcel, then comes back in. Referring to the beggar, who is asleep again)*: Was he awake?

THE PORTER: Yes, just for a second.

THE WIFE: Did he see 'it'?

THE PORTER: I don't know. Why?

The bell rings again.

THE WIFE: Take him into the bedroom.

THE PORTER: I've got to go and let them in or they'll know something's going on.

THE WIFE: Keep them talking outside for a minute. *(Referring to the beggar)*: He did it. In there. When they come in, we don't know anything about it. *(Shakes the beggar.)* Oi, you!

The porter makes to leave. The wife bundles the half-asleep beggar into the bedroom, then comes back in and exits through another door, opposite.

THE PORTER *returning with the two maids from the manor house*: It's cold out today and you ladies haven't even got coats on.

THE HOUSEKEEPER: We've just run over to pick up the parcel.

THE PORTER: We've put it in the bedroom.

THE HOUSEKEEPER: The mistress can't wait to see it – where is it?

THE PORTER: Best I take it over to her myself.

THE HOUSEKEEPER: Don't put yourself out, Mr Fersen.

THE PORTER: I'm happy to do it.

THE HOUSEKEEPER: I know you are, Mr Fersen, but there's really no need. Is it in here?

THE PORTER: Yes – the big parcel. *(She goes in.)* So it's meant to be a good luck god, is it?

THE MAID: Yes. The mistress is livid that the chauffeur didn't bring it straight to her an hour ago – they do it out of spite, she can't rely on anyone, all they ever think of is themselves, no one ever wants to take the blame when something goes wrong, etcetera, etcetera. Yes, well, not everyone's prepared to crucify themselves for an employer like that, am I right?

THE PORTER: Indeed. Everybody's different.

THE MAID: My aunt always says he who sups with the devil needs a long spoon.

THE HOUSEKEEPER *from the bedroom*: This is terrible.

THE PORTER AND THE MAID: What's the matter?

THE HOUSEKEEPER: Someone must have done this on purpose! Someone's gone and snapped the head off!

THE PORTER: Snapped it off?

THE MAID: The good luck god?

THE HOUSEKEEPER: Look at it! As soon as I picked it up I could tell it was broken in half. There I am wondering whether or not I should open it, I undo one corner – and the head falls out!
The porter and the maid run into the bedroom.

THE HOUSEKEEPER: His birthday present – and her so superstitious.

THE PORTER'S WIFE *enters*: What's going on? You all look so flustered.

THE HOUSEKEEPER: I can hardly bear to tell you, Mrs Fersen – I know what a respectable woman you are – but someone's broken the good luck god.

THE WIFE: What? Broken it? In my house?

THE PORTER *coming back with the maid*: I just don't understand it. We're finished. They entrust us with such a precious possession and then this happens! I'll never be able to look the mistress in the face again!

THE HOUSEKEEPER: So who's responsible?

THE MAID: It must have been that beggar – that peddler. He pretended he'd been asleep the whole time and had only just woken up, but he still had the string on his lap. He was probably trying to find out what was in the parcel so he could see if it was worth stealing.

THE PORTER: Damn it, I shouldn't have thrown him out!

THE HOUSEKEEPER: Why didn't you keep hold of him?

THE PORTER: Goodness knows! But how can a man think of absolutely everything at once? It's impossible! My temper just ran away with me. There was the good luck god, and there was the head on the floor a few feet away, and there on the bench was that man, playing the innocent – all I could think of was the mistress.

THE HOUSEKEEPER: The police will pick him up soon enough.

THE WIFE: I feel sick.

THE FISHWIVES' QUARREL
(*Parallel to Schiller's* Mary Stuart, *Act 3*)

1.

A street. Mrs Zwillich and her neighbour, walking.

MRS ZWILLICH: No, Mr Koch, I can't do it. I can't humiliate myself like that. I may not have been left with much, but I do still have my pride. I won't have them point the finger at me in the fish market and say 'She's the bootlicker that went crawling to that two-faced monster Mrs Scheit!'

MR KOCH: You mustn't let yourself get so worked up, Mrs Zwillich. You have to go and see Mrs Scheit – if her nephew testifies against you in court they'll give you four months.

MRS ZWILLICH: But I didn't give false weight. It's all lies.

MR KOCH: Of course, Mrs Zwillich – we know that, but do the police? Mrs Scheit is much craftier than you. You're no match for her.

MRS ZWILLICH: Dirty tricks.

MR KOCH: No one's saying she was right to send that no-good nephew of hers to buy a flounder from you and then take it to the police to get the weight checked! Of course the police know she was just trying get rid of the competition. But the fact remains, I'm afraid, that your two-pound flounder was still that fatal three ounces short.

MRS ZWILLICH: That's because I got chatting to the nephew while
I was weighing it and didn't look carefully at the scales. It's being
friendly to a customer that's got me into this mess!

MR KOCH: We all admire you for your friendliness to customers.
Everybody says as much.

MRS ZWILLICH: Obviously the reason all the customers came to me
and not her is that I'm attentive to them, and I've got the personal
touch. That's what made her see red. But it wasn't enough to get
the market police to take away my stall and stop me trading – she
had to get her nephew to drag me through the courts as well. That's
going too far.

MR KOCH: And now you're going to need to tread carefully, believe
me. Very carefully. Watch what you say!

MRS ZWILLICH: 'Watch what you say!' What's the world coming to
when I have to watch what I say to vermin like her – a woman who
should be locked up for slander!

MR KOCH: But you really do need to! You're lucky she's even letting
me take you to see her, Mrs Zwillich – don't go ruining everything
now with your temper and your righteous indignation.

MRS ZWILLICH: I can't do it, Mr Koch, I just know I can't. All day
I've been waiting to find out whether she's going to deign to listen
to me or not. Pull yourself together, I said to myself – she can land
you behind bars if she wants to. I pictured the whole thing – how
I'd reason with her, and perhaps get her to take pity on me. But now
I just can't do it. All I know is I hate the woman – she's a shameless
hussy and I'd like to scratch her eyes out.

MR KOCH: You've got to control yourself, Mrs Zwillich, I'm begging
you. You've got to grin and bear it. She's left you no choice. Ask her
to be merciful, beg her forgiveness. For God's sake forget your pride
now – this is no time for pride.

MRS ZWILLICH: I know you mean well. And I will go – but no
good'll come of it, believe you me. We're like cat and dog. She's
done me wrong, and I'd like to scratch her eyes … *(They walk
away.).*

2.

*At the fish market in the evening. Mrs Scheit is the only fishwife still there.
She is seated, with her nephew beside her.*

MRS SCHEIT: No, I won't talk to her – why should I? Now that she's
finally out of my hair. What heavenly peace there's been in the fish
market today and yesterday, without her and her la-di-da ways:

'A handsome eel, Madam? Husband keeping well I hope? You're
looking lovely today as usual!' It used to make my blood boil.

THE CUSTOMER: I've been standing around chatting so long I've not
bought anything to cook this evening. Bit small isn't it, that pike?

MRS SCHEIT: Catch yourself a bigger one then, Madam. It's not my
fault it died young – if you don't want it don't take it, it's no skin off
my nose.

THE CUSTOMER: There's no need to take offence – I was just saying
it looks a bit small.

MRS SCHEIT: And it doesn't have a moustache, either – in other
words it's not what you're looking for and that's that. Hugo, pack up
the baskets. We're closing.

THE CUSTOMER: All right, I'll take it. No need to fly off the handle.

MRS SCHEIT: One thirty. *(Hands her the fish. To the nephew)*: People
come strolling up when we've already finished for the day and still
think they can pick and choose! I like that! Come on, let's go.

THE NEPHEW: But you said you'd speak to Mrs Zwillich, Aunt.

MRS SCHEIT: At the end of the day, I said, and do you see her
anywhere?

Mrs Zwillich and Mr Koch appear, and stand a short distance away.

THE NEPHEW: Here she comes now.

MRS SCHEIT *as if she hadn't noticed Mrs Zwillich*: Pack up the
baskets. We haven't done badly at all today – twice as much as last
Thursday. They were practically snatching it out of my hands. 'My
husband always says *this carp's one of Mrs Scheit's, I can tell by the
taste.'* People really are idiots. As if one carp didn't taste exactly like
another!

MRS ZWILLICH *shuddering, to Mr Koch*: No one with a shred of
human feeling could ever talk like that!

MRS SCHEIT: Might the lady and gentleman wish to buy a flounder?

THE NEPHEW: That's Mrs Zwillich, Aunt.

MRS SCHEIT: What? Who told her to come pestering me?

THE NEPHEW: Well she's here now, Aunt. And the Bible does say to
love thy neighbour.

MR KOCH: Please be understanding, Mrs Scheit. An unhappy woman
stands before you. She doesn't even dare speak to you.

MRS ZWILLICH: I can't do it, Mr Koch.

MRS SCHEIT: What did she say? Did you hear that, Mr Koch? An
unhappy woman, you say, who's come to ask my forgiveness, who's
been crying her eyes out day and night? Don't make me laugh!
Haughty, that's what she is! As impudent as ever!

MRS ZWILLICH: Fine – even that I can cope with. *(To Mrs Scheit)*:
   You've got what you wanted. You can thank the Lord for that. But
   don't go too far. Give me your hand, Mrs Scheit. *(Holds out her
   hand.)*

MRS SCHEIT: You've got yourself into this position, you know, Mrs
   Zwillich.

MRS ZWILLICH: Just remember, Mrs Scheit, that people's luck can
   change – even yours. Mine already has. And people are listening.
   And after all, we were fellow traders – nothing like this has ever
   happened in the fish market before! Good God, don't just stand
   there like a rock! I can't bring myself to beg on my knees any more
   than you can! It's bad enough that I'll go to prison if I can't get you
   to take pity on me. But just looking at you makes the words stick in
   my throat.

MRS SCHEIT: Would you mind cutting to the chase? I don't
   particularly want to be seen with you. I only agreed to this out
   of Christian charity. For two years you've been luring away my
   customers.

MRS ZWILLICH: I don't know what to say. If I tell the truth you'll be
   offended, because what you've done to me isn't right. When you
   sent your nephew to buy that flounder you were just trying to get
   me in trouble – I'd never have thought it of you, or anyone. Ever.
   All I did was sell fish here, same as you, and now you're dragging
   me through the courts. Look: I'm prepared to say that the whole
   thing was a misunderstanding – you're not to blame, I'm not to
   blame, we were both just trying to sell fish and the customers came
   between us. People told you one thing and me another. They said
   you said my fish stank, they said I said you gave false weight, or
   vice versa. But there's no one between us now – we might just as
   well be sisters. You the older one and me the younger. It would
   never have come to this if we'd been open with each other from the
   start.

MRS SCHEIT: Oh, yes – and a fine viper I'd have been nourishing in
   my bosom! You don't belong in the fish market! You don't play fair!
   You hog all the business! You've poached one after another of my
   customers with your posturing, your affectations, your simpering
   "Just one more little perch, Madam?" – and when I told you so you
   threatened to have me up for slander. But now the boot's on the
   other foot!

MRS ZWILLICH: I'm in the hands of God, Mrs Scheit. Surely you
   wouldn't want to commit such a sin—

MRS SCHEIT: And who's going to stop me? You were the one who first brought the police into it when you accused me of slander! If I let you off and tell my nephew not to press charges after all, you'll be right back here tomorrow. I know you. You won't show any remorse, oh no – you'll go out and buy some lipstick to get the waiter from the Red Lion to buy your haddock! That's what'll happen if I put mercy before justice.

MRS ZWILLICH: Oh for God's sake, keep your fish market! Sell fish on your own! I'm giving up my stall for good. You've got what you wanted. You've broken me. I'm only a shadow of the Mrs Zwillich I used to be. But stop persecuting me now. Say: Go in peace – I've shown you what's what, and now I'm going to show you how a Christian woman behaves. If you say that, I'll say thank you and truly mean it. But don't make me wait too long for those little words. If you don't say them – if you go to the police – I wouldn't want to have to face people in your shoes for all the world!

MRS SCHEIT: So you've finally realized you're beaten? Have you run out of tricks now? Has the market policeman gone off you? Haven't you got any more admirers? You'd go to the pictures with anyone you thought would be good for business, if he'd been married ten times over!

MRS ZWILLICH: You're really pushing it now. That's going too far.

MRS SCHEIT *after giving her a long, contemptuous look*: Hugo, is this the same Mrs Zwillich who's always so friendly to everyone? Who they all go running to as if yours truly was just a horrible old bag, a heap of shit in the marketplace that everyone goes out of their way to avoid? She's nothing but a common whore.

MRS ZWILLICH: This is too much!

MRS SCHEIT *laughing scornfully*: Ah, now she's showing her true colours! Now her pretty mask has slipped!

MRS ZWILLICH *incandescent with rage, but dignified*: Mr Koch – I admit that I'm young and I have my flaws. I may have given a man a friendly glance now and again when he came to buy my fish, but I've never done anything behind closed doors. If that's my reputation then all I can say is I'm better than my reputation. You'll see what it's like yourself soon enough, Mrs Scheit! You keep your pleasures secret. Everyone on the market knows you're a bad lot. Your mother didn't get locked up for nothing!

MR KOCH: For God's sake! That's blown it! You didn't control yourself as you promised, Mrs Zwillich.

MRS ZWILLICH: Controlled myself is right, Mr Koch. I've stood

as much as a woman can stand. Now I'm going to talk – now I'm
going to let it all out, all of it …

MR KOCH: She's lost her mind – she doesn't know what she's saying,
Mrs Scheit!

THE NEPHEW: Don't listen to her, Aunt! Come on, let's go! I'll take
the baskets.

MRS ZWILLICH: It stank, that fish she sent to the Red Lion! She's a
disgrace to the whole fish market! She only got her stall because her
no-good brother goes drinking with one of the market policemen!

(ii) Intercalary Scenes

The intercalary scenes for Shakespeare's *Hamlet* and *Romeo and Juliet*
are not intended to feature in performances of the plays but simply to be
run through by the actors during rehearsals. The *Hamlet* ferry scene (to
be inserted between Scenes 3 and 4 of Act 4) and the recitation of the
concluding report are designed to prevent a heroizing portrayal of Hamlet.
Bourgeois criticism of *Hamlet* tends to view Hamlet's hesitation as the interesting new element in this play, yet treats the massacre in Act 5 – where
Hamlet abandons reflection in favour of 'doing the deed' – as a positive
resolution. The massacre, however, represents a regression, because the deed
is in fact a misdeed. The short practice scene provides an explanation for
Hamlet's hesitation: it is consistent with the new bourgeois attitudes that are
already well established in the political-social sphere. The intercalary scenes
for *Romeo and Juliet* are not, of course, designed to illustrate the simple
maxim 'One man's joy is another man's sorrow', but to enable the actors
playing Romeo and Juliet to develop the characters in a contradictory way.

HAMLET
Ferry scene
(To be played between Scenes 3 and 4 of Act 4)

A ferry. Hamlet and the ferryman. Hamlet's confidant.

HAMLET: What's that building on the shore over there?
FERRYMAN: A fort, your Highness. It was built for the coast guard.
HAMLET: But what's that wooden chute running down to the sound?
FERRYMAN: It's for loading the fish on to the boats bound for
Norway.
HAMLET: Funny kind of fort. Do the fish live there?

FERRYMAN: It's where they get salted. His Highness your father, the
new king, has signed a trade agreement with Norway.

HAMLET: We used to send our soldiers to Norway. So they've been
salted away now? Funny kind of war.

FERRYMAN: We're not at war any more. We backed down and let them
have the coast, and they agreed to buy our fish. Since then we've had
more influence there than we did before – indeed we have, sire.

HAMLET: So the fish must be all in favour of the new king?

FERRYMAN: They say the alarums of war don't fill the belly, sire.
They're for the king.

HAMLET: But I hear the ambassador of my noble first father – whom
you must distinguish from my second one – was slapped in the face
at the Norwegian court. Has that all been forgotten about now?

FERRYMAN: His Highness your second father, so to speak, sire,
apparently said that the ambassador had too much face for the
ambassador of any country with so much fish.

HAMLET: Wise restraint.

FERRYMAN: For half a year we were worried sick here on the coast.
The king hesitated to sign the treaty.

HAMLET: Really? He hesitated?

FERRYMAN: He hesitated. They even sent more men to man the
fort. Everyone said, 'There'll be war and no fish trade.' Oh, how we
lurched between hope and despair! But God guided the good king,
and he signed.

HAMLET'S CONFIDANT: And what of honour?

HAMLET: I see no violation of honour in it, quite frankly. The new
methods, friend – they're everywhere now. People don't like the
smell of blood any more. Tastes are changing.

HAMLET'S CONFIDANT: Unwarlike times – a feeble generation.

HAMLET: Why unwarlike? Perhaps it's the fish doing the fighting now?
An amusing idea, that – salted soldiers. A little disgrace and a lot of
honour. And he who slaps the ambassador in the face has to buy the
fish. Disgrace digs his grave and honour feasts on fish. And in the
same way the murderer improves his reputation by rubbing his face
with a smile, and the unworthy son points to the money brought in
by good fish sales. His scruples towards the murderer, not towards
the murdered, are what do him honour now; his cowardice is his
best feature; he would be a villain if he wasn't a villain, and so on.
And so to bed, to be sure we don't interfere with the fishing.

    As commerce thrives, the splendid tombstone crumbles.
    And crumbling how much more it points the finger!

One bit of business yet unfinished, but,
Drawing a line, you draw it through another
Prematurely – is there a postmaturely?
And yet a villain breathes a sigh? Becomes
A good man almost – not only seems but is!
And you, tear down what has been built, because
It stands on ruins (and grows, and bears good fruit).
Fill up the fort again with butchers, and turn back
To bloody deeds – that's how *he* got his start!
Oh, had he but hesitated! Oh!

Concluding Report

And so – carefully exploiting the beating of chance drums
Eagerly taking up the battle cry of unknown butchers
Freed at last, by this chance, from his
So sensible and human inhibition –
In one horrific killing spree
He slaughters the king, his mother and himself
Thus justifying his successor's view
That he was likely, had he been put on,
To have proved most royal.

ROMEO AND JULIET
The Servants
(To be played between Scenes 1 and 2 of Act 2)

1
Romeo and one of his tenants.

ROMEO: I've already told you, old fellow – I need the money. It's for a
very good cause.

TENANT: But where are we supposed to go if your lordship sells the
land so suddenly? There are five of us.

ROMEO: Can't you go and hire out somewhere? You're a good worker,
and I'll give you an excellent reference. I've got to have the money
– I have obligations. You don't understand these things. Or do I
have to explain that when a lady has given herself to me I can't just
put her out in the street without a gift of any kind? Just an 'Adieu,
my love' and nothing more? Do you want me to do something so
ignoble? Then you're nothing but a miserable wretch, a selfish cur.
Parting gifts cost money. And you have to admit they're completely
selfless – you never get anything in return. Isn't that right, old

friend? Don't be a spoilsport. Are you not the one who bounced me on his knee and whittled my first bow? Has it come to this – even Gobbo doesn't understand me any more, lets me down, wants me to behave like a cad? I'm in love, man! I'd sacrifice anything in the world. I'd even commit a crime for the girl I love – a murder. And I'd be proud of it. You won't understand that. You're too old, old Gobbo – you're all dried up. Don't you see, I need to get the other girl out of the way. And now I've taken you into my confidence, I ask you: are you still the same old Gobbo you used to be or not? Answer me.

TENANT: I'm no good at making fine speeches, my lord. But I don't know where my family and I will go if you drive us off your land.

ROMEO: Poor old Gobbo. He's too old to understand. I tell him my heart is aflame, and he mumbles something about land. Do I own land? I've forgotten. No, I have no land – or rather, I do, but it's got to go. What do I care about land? I'm burning with love – burning!

TENANT: And we're starving, my lord.

ROMEO: Imbecile. It's impossible to have a sensible conversation with you! Do you animals have no feelings? Then off with you – the sooner the better.

TENANT: Yes, off with us. Here, do you want my coat too? *(He takes it off.)* My hat? My boots? Animals, are we? Even animals need to eat.

ROMEO: So it's like that is it? This is your true face? The one you've kept hidden for twenty-five years like a leprous spot? This is what I get for trying to speak to you like a human being? Get out of my sight or I'll thrash you, you animal.

He chases him off, but during the love scene the tenant continues to lurk in the background.

ROMEO: He jests at scars that never felt a wound.

2

Juliet and her maid.

JULIET: And you love your Thurio? How much do you love him?

MAID: At night, once I've said my Our Father and the nurse has started snoring, begging your pardon, mistress, I get back out of bed and go over to the window in my bare feet.

JULIET: Just because he might be standing outside?

MAID: No – because he stood there once before.

JULIET: Oh, how I know that feeling. I like to look at the moon because we've looked at it together. But tell me more about how you love him. If he was in danger, for instance …

MAID: You mean for instance if he was dismissed? I'd run straight to his master.

JULIET: No – if his life was in danger …

MAID: Oh, you mean if there was a war? Then I'd keep on and on at him till he pretended to be ill and took to his bed.

JULIET: But that would be cowardly.

MAID: I'd make a coward of him all right. He definitely would stay in bed if I got in there with him.

JULIET: No – I mean if he was in danger and you could save him by sacrificing your own life.

MAID: If he got the plague, you mean? I'd stick a rag soaked in vinegar in my mouth and take care of him, of course.

JULIET: But would you even be thinking about the rag?

MAID: How do you mean?

JULIET: And it doesn't help anyway.

MAID: Not much, but it does a bit.

JULIET: But anyway you'd risk your life for him, and so would I for my Romeo. But one more thing: what if for instance he went off to war and then when he came back he was missing something?

MAID: What?

JULIET: I can't say it.

MAID: Oh, that! Then I'd scratch his eyes out.

JULIET: Why?

MAID: For going to war.

JULIET: And then it would be over between you?

MAID: Well yes, wouldn't it?

JULIET: You don't love him at all.

MAID: What – don't you think it's love that I like being with him so much?

JULIET: That's physical love.

MAID: And isn't physical love nice?

JULIET: Yes – but I love my Romeo more, I assure you.

MAID: Do you think because I like being with my Thurio so much it means I don't really love him? But maybe I'd even forgive him for what you said. Once I'd got over the initial shock, I mean. Definitely. I love him too much.

JULIET: But you hesitated.

MAID: That was out of love.

JULIET *embraces her*: It's true. You must go to him tonight.

MAID: Yes, because of that other girl. I'm so glad you're letting me go early. If he meets her it'll all be over.

JULIET: And you're sure you'll be able to catch him at the back door in the wall?

MAID: Yes – that's the only way he can go. And he's not supposed to be meeting her till eleven.

JULIET: If you leave now you can't miss him. Here, take this shawl, it's pretty – and which stockings have you got on?

MAID: My best ones. And I'll put on my sweetest smile and be nicer to him than I've ever been. I love him so much.

JULIET: Was that a twig cracking?

MAID: It sounded like someone jumping down from the wall. I'll go and look.

JULIET: But don't miss your Thurio.

MAID *at the window*: Who do you think has jumped over the wall and is standing right here in the garden?

JULIET: Romeo! Oh Nerida, I have to go out on the balcony and speak to him.

MAID: But the gatekeeper's room is right below yours, mistress. He'll hear everything. All of a sudden there won't be any footsteps in your room any more and there'll be voices from the garden and the balcony.

JULIET: Then you'll have to walk up and down in here and rattle the basin so it sounds like I'm washing.

MAID: But then I won't be able to meet my Thurio and it will all be over for me.

JULIET: Maybe he'll have been kept in as well tonight – he's a servant too, after all. Just walk up and down and rattle the basin. Dear, dear Nerida. Please don't let me down. I have to speak to him.

MAID: Can you make it quick? Please make it quick.

JULIET: I'll be quick, Nerida, I'll be very quick. Walk up and down in here. (*She goes out on to the balcony. Nerida walks up and down and rattles the basin during the love scene. When the clock strikes eleven, she faints.*)

[BFA 22, pp. 830–46]

Brecht gathered these 'Practice Pieces' for publication as an extract 'from the *Messingkauf*' in his *Versuche* series (volume 11, 1950). They date back, in their original form, to 1940 and were composed to support Helene Weigel's work at a Stockholm drama school. They seem at one point to have been conceived as part of the 'Third Night' of *Buying Brass*. The scenes make extensive use of quotation and pseudo-quotation from Schiller's original German and the standard German translations of Shakespeare.

To these, Brecht added a dialogue, written in 1950, between Homer and Hesiod, which we have excluded from our selection, and the quaint popular song in (iii) below. This latter was first quoted by Brecht in fragmentary form in his 1922 play *Drums in the Night* (there as an expression of the antihero's fatalism). Intriguingly, a version of the same ditty features in Samuel Beckett's *Waiting for Godot*, sung and pondered over by Vladimir in Act 2. We have used Beckett's version by way of translation.

(iii) Circular Poems

Another useful exercise is to recite circular poems such as:

A dog came in the kitchen
And stole a crust of bread.
Then cook up with a ladle
And beat him till he was dead.
Then all the dogs came running
And dug the dog a tomb
And wrote upon the tombstone
For the eyes of dogs to come:
A dog came in the kitchen, etc.

These eight-line poems are recited using a different type of gestus each time, as if by different characters in different situations. The exercise can also be used to help actors practise consistent delivery.

Part Two

Modelbooks

Introduction

It is well known, although less widely understood, that Brecht created so-called 'models', holding fast those otherwise fleeting experiences of theatre rehearsal and production, and with a view to enabling both imitation and critical analysis on the basis of the pictorial and documentary record. Part Two contains extracts from Brecht's *Modelbooks*, by way of illustration of this practice. Of three of the models illustrated and discussed here, there is in fact a whole book, or at least a pamphlet volume (published first in East Berlin by Gebrüder Weiss in the case of the *Antigone Model*, 1948, and by the Henschel Verlag in the case of *Constructing a Role: Laughton's Galileo*, 1956–8 and the *Courage Model*, 1958). To these we have added a handful of especially pertinent essays from the Berliner Ensemble's large-format illustrated volume *Theaterarbeit* (*Theater Work*) (Dresden 1952) and extracts from the *Katzgraben Notes 1953*, which remained largely unpublished until rather later. What follows is thus to some degree just a 'taster' drawn from the far more voluminous material which is available in print in German. As well as the original East German publications, most of the material is now also contained in the Berliner und Frankfurter Ausgabe of Brecht's works, volume 25 (Frankfurt/Main: Suhrkamp, 1994). These, and original material in the Brecht Archive in Berlin, have been our sources. It is perhaps regrettable that we have not been able to undertake a comprehensive English edition of these remarkable documents of theatre history and resources for understanding Brecht's theatrical and directorial practice. But, in supplement to what follows, the texts to both the *Courage* and the *Galileo* models are contained, in almost complete form, in the Methuen Drama volume *Collected Plays: Five*, and of the photographs a very wide selection is readily accessible in those German publications.[1] The sub-sections of Part Two are organized chronologically in terms of the productions to which they refer.

---

[1] It is above all the prohibitive cost of acquiring permission and then reproducing the photos (all of which are still under copyright) that has inhibited fuller publications, in English, German or any other language.

Back in 1928 Carl Koch filmed parts of the original production of *The Threepenny Opera*, and it appears that Brecht was interested in the still photos that could be extracted, more so than in the film as such.[2] Koch later went on to make a 16mm film of the 1931 production of *Man Equals Man*. The theatre photographer, Willi Saeger, who was employed by Max Reinhardt at the Deutsches Theater in the 1920s and remained there well into the post-war period, also worked on several Brecht productions, including again *The Threepenny Opera* and the 1931 *Man Equals Man* in Berlin – which thus became one of the most extensively photographed of all of Brecht's earlier plays. One could argue that those first experiments in creating a photographic record, in the period around 1930, along with the extensive notes Brecht made on such productions as *Mahagonny* and *Man Equals Man* – and the painstaking way in which the elements (textual, visual, musical) were related to one another – amount to prototypes of what were later to be the *Modelbooks*. Brecht himself, however, singled out as the very first experiment with 'Models' the use Ruth Berlau made of photographs of earlier productions in her own Copenhagen stagings of *The Mother* and *Señora Carrar's Rifles* in 1935 and 1937, amateur productions in which Brecht was also personally involved. Berlau apparently showed photographs of Weigel playing both Pelagea and Carrar (the latter including Josef Breitenbach's recent photos of the Paris premiere) to the actress Dagmar Andreasen, who was also to play the lead roles in these plays. However different the two performances turned out in the end, commented Brecht, 'the experiment was a tribute to Andreasen and to Weigel, who had created something that could be both imitated and changed' (BFA 25, p. 77).

Thereafter Berlau undertook extensive photo-documentations of a number of Brecht's plays in the theatre: *The Private Life of the Master Race* in New York (1945), *The Life of Galileo* in Beverly Hills and New York (1947 and 48), *The Antigone of Sophocles* and *Mr Puntila and His Man Matti* in Switzerland (1948), *Mother Courage* in Berlin (1949), and then a whole series of Berliner Ensemble productions. In Berlin she assumed special responsibility for matters visual and pictorial, gathered and archived pictorial material and sources, and edited and prepared for publication the four *Modelbooks* (of, in order of publication, *Antigone, Señora Carrar's Rifles,*[3] *Galileo* and *Mother Courage*), as well as the *War Primer* and *Theatre Work*.

[2] 'I'm waiting in anticipation for Koch's *Threepenny*-photos', letter to Weigel, end of September/October 1928 (not in the English edition). The film is lost.

[3] The *Carrar* model (not published until 1952 in the VEB Verlag der Kunst, Dresden) was more Berlau's project than Brecht's. Unlike the others, it has not been reprinted and is not represented in this volume.

In many cases we cannot be entirely sure what her precise contribution was, but we can be sure that it was significant.

By 1944 and the time of Brecht's collaboration with Charles Laughton on the translation and production of *Galileo* in the States, the idea of using pictures to record rehearsals, to enable critical reflection and to help develop a production was already quite well established, if never fully realized in practice. Now, with Berlau's help, there was the opportunity to do something more complete and purposeful than had been achieved hitherto. Brecht charged her to document the rehearsals and the whole process of preparing the production as fully as she possibly could. She even photographed the celebrities in the audience at the eventual premiere at the Coronet Theatre in Beverly Hills. And she resumed her painstaking documentation when the play was re-staged at the Maxine Elliott Theatre on Broadway. Brecht was delighted; now back in Zurich he wrote: 'The photos are splendid! Now you're a specialist' (mid-December 1947 – not in the English edition); and he immediately proposed she do the same for the production of *Antigone* that he was planning in Switzerland. So Berlau returned to Europe, now more or less entirely dependent on Brecht, as she had never been in Scandinavia or the States. Under Brecht's direction Berlau took literally thousands of pictures of this *Antigone* production, including some at specially organized extra rehearsals with brighter lighting, and some even in colour. Now the *Modelbook* project – detailed accounts of the productions, critical commentaries and, of course, all those photographs – was properly underway.

Although Berlau also took pictures of individual actors, and even of props and all sorts of other matters associated with the production, when it came to the play itself, her practice from the mid-1940s onwards and for the *Modelbooks* was to photograph the stage for the most part in its entirety. The camera was situated just to one side of the centre and in a slightly raised position, offering, as it were, the ideal spectator perspective, the angles revealing a depth to the field of play, and not an entirely flat stage picture. From picture to picture the perspective and distance were often slightly modified, again giving more of a sense of space. The figures are always full-length, even if less than the whole stage is shown. The inadequate lighting has as a consequence that the background nearly always appears dark. Equally, because of the shutter speeds necessary, movement tends to appear blurred. Berlau and Brecht both quite liked that effect: it was not so much the crispness of the image that mattered as the overall shape, sense of distribution and movement. The illustrations in the published *Modelbooks* are only a small extract from the vast collection of available images. By the end of the decade the practice had developed so that they could use several camera angles simultaneously, or at successive dress rehearsals or performances, making exposures rhythmically with sometimes only seconds between them. Of some productions enough photographs survive to construct a flip-book of an entire play. In the case of the last of the models, devoted to the Berlin and Munich productions of *Mother Courage*, several thousand photographs were taken, by Berlau and others, 800 of which were archived at the Berliner Ensemble (BFA 25, p. 172), of which again a mere 226 were selected for the published *Modelbook*. (We have only 34 in the present volume.)

There are also significant differences between each of the books; indeed the whole genre of *Modelbook* was clearly evolving as they worked. In the Laughton *Galileo* there are far fewer pictures, and there is really no continuous narrative sequence for the whole play. There is also a great deal of intervening textual material by way of commentary. In the *Antigone Model* there are only photographs organized in narrative sequence (plus a few examples of Neher's work at the end), and that sequence is introduced and then accompanied by further commentary. The textual material includes descriptions of the set-up, apposite quotations as captions to the pictures, and a question-and-answer commentary as if between a naive would-be director and a knowing authority on epic theatre and this production (Brecht). The *Courage Model* has, again, more paratextual material by way of essays on aspects of the productions and the use of the model. The pictures chosen here can be divided into, on the one hand, those that depict particular details (notable instances of gestus, movements, interesting sequences, or comparisons between the two productions) and, on the other, those that show us how the plot unfolded. Those in the latter category are organized in narrative sequence, with short descriptive captions, and could virtually all be said to reveal some sort of essential organization or blocking of the actors on stage (what Brecht called the *Arrangement*). They are not, however, by any means all turning points in the narrative or changes in the set-up. On the contrary, on occasions the photos seem to have been chosen precisely to reveal how little has changed from one moment to the next.

Brecht seems to have developed a surprising and un-ironic faith in the power of these photographs to render something essential about the productions. Surprising because we see elsewhere how sceptical he could be about all sorts of processes of representation. The camera is a far from neutral observer, and Brecht was surely aware of it as a medium of construction as well as of notation. Notwithstanding, he instructed Berlau to make similar photographs of other theatres' work, simply 'so that I can see what they can achieve'.[4] And he recommended, in a text for the publisher of the *Antigone*

---

[4]   Letter of 14 April 1950 (not in the English selection).

Model, that readers might read his plays alongside the accompanying photographic documentation, 'because the reader of plays can generally only
imagine the events in relation to the theatre productions that he has already
seen, and they will not always have been much good' (BFA 25, pp. 507–8).
He was unstinting in his praise of Berlau's efforts, and paid regular tribute
to her application and pioneering achievement.[5] But it is a letter to Gerda
Goedhart, an exile acquaintance and close friend of Berlau's who also came
to work at the Berliner Ensemble as a photographer, that betrays the almost
sensuous pleasure that theatre photographs could occasion for Brecht: 'On
my table your *Chalk Circle* and *Courage* photos are spread out. I rummage
around in them like Monsieur Harpagon in his money.'[6]

Sometimes it was the production itself that was thought of as the 'model'.
In an ambitious sketch entitled 'Theaterprojekt B', probably from the end of
1948, so even before the Ensemble was founded, Brecht argues that his new
company should produce 'model productions [...] with which it could tour
Germany.'[7] In other words, Brecht, with half an eye already on posterity,
was proposing an imitable product, by which his new methods could be
passed on to other theatre practitioners as a basis for their own work. But he
could not assume that all future directors would have witnessed the model
production live in the theatre. So now, having fulfilled its function as a directorial aid in the development of a production, photography came once more
into its own as a tool of documentation – in the first instance again for Brecht
and for the Ensemble themselves. If they were to know what they had done
last time, if they were to be able to recreate a production, vary it, continue to
develop it, then they needed a record. After that the documentation could
be used for the guidance of others. Of *Mother Courage*, there survive over 20
original 'scrapbook' *Modelbooks* (some of them now in the Brecht Archive,
some in the Berliner Ensemble and some in private hands). The first, which
precede the published version, have the script of the play typed in beneath
the photographs (sometimes with handwritten annotations). Later versions,
made to give to theatres and other interested parties, were made by sticking
extracts from the published text under the pasted photos. These *Modelbooks*
may vary considerably in what they choose to show. They mostly exclude the
essays and commentary material, but they are far more generous (they can
afford to be) in terms of photographs. They are all in large format (of various
sizes) and more detailed than the published version. Again it becomes clear

---

[5] E.g. the letter of 14 March 1950 (not in the English selection).
[6] Quoted in Goedhart, *Bertolt Brecht Porträts* (Zurich: Arche, 1964), p. 106.
[7] 'Theaterprojekt B', undated, n.p., LAB C Rep 120 1504, in the Berliner Ensemble
Archive.

that, whatever one looks at, one is looking at only a fraction of the entire enterprise of documenting the 'model'.

Painstaking documentations were part of the scientific and experimental method to which Brecht aspired. Besides, he had a mania for preserving records. He felt that his achievement, in these dark times, was an endangered thing, and he also enjoined Berlau (in parallel with his work with Laughton) to photograph his own manuscripts and typescripts, so as to create a compact and durable archive that could be stored apart from the fragile originals themselves.[8] The new technological media could serve him here. At the Berliner Ensemble he encouraged Hans Bunge to make sound recordings of rehearsals. The photographs of the model productions were to be another such durable record, this time of the inevitably ephemeral processes of the theatre itself – another sort of achievement which, without such a documentation, could all too easily be lost and forgotten for ever. So the books of photographs and texts themselves became the 'models'.

They were to be a documentation of epic theatre in practice, a practical deictic parallel to the potentially dry theory of the *Short Organon*. It is no accident that both that theoretical essay and the first models date from about the same time, before and just after Brecht's return to a devastated Europe, uncertain of his reception and his opportunities. Both were designed to uphold epic theatre and to defend it, both against the old complacency and against the new wave of Stanislavsky-inspired theatre work. Brecht felt, with some justification, peculiarly embattled, even after the foundation of the Berliner Ensemble in November 1949, beset by Stalinist bureaucrats and pursued by accusations of formalism.[9] The photographs were to make clear, in a way that the theory alone perhaps never really could, that he was working concretely, historically and with reality, and not in some rarefied formalist art-world. Indeed, it is striking how, in these publications, as in his daily directorial work in the theatre, Brecht skirted round his own carefully evolved terminology: the word *Verfremdung* is very sparingly used, and occurs only twice in our extracts from these writings – in the introduction to the *Antigone Model* and in one of the rehearsal notes to *Katzgraben*.

By publishing and distributing these handbooks of epic theatre, Brecht of course implied other claims too. The *Modelbooks* have been dogged since their very first appearance by accusations that Brecht was being authoritarian, restrictive, laying down performance styles, fetishizing a certain look, crippling creativity and so on. They have been widely understood as

---

[8] *Journals*, undated entry between 20 and 22 December 1944; compare the photograph of the contact prints of this process on p. 340 (in the English edition of the *Journals*), and the letter to Berlau of 18 May 1944 (not in the English edition).

[9] See *Brecht on Theatre*, Part Three, for a further elucidation of this context.

setting a prescription for the production of these plays in particular. That was probably inevitable. Brecht was indeed mistrustful of other directors' efforts – possibly with some justification, and he was keen to maintain some measure of control. Above all, he was keen to raise the standard of a theatre which he thought had been horribly corrupted by fascism, and he was trying to promulgate a new kind of theatre in a post-war Europe that, he felt, urgently needed a different, post- and anti-fascist theatre. He was writing, very consciously, for example in the opening sentences of the *Courage Model*, 'in our ruined cities after the great war'. The last thing he wanted to see was theatres slipping back into some pseudo-naturalistic psychologizing drama, and – horror of horrors – using his own texts to do it. Nonetheless, the avowed intention, expressed clearly enough in the *Modelbooks* themselves, was not to fix the look of a production for all time, but to offer a handbook for directors and actors (and the reading public), to elucidate what they needed to bring to a productive interaction with a work of epic theatre, and to initiate them into the processes of 'rational' directing.

> For the model is not constructed in order to fix for all time the way the production should work, quite the contrary! The prime emphasis is on development: changes are to be provoked and made perceptible; sporadic and anarchic acts of creation are to be replaced by creative processes whose changes proceed by steps or leaps. The model [...] must be regarded as by definition incomplete. The very fact that its shortcomings cry out for improvement should stimulate the theatres to use it.

If 'progress' was to be made from one production to the next, Brecht argued, then it could only be done on the basis of a clear record. The very insistence on the historical context in which his own work was produced (in, for example, the last sentences of the *Galileo Model* or the first sentences of the *Antigone* or *Courage Models*) implies that in another historical context a new approach might be necessary. You have to know what you are doing differently, and why. Besides, the *Modelbooks* did not prescribe a single approach. Both the *Galileo* and *Courage Modelbooks* include photos and accounts from more than one production. And the whole convolute of instructions, reports, photos and commentaries was intended to set up dialogical relationships, both within the *Modelbooks* themselves, and between them and their readers. After all, 'the act of creation has become a collective creative process, a continuum of a dialectical sort in which the original invention, taken on its own, has lost much of its importance'.[10]

---

[10] This and the preceding quotation come from §3 of the *Antigone Model* Foreword.

There are, nevertheless, evident tensions between Brecht's controlling, rationalizing instincts, on the one hand, and his avowed belief, on the other, in the contingency of the artwork and in free collective creativity. The overwhelming desire, felt as a 'need', to assert the epic over other models of theatre, the experience of himself and his art as marginalized and threatened, and that strange faith in processes of documentation and archivization perhaps conspired to create a 'model' record that fell oddly short of his own aspirations. As he himself feared, 'meant to simplify matters, they are not simple to use' (opening paragraph of the *Courage Model*). In a piece published first in *Theatre Work* in 1952 and entitled 'Bertolt Brecht's Stage Direction' (see below), he claimed of himself, 'Brecht is not one of those directors who always know better [...]. The attitude he takes to the play is one of "not knowing"; he waits and sees.' Working with Brecht could evidently really sometimes be like that, for the actors and for all the other professionals involved in a production: designers, musicians, technicians, other directors. But there were equally instances where it might be made very plain to a co-worker that the line, the train of thought they were developing, contradicted Brecht's vision and was not to be pursued. Similarly, the *Modelbooks* could be made to cut both ways, as enabling or as restricting the creativity of others. The international reception of *Mother Courage*, for example, even long after Brecht's death, has probably been unhelpfully dependent on the famous images from the published model and on Teo Otto's striking designs: the bleached colours, the famous wagon, the open revolve. Theatres and directors have not always found it easy to make the distinction that Brecht calls for in an appendix to the *Courage Model* between 'slavish imitation and masterful imitation'.

However, hard as it is to re-imagine a production from a mere photographic record, something else can also emerge from a study of the *Modelbooks*. That is the clarity, lightness and humour of Brecht's own productions. 'A theatre imbued with imagination, humour and meaning', he calls it in the *Katzgraben Notes*: 'It is not enough merely to demand insights from the theatre, to look to it for instructive depictions of reality. Our theatre has to make people *desire* insight; it must illustrate the *pleasure* to be had in changing reality.' If we can distil a sense of that pleasure from these *Modelbooks*, then they will have achieved an important task.

Tom Kuhn

On *Life of Galileo* (1947–8) from *Constructing a Role: Laughton's Galileo*

Introduction

In the spring of 1944, living in Santa Monica, Brecht got to know the great Hollywood star Charles Laughton, whose performance as the king in Alexander Korda's *The Private Life of Henry VIII*, admired by Brecht, had garnered him one of the first Oscars (in 1933). The admiration was mutual. In the course of the year they discussed a range of possible projects, eventually fixing on a new English translation of Brecht's *Life of Galileo* with a view to a production in which Laughton would star. The play had originally been written in 1938–9 in Denmark, and that version had been premiered in Zurich in September 1943 under the title *Galileo Galilei*. But of course Brecht himself, in the States since the summer of 1941, had had nothing to do with the Zurich production. Indeed he had not been able conscientiously to develop a production of one of his own plays since 1932 (although he had been at least peripherally involved in several more rushed pieces of work). Now he was determined to get it right. Playwright and actor worked together closely for months, in probably one of the oddest and most remarkable artistic collaborations of all modern theatre history. Laughton knew no German, and Brecht was not confident that his English was even nearly good enough to judge the appositeness of a translated phrase. So Laughton acted out their rough script, and they fiddled and turned and polished it until things started to sound right and seemed to express the right gestus. When there was eventually the prospect of a production in Hollywood and it came to the rehearsals, the collaboration continued, no less intensely. By now it was June 1947: they had been working on the play for two and a half years. Carl Weber, one of a younger generation of Brecht's assistants at the Berliner Ensemble and himself a notable theatre scholar, writes in the *Brecht-Handbuch* (4, p. 290) that there can hardly have been a comparable cooperation between a dramatist and his leading man since Shakespeare and Richard Burbage. Brecht, who gives his own account in the first text below, later referred to the whole affair as 'two years of fun'. The play, in this English version, was eventually premiered in the Coronet Theatre in Beverly Hills (Los Angeles) in August 1947, with Laughton in the title role, alongside Frances Heflin and Hugo Haas (among others). Joseph Losey directed, although of course Brecht himself was much involved; the set was by Robert Davison and the music by Hanns Eisler. The production was subsequently reprised at the Maxine

Elliott Theatre on Broadway in New York, after Brecht's return to Europe, in the following year.

Ruth Berlau took hundreds of photographs especially of the New York production, which Brecht – envisioning it for himself from distant Zurich – opined was of greater clarity. He started to put together the texts and commentary that would make a *Modelbook* of the whole experience. This material from the American productions was then left on the back burner for a number of years, and it was not until 1955, when Brecht was planning another *Galileo* production, at the Berliner Ensemble with Ernst Busch in the title role, that publication plans became more concrete. The idea was to incorporate photographs and accounts of the new production as well as of the Laughton version, but Brecht died (on 14 August 1956) before either the new production itself or the publication could be finalized. In the end the *Modelbook* was printed in 1956 as *Aufbau einer Rolle. Laughtons Galilei* (Berlin: Henschel),[1] without the new material, as number two (after the *Antigone Model*) in Ruth Berlau's series of 'Modelbooks of the Berliner Ensemble'. However, distribution was delayed. The Busch *Galileo* opened on 15 January 1957, directed by Erich Engel. Hanns Eisler took on editorial responsibility for a second pamphlet volume representing the new Berliner Ensemble production. And eventually the *Modelbook* was distributed in 1958, with three slim volumes in a cassette – *Laughtons Galilei, Buschs Galilei* and the play text.

We present here only a fragment of the first of those publications. The English play text is of course available elsewhere, the volume devoted to Ernst Busch's performance contains no new texts by Brecht (although it does have wonderful photographs of the Berliner Ensemble production), and most of the rest of the texts that belong in the Laughton pamphlet volume (although not the photos) are in *Collected Plays: Five*, pp. 206–31. Together, these various published sources provide a full and important documentation about the play, about the context of its revision, and about the two American and one Berlin productions.

---

[1] The title, *Aufbau einer Rolle*, has sometimes been translated as *Building up a Part*, but Brecht means with 'Aufbau' to imply a more engineering approach, and certainly not a psychological one, hence our version, *Constructing a Role*.

Constructing a Role: Laughton's Galileo

Foreword

With his description of Laughton's *Galileo*, the playwright is setting out, not so much to try to give a little more permanence to one of those fleeting works of art that actors create, as to pay tribute to the pains a great actor is prepared to take over a fleeting work of this sort. This is no longer at all common. It is not only the under-rehearsing in our hopelessly commercialized theatre that is to blame for vapid and stereotyped portraits – give the average actor more time and he would hardly do any better. Nor is it simply that this century has very few outstanding individual personalities with rich characteristics and grand contours – if that were all, care could be devoted to the portrayal of 'lesser' figures. We seem above all to have lost any understanding and appreciation of what we might call a *theatrical conception*: what Garrick did when, as Hamlet, he met his father's ghost; Sorel when, as Phèdre, she knew that she was going to die; Bassermann when, as Philip, he had listened to Posa. These were all moments of high invention.

The spectator could isolate and detach such theatrical ideas, but they also merged to form a single rich texture.

Odd insights into the nature of mankind, glimpses of their particular way of living together, were brought about by the actors' ingenious contrivances.

There is even more secrecy about how works of art are made than how philosophical systems are developed. Those who produce them work hard to give the impression that everything happens with ease, as it were of its own accord, as though an image were forming in a clear mirror that is itself inert. Of course, this is deceptive, and the assumption seems to be that, if the deception is successful, it will increase the spectator's pleasure. But this is not the case. What the spectator – the experienced spectator, in any case – enjoys about art is the making of art, the active, creative element. In art we view nature herself as if she were an artist.

The ensuing account deals with this aspect, with the process of production rather than with the result. It is therefore more about the conception of reality that the artist has *and communicates* than about temperament; more about the observations that go into an artist's creations and can be derived from them than about that artist's vitality. This means neglecting much that seemed to us to be 'inimitable' in Laughton's achievement, and instead moving on to what can be learned from it. For we cannot create talent; we can only set it tasks.

It is unnecessary here to examine how the artists of the past used to surprise their audiences. Asked why he acted, L answered: 'Because people don't know what they are like, and I think I can show them.' His collaboration in the rewriting of the play showed that he had all sorts of ideas which were begging to be disseminated, about how people *really* live together, about the motivating forces that need to be taken into account. L's attitude seems to the playwright to be that of a realistic artist of our time. For whereas in relatively stationary ('quiet') periods artists may find it possible to merge wholly with their audience and faithfully 'embody' general notions, our profoundly unsettled time forces them to take special measures to penetrate to the truth. Our society will not itself admit what moves it. It can even be said to exist purely through the secrecy with which it cloaks itself. What attracted L about *Galileo* was not only one or two formal points but also the subject matter; he thought this might become what he called a *contribution*. And so great was his desire to show things as they really are that despite all his indifference, indeed timidity, in political matters, he suggested and even demanded that several of the play's points should be sharpened, simply because these passages seemed 'somehow weak' to him, by which he meant that they did not do justice to things as they are.

We usually met in L's large house above the Pacific, as the dictionaries of synonyms were too bulky to lug around. He had continual and inexhaustibly patient recourse to these tomes, and would in addition fish out the most varied literary texts in order to examine this or that gestus, or some particular form of speech: Aesop, the Bible, Molière, Shakespeare. He gave readings of Shakespeare's works in my house, to which he would devote perhaps a fortnight's preparation. In this way he read *The Tempest* and *King Lear*, simply for me and one or two guests who happened to have dropped in. Afterwards we would briefly discuss what seemed relevant to us, an 'aria' perhaps or an effective scene opening. These were exercises, and he would pursue them in various directions, incorporating them into the rest of his work. If he had to give a reading on the radio he would have me hammer out the syncopated rhythms of Whitman's poems (which he found somewhat strange) on a table with my fists, and once he hired a studio where we made records with half a dozen ways of telling the story of the creation, in which he was an African planter telling the Negroes how he had created the world, or an English butler ascribing it to His Lordship. We needed such broad studies because he spoke no German whatsoever, and we had to decide the gestus of dialogue by my acting it all in bad English or even in German and his then acting it back in proper English in a variety of ways until I could say: that's it. He would write the result down sentence by sentence in longhand. Some sentences, indeed many, he carried around for days, changing them continually. One immense advantage of this system of performance-and-repetition was that we avoided psychological discussions almost entirely.

Even the most fundamental instances of gestus, such as Galileo's way of observing, his showmanship, or his addiction to pleasure, were established in three dimensions by actual performance. Our primary concern throughout was for the smallest fragments, for sentences, even for exclamations – each treated separately, each demanding the simplest, most appropriate form, giving a certain amount away, hiding or leaving a certain amount open. More radical changes in the structure of entire scenes or of the work itself were intended to help the narrative to move along and to bring out our rather general conclusions about people's attitudes to the great physicist. But this reluctance to tinker with the psychological aspect remained with L throughout our long period of collaboration, even when a rough draft of the play was ready and he was giving various readings to test reactions, and even during the rehearsals.

The awkward circumstance that one translator knew no German and the other scarcely any English compelled us, as can be seen, to use acting as our means of translation from the outset. We were forced to do what better equipped translators should do too: to translate instances of gestus. For language is theatrical above all when it expresses the behaviour of the speakers to each other. (When it came to the 'arias', as has been mentioned, we also brought in the playwright's own gestus, by observing the songs of Shakespeare or the writers of the Bible.) L showed his lack of interest in the 'book' in a most striking and occasionally brutal way, to a degree that the playwright could not always share. What we were making was a text; the production was all that counted. It was impossible to lure him to translate passages which the playwright was willing to cut for the proposed production but wanted to keep in the book. The theatrical occasion was what mattered, the text was only there to make it possible; it would be expended in the production, would be consumed in it like gunpowder in a firework. Although L's theatrical experience had been in a London which had become thoroughly indifferent to the theatre, the old Elizabethan London still lived in him, the London where theatre was such a passion that it could swallow immortal works of art greedily and barefacedly simply as 'texts'. In fact these works which had outlived the age were like improvisations made for an all-important moment. Printing them at all interested only a few, and probably only happened so that the spectators – in other words, those who were present at the actual event, the production – might have a souvenir of their enjoyment. And the theatre seems to have been so potent in those days that the cuts and interpolations made in rehearsal can have done little harm to the text.

We used to work in L's small library, and in the mornings. But often L would come and meet me in the garden, walking barefoot over the damp grass in shirt and trousers, and would show me some improvements to his flowerbeds, for his garden always occupied him, harbouring many refinements and challenges. The gaiety and beautiful proportions of this garden world entered into our work in a most pleasing way. For quite a while we gathered everything into our work. If we discussed gardening it was only really a digression from one of the scenes in *Galileo*; if we were combing a New York museum for technical drawings by Leonardo to use as background pictures in the performance, we would digress to Hokusai's graphic work. I was able to observe how L would make only light use of such material. The parcels of books, or photocopies from books, which he constantly ordered, could not turn him into a bookworm. He obstinately sought the external: not physics, but the behaviour of physicists. It was a matter of putting together a bit of theatre, something slight and superficial. As the material piled up, L became intent on the idea of getting a good draughtsman to produce entertaining sketches to expose the anatomy of the action, as Caspar Neher tended to do. 'Before you amuse others, you have to amuse yourself,' he said.

For this no trouble was too great! No sooner had L heard of Caspar Neher's delicate stage sketches, which allow the actors to group themselves according to a great artist's compositions and to employ gestures that are both exquisite and true, than he commissioned a distinguished draughtsman from the Walt Disney Studios to make similar sketches. They turned out a bit mischievous; L used them, but with caution.

What pains he took over the costumes; not only his own, but those of all the actors! And how much time we spent casting the many parts!

First we had to look through books of costumes and old pictures to find costumes that had nothing of what our age might consider fancy dress. We sighed with relief when we found a small sixteenth-century panel that showed long trousers. Then we had to distinguish the classes from each other. There Breughel the Elder was of great service. Finally we had to work out the colour scheme. Each scene had to have a basic tone: the first, for example, a delicate aubade of white, yellow and grey. But the entire sequence of scenes had to develop in terms of colour. In the first scene a deep and distinguished blue made its entrance with Ludovico Marsili, and this deep blue remained, set apart, in the second scene with the haute bourgeoisie in their blackish-green coats of felt and leather. Galileo's social ascent could also be discerned in the colours. The silver and pearl-grey of the fourth (court) scene led into a nocturne in brown and black (where Galileo is jeered by the monks of the Collegium Romanum), then on to the seventh, the cardinals' ball, with delicate and fanciful individual masks (ladies and gentlemen) moving among the cardinals' crimson figures. There colour was able to burst out, but it still had to be fully unleashed, and this occurred in the tenth scene, the carnival. Like the nobility and the cardinals, the poor people too had their masked ball. Afterwards came the descent into dull and sombre colours. The difficulty of such a scheme of course lies in the fact that the costumes and their wearers wander through several scenes; they always have to fit in and contribute to the colour scheme of the new scene.

We cast mainly young actors. The speeches posed certain problems. The American stage shuns speeches except in (and perhaps because of) its frightful Shakespearean productions. In its eyes speeches just mean a pause in the action; and, as they are commonly delivered, that is what they are. L worked with the young actors in a masterly and conscientious manner, and the playwright was impressed by the freedom he allowed them, by the way in which he avoided anything Laughtonish and simply taught them the structure. To those actors who were too easily influenced by the Laughtonish personality he read passages from Shakespeare, without rehearsing the actual text at all; he did not read the text itself to any of them. Incidentally, the actors were asked on no account to prove their suitability for the part by putting something 'impressive' into it.

We jointly agreed the following points:

1. The set should not make the audience believe that they are in a medieval Italian room or the Vatican. The audience should be fully conscious of being in a theatre.
2. The background should show more than Galileo's immediate surroundings; it should show the historical setting in an imaginative and artistically appealing way. At the same time, it should remain background. (This can be achieved, for example, if the scenery is not itself colourful, but complements the actors' costumes by enhancing the roundedness of the figures, by giving a two-dimensional impression even if it contains three-dimensional elements, etc.)
3. Furniture and props (including doors) should be realistic and above all of social and historical interest. Costumes must be individualized and show signs of having been worn. Social differences are to be emphasized as we find it difficult to distinguish them in ancient fashions. The colours of the various costumes should harmonize.
4. The character groupings must have the quality of historical paintings (but not so that they bring out the historical aspect as an aesthetic attraction; this directive is equally valid for contemporary plays). The director can achieve this by inventing historical titles for the episodes. (Example: in the first scene such titles might be:
   'Galileo the physicist explains the new Copernican theory to his

subsequent collaborator Andrea Sarti and predicts the great historical importance of astronomy. To make a living the great Galileo teaches rich pupils. Galileo, who has requested support for his continued investigations, is urged by the university authorities to invent profitable instruments. – Galileo constructs his first telescope based on information from a traveller.')

5. The events must be presented calmly and in a grand sweep. Frequent changes of position, whereby the characters make insignificant movements, must be avoided. The director must not for a moment forget that many of the actions and speeches are hard to understand and that it is therefore necessary to express the underlying idea of an incident by the positioning. The audience must be assured that when someone walks, or gets up, or makes a gesture, it has meaning and deserves attention. But groupings and movements must remain absolutely natural and realistic.

6. Realism is of particular importance in casting the ecclesiastical dignitaries. A caricature of the church is not intended, but the refined manner of speech and the 'edification' of the seventeenth-century hierarchy must not mislead the director into picking otherworldly types. In this play, the church principally represents authority; as types, the dignitaries should resemble our present-day bankers and senators.

7. The portrayal of Galileo should not aim at rousing the audience to sympathy or empathy; they should rather be encouraged to adopt an attitude of astonishment, criticism and evaluation. Galileo should be portrayed as a phenomenon of the order of Richard III, whereby the vitality of this strange figure brings out emotions of approval in the audience.

8. The more profoundly the historical substance of a production is established, the more humour can be brought to the fore. The more sweeping the overall arrangement, the more intimately individual scenes can be played.

9. There is no reason why *Life of Galileo* cannot be performed without drastically changing the present-day style of production, as a historical 'war-horse', for instance, with a star part. Any conventional performance, however (which need not seem at all conventional to the actors, especially if it contained interesting inventions), would weaken the play's real strength considerably without making it any easier for the audience. The play's main effects will be missed unless the theatre changes its attitude. The stock reply, 'Won't work here', is familiar to the author; he heard it at home too. Most directors treat such plays as a coachman would have treated an automobile when it was first invented. On the arrival of the

machine, mistrusting the practical instructions accompanying it, this coachman would have harnessed the horses in front – more horses, of course, than to a carriage, as the new car was heavier – and then, his attention being drawn to the engine, he would have said, 'Won't work here.'

The production was put on in a small theatre in Beverly Hills, and L's chief concern was the prevailing heat. He asked for trucks full of ice to be parked against the theatre walls and for fans to be set in motion, 'so that the spectators can think'.

[BFA 25, pp. 9–20]

This was first published, along with John Hubley's arrangement sketches, as the introduction to the *Modelbook*, *Aufbau einer Rolle*, in East Berlin in 1956. Point 9 was added later.

As examples of great actors, Brecht mentions an Englishman, David Garrick (1717–79), a French woman, Cécile Sorel (born 1873 – he is possibly confusing her with Sarah Bernhardt, born 1844, who was indeed renowned for her embodiment of Racine's Phèdre) and a German, Albert Bassermann (born 1867). Bassermann was now, like Brecht, in exile; he had been famous for his portrayal of the Spanish King Philipp II in Schiller's *Don Carlos*, first in Max Reinhardt's 1907 Berlin production and subsequently in Munich and Zurich. Among the artists who inspired Brecht's and Laughton's work he names Leonardo da Vinci, Breughel (Bruegel) the Elder and the eighteenth-/nineteenth-century Japanese painter and printmaker Katsushika Hokusai.

What now follows is merely an extract from the very beginning of the material of this *Modelbook*.

A Sequence from Scene 1

Rotation of the Earth and Rotation of the Brain

L arranges the little demonstration of the earth's rotation quickly and casually from his high desk, where he has started to read, running to and from it. He avoids any sense of urgency, seeming to pay no attention at all to the child's capacity to understand and just leaving him sitting there with his thoughts.

As well as reflecting that Galilei is pressed for time, this casual manner also admits the boy to the community of scholars. It is in precisely this way that L established that learning and teaching are one and the same thing for Galilei – which is what makes his subsequent betrayal so terrible.

Andrea's mother interrupts Galilei during his demonstration of the earth's rotation. Taken to task for the absurd idea that he is teaching the child, he answers: 'Apparently we are on the threshold of a new era, Mrs Sarti.' It is enchanting to see how tenderly L drains his glass of milk as he utters these words!

[BFA 25, pp. 23–5]

These are notes on the opening of the play. There are similar notes and photographs for each sequence and scene. The notes are contained in *Collected Plays: Five*. The *Modelbook: Constructing a Part* ends with some more generalized reflections, as follows.

Background to the Performance

It is important to realize that our production took place at the time and in the place where the atom bomb had just been produced and put to military use, and where nuclear physics was shrouded in deepest secrecy. Anybody who was in the States at the time will struggle to forget the day the bomb was dropped. It was the Japanese war that really cost the States sacrifices. The troop ships left from the west coast, and the wounded and victims of tropical diseases returned to its ports. When the news first reached Los Angeles, it was at once clear that this was the end of the dreadful war, and that sons and brothers would soon return. But the great city lifted itself up in an astonishing display of mourning. The playwright heard bus conductors and saleswomen in the fruit markets express nothing but horror. It was victory, but it was the shame of a defeat. Then there was the fact that the tremendous energy source had been kept secret by the military and politicians, which upset the intellectuals. Freedom of inquiry, the exchange of scientific discoveries, the international community of scholars: all were closed down by authorities who were massively distrusted. Great physicists fled from the service of their bellicose government; one of the most renowned took a teaching post that forced him to waste his working hours on teaching the most rudimentary essentials, just to avoid working for these authorities. Making discoveries had become shameful.

[BFA 25, pp. 65–6]

On *The Antigone of Sophocles* (1947–8) from *Antigone Model 1948*

Introduction

Brecht returned to Europe from the United States in November 1947 and made his way to Zurich, partly explicitly to make contact once more with his pre-war designer and oldest collaborator, Caspar Neher, and partly because the Zurich Schauspielhaus had been the only prominent German-speaking theatre to interest itself in Brecht's work during the Nazi years. An encounter there with Hans Curjel, a Berlin theatre man whom he knew from the 1920s and now the director of the Stadttheater in Chur, led to his first theatre project back on European ground. *Antigone* (in Chur and then in Zurich) was a crucial project for Brecht. It gave him the opportunity to work together once more with Neher, it offered a starring role for the first time in years to his wife Helene Weigel, it was a return to the German language for both writer and actor, and it was exceptionally (even perilously) experimental in its conception. Sophocles' *Antigone* dates from around 441 BC, and Brecht used Hölderlin's strange and somewhat tortured 1804 translation. His text, completed swiftly in December 1947, was designed to enable an audience and readership to see and hear through these layers, in a dizzying historical abyss of references to tyranny and war. As for the theatrical realization, we must recall that at exactly the same time as the preparation of this play Brecht was also working on the summary of his theoretical ideas which was to become the *Short Organon* (see *Brecht on Theatre*). This was an opportunity for some properly experimental work in the theatre, such as he had not been able to essay since the early 1930s.

Rehearsals began in January 1948. From the very start Brecht considered Neher's designs and the whole look of the production to be so 'exemplary' that they must somehow be preserved. In February Ruth Berlau came back from New York to photograph proceedings. The premiere took place on 15 February, with Weigel in the title role and a relatively young and inexperienced actor, Hans Gaugler, as Creon. Despite the presence of friends and guests, excited about Brecht's return, the production was not a success. There were only five performances, one a matinee in Zurich. Almost immediately, however, Brecht, Berlau and Neher discussed the possibility of creating a *Modelbook*, which the relatively small West Berlin publisher Gebrüder Weiss was interested in publishing. The pamphlet volume appeared in August 1949, and was revised and republished by the East German Henschel publishing house in 1955 (by which time the play had also been staged in the small Thuringian town of Greiz, south of Leipzig). The publication also did not meet with much resonance, and questions about the creative freedom of theatres and directors were immediately raised.

Antigone Model 1948

Foreword

Thanks no doubt to its total moral and material collapse, our unfortunate land, source of so much misfortune, has acquired a vague appetite for novelty; and where art is concerned it is apparently being encouraged now and then to try something new. But because there seems to be a good deal of confusion as to what is old and what is new, and the fear that the old will return has been mixed with the fear that the new will set in; and because the vanquished are frequently being instructed that they must simply rid themselves of all intellectual and emotional traces of Nazism, artists would be well advised not to rely blindly on the assurance that novelty is welcome. Yet art can only find its bearings by progressing, and it must do so in company with the progressive elements of the population and not in divergence from them. Together with them it must stop waiting to be acted upon and act itself, and it must find some starting point in the general decay. It is not going to be at all easy for art to regain control of its ways and means and to augment them with new ones. The rapid decline of artistic methods under the Nazis seems to have taken place almost unnoticed. The damage done to the theatre buildings is far more conspicuous than that done to performance. This is partly because the former took place with the fall of the Nazi regime, but the latter during its rise. And so even today people actually speak of the 'brilliant' technique of the 'Göring theatre', as if such a technique could be adopted regardless of where that brilliance had shone. A technique which served to hide the causality at work in society can hardly be used to reveal it. And it is high time for a theatre of the inquisitive! Bourgeois society, with its anarchic system of production, only becomes aware of its own laws of motion in a catastrophe: as Marx says, it is only the roof falling in on their heads that reveals the law of gravity to them. But mere misfortune is a bad teacher. Its pupils learn hunger and thirst, but seldom hunger for truth and thirst for knowledge. No amount of illness will turn a sick man into a physician; neither close inspection nor a view from a distance makes the eyewitness into an expert. If the theatre is capable of showing reality, then it must also be capable of making the sight of it a pleasure. How then can such a theatre be created? The problem with ruins is that the house has gone, but the site is no longer there either. The construction plans, on the other hand, never get lost. So reconstruction resurrects the old dens of iniquity and centres of disease. Fevered life masquerades as vitality: no one steps out so firmly as the victims of spinal damage who have lost all feeling in the soles of their feet. Yet the difficult thing about art is that it has to conduct all its affairs with complete ease, however futile they may seem.

And so it may not be exactly easy to create progressive art in a period of reconstruction. This should spur us on.

2

The Antigone drama was selected for the present theatrical undertaking because it provided a certain topicality and raised some interesting formal issues. In terms of its political content, the streamlining process brought the present-day analogies out in an astonishingly powerful way, although on the whole they were a handicap: the great figure of resistance in the ancient drama does not represent the German resistance fighters, although it is they who necessarily seem most important to us. This was not the occasion for a poetic tribute to them; and this is all the more regrettable as these days so little is done to preserve their memory and so much to erase it. Nor will it be clear to everyone that it is not these fighters who are talked of here, but only those who realize this will be able to summon up the degree of strangeness that is needed if the truly remarkable element of this Antigone play – namely, the role of force in the collapse of a head of state – is to be usefully remarked upon. Even the prologue could do no more than to establish the topicality and sketch out the subjective problem. The Antigone drama then unfurls the action in its entirety, objectively, on the unfamiliar level of the rulers. It was possible to portray such grand-scale intrigue in an objective manner precisely because (and this was in other respects fatal) the old play was historically so remote that identification with its principal figure was impossible. Here too its elements of epic form were an aid, and in themselves provided something of interest to our theatre.

Greek dramaturgy uses certain forms of *Verfremdung*, notably interventions by the chorus, to try to rescue some of that freedom of calculation which Schiller is uncertain how to secure.[1] For the rest, this is in no way about using the Antigone drama as a means or pretext for 'conjuring up the

---

[1] A dramatic plot will move before my eyes; an epic seems to stand still while I move around it. In my view this is a significant distinction. If a circumstance moves in front of me, then I am bound strictly to the sensory present, my imagination loses all freedom, I feel a continual restlessness develop and persist in me, I have to stay rooted to the object, any reflection or retrospection is forbidden me, for I am led by an unfamiliar power. But if I move around a circumstance, which cannot get away from me, then my pace can be irregular, I can linger or hurry on according to my own subjective needs, can take a step backwards or leap ahead, and so forth.

Schiller–Goethe correspondence, 26 December 1797

spirit of antiquity'; philological interests were not the point. Even if we felt obliged to do something for a work like *Antigone*, we could only do so by having the play do something for us.

3

We did not so much develop a new dramaturgy as try out a new type of performance on an ancient play, and so the new adaptation cannot be handed over to theatres in the usual way, for them to deal with freely. A binding production model has been put together, which is made up of a collection of photographs accompanied by explanatory instructions.

Such a model will of course stand or fall according to the ease with which it can be imitated and varied. It is possible that the whole, or certain parts, may achieve no life when reproduced; in that case the whole or the parts in question must be discarded. A model cannot depend on cadences whose charm is due to particular voices or on gestures and movements whose beauty springs from particular physical characteristics: that sort of thing cannot serve as a model, for it is not exemplary so much as unparalleled. If something is to be usefully copied, it must first be shown. What is actually achieved when the model is put to use can then be a mixture of the exemplary and the unparalleled.

The idea of using models represents an obvious challenge to the artists of an era that applauds only that which is 'original', 'incomparable', 'never seen before', and encourages all that is 'unique'. They may well realize that a model is not a blueprint, and yet find that the way they work does not at all help them to use the models. It is hard enough for them to forget the role models of their youth, but by now they have learned to create everything out of the roles themselves, entirely from within the resources of the self. What, they will ask, is in any way creative about the use of models? The answer is that today's division of labour has altered creativity in many important areas of life. The act of creation has become a collective creative process, a continuum of a dialectical sort in which the original invention, taken on its own, has lost much of its importance. The initial invention of a model need not really count for all that much, for actors who use it immediately make their own personal contribution. They are free to invent variations on the model, that is to say variations that will make the image of reality that the model is to provide truer and richer in its implications, or artistically more satisfying. The choreographic figures (positions, movements, groupings, etc.[1]) can be

---

[1]   Neher's sketches served as the basis for the grouping and the masks, so that the model's inventors themselves were already, as it were, working to a pattern.

treated either slavishly or masterfully; masterfully, that is, only if reality enters into them freely. If the variations are undertaken in the right way, they too take on the qualities of a model; the learner becomes the teacher, and the model itself changes.

For the model is not constructed in order to fix for all time the way the production should work, quite the contrary! The prime emphasis is on development: changes are to be provoked and made perceptible; sporadic and anarchic acts of creation are to be replaced by creative processes whose changes proceed by steps or leaps.[1] The model was worked out in a dozen and a half rehearsals at the municipal theatre in Chur, and must be regarded as by definition incomplete. The very fact that its shortcomings cry out for improvement should stimulate the theatres to use it.

4

Neher's stage for 'Antigone'. Long benches, on which the actors can sit and wait for their cues, are placed in front of a semicircle of screens covered in red-coloured rush matting. There is a gap in the middle of the screens, where the record player sits and is visibly operated; the actors can go off through this gap when their part is done. The acting area is bounded by four posts, from which horses' skulls hang suspended. In the left foreground is a board for props, with Bacchic masks on sticks, Creon's laurel wreath made of copper, the millet bowl and the wine jug for Antigone, and the stool for Tiresias. Subsequently Creon's sword is hung up here by one of the elders. On the right is a framework with a sheet of iron on which an elder beats with his fist during the chorus song 'Spirit of joy, pride of the waters'. For the prologue a white wall is lowered on wires. There is a door and a cupboard in it. A kitchen table and two chairs stand in front of it; a sack lies in the right foreground. At the beginning a board with the time and the place written on it is lowered over the wall. There is no curtain.

The actors sit openly on the stage and only adopt the attitudes proper to their roles once they enter the (very brilliantly lit) acting area. The reason for this is that the audience must not believe that they have been transported to the scene of the action, but must instead be invited to witness the delivery of an ancient poem, irrespective of how it has been restored for the occasion.

There was a first and a second concept for the stage set. In the first, the

[1] The first attempt to use models of epic theatre was made by R. Berlau in Copenhagen. She used photographs of previous productions for Dagmar Andreasen's performances of *Die Mutter* and *Señora Carrar's Rifles*. Andreasen's Vlassova and Carrar were completely different from Weigel's figures. The attempt was a credit both to her and to Weigel, who had created something that could at the same time be both imitated and altered.

actors' benches formed the site of the old poem, as it were. The screen behind them consisted of ox blood-coloured canvases reminiscent of sails and tents, and the posts with the horses' skulls stood in between. The acting area was just lit very brightly and marked out by little flags. In this way the old poem would have been visibly separated from its secularized version. But we became more and more dissatisfied with this concept, until we eventually decided to situate the modern part of the action among the barbaric emblems of war as well.

A third possibility would be to cut the prologue and replace the screens behind the benches with a screen showing bomb damage in a modern city.

Costumes and props. The men's costumes were made of unadorned sackcloth, the women's of cotton. Creon's and Hamon's costumes had inserts of red leather. Antigone's and Ismene's were grey.

Particular care was taken over the props: good craftsmen worked on them. This was not so that the audience or the actors would imagine that they were real, but simply so as to provide the audience and the actors with beautiful objects.

5

As for the style of the portrayal, we follow Aristotle in maintaining that the plot is the kernel of the tragedy, even if we disagree about the purpose for which it should be performed. The plot ought not just to be a starting point for all kinds of excursions into the psyche or elsewhere, but should contain everything; and everything should be done for the plot so that once it has been told, everything has happened. The blocking and movement of the figures must narrate the plot, which is a chain of incidents, and this is the actor's sole task. The stylization which turns the actor's performance into art must not in the process destroy the naturalness, but should on the contrary heighten it. Obtrusive shows of temperament and conspicuously clear speech are to be discouraged. Stylization means a general elaboration of what is natural, and its object is to show the audience, as part of society, what is important for society about this plot. Thus the so-called 'poet's own world' must not be treated as isolated, authoritarian and 'obeying its own logic'; instead whatever it contains of the real world must be brought out and made effective. The 'poet's word' is only sacred in so far as it is true; the theatre is not the handmaiden of the poet but of society.

6

To keep the portrayal subordinate to the plot, *bridge verses* were given to the actors at rehearsals, which they were to deliver with the attitude of a narrator. Before stepping into the acting arena for the first time Weigel said (and in subsequent rehearsals heard the prompter saying):

> But Antigone went, King Oedipus' child, with her pitcher
> Gathering dust to cover the body of dead Polynices
> Which the wrathful tyrant had thrown to the dogs and the vultures.

The actress playing Ismene, before entering, said:

> To her, gathering dust, there appeared her sister Ismene.

Before verse 1 Weigel said:

> Bitterly the gatherer mourned the fate that had come to her brothers.

And so on. Each speech or action that is introduced by such verses then comes to seem like their realization in practice, and the actors are prevented from transforming themselves completely into the character: instead, the actors show. The bridge verses are printed under the photographs, and must be lifted out as appropriate.

More make-up than usual was used for the masks, and these too were meant to tell a story: in the case of the elders, for instance, the ravages left on the face by the habit of commanding, and so forth. As the photographs show, this did not entirely come off.

The tempo of the production was very fast.

7

The present model is to some extent difficult to study because it contains much that is unintentional and provisional; this has to be located and eliminated. This includes the entire field of mimicry, which all the actors, apart from Weigel, use in their own way to get by, so to speak. This field brings one up against the almost inextricable tangle of styles that defines our bargain-basement era, which puts on the plays of every era and country and invents the most disparate styles for them without having any style of its own. Of course such efforts then fail, and in a single production one finds both the resonant pathos and the quaintness which would make, say, Aeschylus or Gozzi respectively so unbearable; meanwhile the actors quite obviously all act with completely different purposes. This unhappy state of affairs is also bound to affect the model's proper sphere of competence, that is attitudes and blocking. Generally speaking it was the blocking to which most care was devoted. Economy in the movements of the groups and figures was intended to ensure that these movements had meaning. The separate constellations, even the distances between them, have dramatic significance, and at certain moments a single movement of one of the actors' hands may be enough to transform a situation. It was also hoped that the producers' and actors' inventions would be clearly visible as theatrical ideas – in this we have lost all sight of proper standards, so that it is no longer possible to distinguish great from small. Here as elsewhere the study of the pictures and notes is chiefly aimed at nurturing those senses of beginning and differentiating, which simply must be established in the confused and constipated realm of our current practice of art, tending as it does towards the conclusive, the complete and the general.

Moreover, if the whole experiment is not to be dismissed as unimportant, irrespective of whether it is thought to have been properly carried out, then nobody must be put off by the fear that it might mean we have to sacrifice all our practical experience to date. Theatre is simple-minded if it is not multifaceted. And dance often reaches its climax when someone dances out of line. Working with models need not be pursued with greater seriousness than is necessary for any kind of performance. Indeed, it may reasonably be considered to have something in common with Bach's *Well-Tempered Clavier*.

Brecht. Neher
[BFA 25, pp. 73–81]

The Foreword and the following pages closely mimic the opening of the published *Antigone Model*.

The Well-Tempered Clavier is the title given to two collections of preludes and fugues for keyboard instrument in all the major and minor twenty-four keys, the first book written, said Bach, 'for the profit and use of musical youth desirous of learning, and especially for the pastime of those already skilled in this study'.

Ruth Berlau's Prefatory Note

The production of *Antigone* took place in February 1948 in the municipal theatre in Chur, run by Hans Curjel. It was recorded in a series of photographs that were taken during the performance. A Leica, Hectar lens 1:1.9 and Superpan film were used. The photographic equipment was set up in the middle of the auditorium to the side, and it was raised very high so that it had a good view of stage. This is the only way to gain a vivid image of the groupings and movements, and when new theatres are built the first row of seats in the auditorium should be higher than the stage.

The Chur theatre has a normal lighting rig, and it became clear that, as had already been the case in Paris, Copenhagen, New York and Zurich, the 'very brightly lit acting area' demanded by Brecht cannot be produced by normal lighting rigs. Photometers and photographs revealed the irregularity of the light, which must be of more general interest. The actors move in uncontrollable corridors of shadow and hazy light, which must surely affect the audience's impressions unfavourably. (It is well known, for example, that comic passages require strong light.) It is therefore essential that modern theatres improve their lighting apparatus.

As far as the photography was concerned, it was also awkward to have to do without forestage lighting, because to do so would have illuminated the patchy cyclorama.

Under these circumstances, the photographs could do little more than show the groupings and individual attitudes.

Ruth Berlau
[BFA 25, pp. 82–3]

Prelude and Bridge to Scene 1

PRELUDE

At the front of the Antigone stage there is a wall with a door and cupboard in it. A table, two chairs. In the right-hand corner a sack.

A board with the inscription BERLIN. APRIL 1945. DAYBREAK is lowered. A stage hand hits the gong in the right foreground once, and the two sisters climb out of the orchestra pit.

Lines 1–4 are spoken to the audience.

After line 10 the Second Sister goes to the sack and looks inside it.

Lines 17 and 18 are once again spoken to the audience, after which the pair goes to the table and sits down, continuing with the action at line 21.

Sister, why is our door open wide?

A joint of bacon, sister, and a loaf of bread.

The narration must be recited in a plain and poetic tone, not as if the narrator is impressed by what has happened, but as if she has been summoned to report what has happened frequently and to many listeners. The narrator should be particularly careful to ensure that her report is not emotionally burdened by the preceding sections. The performance itself must have the clear character of showing.

From line 34 onwards the actions portrayed in the lines are carried out. After 41 the Second Sister proceeds to the cupboard, and after 42 she shows the First Sister the army coat. At line 50 the army coat is hung back up in the cupboard.

But there was no noise of fighting to be heard.

Sister, he isn't in the fight / He's run for it, he's cleared out.

After 62 both go to the table and pick up the dishes. Then the First Sister leads the way to the door, looks out and turns back to the Second Sister with line 63.

After 66 the Second Sister also looks out of the door, turns back and after 74 walks to the table, followed by her sister.

After line 93 the stage is bathed in half-light. The prelude wall is raised. Stage hands clear away the table and chairs.

The pair goes to the back of the stage, handing over their coats to the wardrobe attendants.

At the same time the actors climb out of the orchestra pit to the left and right and proceed to their benches in the background.

Full light illuminates the acting area, which is framed by the posts with the horses' skulls.

They have hanged him, sister. That was / Why he cried out loud for us.

I'll not leave my brother hanging there / Because he's walked and left your war.

ANTIGONE

The gong is beaten twice. Those portraying Antigone and Ismene stand up and move quickly to the edge of the acting area, which lies between the four posts. The Antigone figure picks up the iron jug off the bench and takes it with her. The Antigone figure then places the jug on her left hip in a calculated manner, turns her head to indicate the secrecy of the movement, and moves with long strides across the acting area. Although it is brief, this walk with the jug must be conspicuous in its freedom, so that her freedom is all the more lacking when the board is tied to her during the quarrel scene.

The gathering of dust under the skull post proceeds for a while; then the person portraying Ismene steps into the acting area.

Question: The person portraying Ismene seems to have performed without any change of position or any particular gesture in this scene. But shouldn't there at least be a difference in her attitude outside of the acting area and within it, since otherwise the difference between waiting for her entrance and waiting for Antigone's request cannot be expressed?

Answer: Yes. Ismene could, from line 21 onwards, veil her face as she steps into the acting area.

Question: So what you did was incorrect?

Answer: Yes.

But Antigone went, King Oedipus' child, with her pitcher
Gathering dust to cover the body of dead Polynices
Which the wrathful tyrant had thrown to the dogs and the vultures.

To her, gathering dust, there appeared her sister Ismene.

[BFA 25, pp. 84–91]

The line references are to the lines of verse as they appear in the published play (the English edition mirrors the German) with the exception of the last lines of the Prologue, for which Brecht made some changes in the Chur production.

The remainder of the *Modelbook* continues in the same detailed vein, with notes, questions and answers on the left-hand page, and photographs and quotations from the play on the right. At the end of the *Modelbook* there are some further photographs and reproductions of Neher's sketches.

Neher's second design for the Antigone *stage*

On *Mother Courage and Her Children* (1949–51)
from *Courage Model 1949*

Introduction

Mother Courage and Her Children was another of the plays premiered in Zurich in Brecht's absence, this time in April 1941 when Brecht himself was in Finland preparing his imminent departure for the United States. When he returned to Europe in 1947–8 he more or less immediately began revising the text in order to counter the widespread reception of that first production as 'a hymn to the inexhaustible vitality of the mother creature' (*Journal*, 7 January 1948). He had had something much more bitingly socially critical in mind. The new German premiere, at the Deutsches Theater in East Berlin, directed by Erich Engel and Brecht himself, and with Helene Weigel as Mother Courage, was on 11 January 1949. Two actors familiar from the theatre of the Third Reich, Paul Bildt and Werner Hinz, played the cook and the chaplain respectively. The production as a whole was, however, programmatically designed to counter the ethos of the National Socialist theatre, which was still very much in the audience's mind. Brecht and Engel leaned heavily on Teo Otto's designs for the Zurich Schauspielhaus and developed a strict, anti-illusionist epic style. Perhaps surprisingly, in view of the production's relative austerity of its message, it was a huge success. It is not too much to say that this one event established the importance of epic theatre in Germany, and enabled Brecht and Weigel to pursue their plans for their own theatre: the Berliner Ensemble was founded later in the same year.

Berlau had of course been hard at work, and this time she was not alone: Hainer Hill, who was later to become a designer at the Berliner Ensemble, had also been taking photographs. A selection of their photographic material and Brecht's directorial notes was assembled into one of those scrapbook *Modelbooks* (see Introduction) in the spring. Brecht went so far as to intervene to prevent a production in Dortmund that was taking no account of the Berlin 'model', and there was then an angry reaction to the whole idea of 'models' when the play was given its West German premiere in Wuppertal in September/October 1949, directed by Willi Rohde. The Suhrkamp publishing house, which managed the rights on Brecht's behalf outside the Soviet countries, instructed theatres that a special 'directorial score' was in preparation, of which future productions would have to take account. The next autumn Brecht himself went on to make triumphant use of the model at a production at the Kammerspiele in Munich, with Therese Giehse as Mother Courage (photographed by Berlau again, with Ruth Wilhelmi); and the following year he returned to it again when a new production of the play was developed for the Berliner Ensemble, again with Weigel, and this time with two decidedly antifascist actors, Ernst Busch and Erwin Geschonneck, who had both worked with Brecht before 1933, as cook and chaplain. It was this staging that went on tour in the years that followed and was so enthusiastically received wherever it went, throughout Germany and Europe and even in America. The Berliner Ensemble production did more than anything else to win converts to epic theatre and to confirm Brecht's importance as one of the theatre greats of the twentieth century.

Some of the *Modelbook* texts had already been published by this time, in the GDR monthly *Aufbau*, and in 1952 further extracts appeared in the Berliner Ensemble's own *Theatre Work* (see below), but other plans for a publication came to nothing – until the contract for a series of *Modelbooks* was signed with the Henschelverlag in 1954. For the published *Modelbook* Brecht wanted to make use of the experience of the further productions that had followed the Deutsches Theater premiere, in particular the Giehse-*Courage* in Munich. In 1956, the last year of his life, he reviewed the texts and made the final selection of photographs from the vast amount of material that had by now accumulated. The *Courage Model 1949* appeared in 1958 as the third in the series. As with *Galileo*, it was a cassette with three pamphlets, this time divided into *Text*, *Production* (with the photos) and *Notes*. As we are presenting here just a fragment of the published material – the remainder of the notes on individual scenes is in Brecht, *Collected Plays: Five*, pp. 277–323 – we have chosen to integrate the photographic material with the notes.[1]

---

[1] The original publication put the photos first, whereas the Berliner und Frankfurter Ausgabe (vol. 25) chooses to put the notes before the photos. For our own publication we have brought them together. In a couple of instances we have substituted non-identical but very similar images of the relevant scene, as it was not always possible to identify good copies of the original photos.

Courage Model 1949

Opening Remarks

Models

If life goes on in our ruined cities after the great war, then it is a different life, the life of different or differently composed groups, inhibited or guided by the new surroundings, new because so much has been destroyed. There are heaps of rubble piled high, but underneath them lie the city's invaluable infrastructures, the water and drainage pipes, the gas mains and electric cables. Even those large buildings that have remained intact are affected by the damage and rubble around them, and may become an obstacle to planning. Temporary structures have to be built and there is always a danger that they will become permanent. All of these things are reflected in art, for our way of thinking is part of our way of living. As for the theatre, we deliver these models into the breach. They immediately meet with strong opposition from all supporters of the old ways, of the routine that masquerades as experience and of the convention that calls itself creative freedom. And they are endangered by those who take them up without having learned to use them properly. For although they are meant to simplify matters, they are not simple to use. And they were designed not to make thought unnecessary but to provoke it; not to replace but to compel artistic creation.

First of all we must simply imagine that the information which the printed text provides about certain events – in this case the adventures of Mother Courage and the losses she incurs – has to some extent just been rounded out; it has now been established that when the woman's dead son was brought to her she was sitting beside her mute daughter, and so on – the kind of information which an artist painting some historic incident can arrive at by questioning eyewitnesses. Later he can still change certain details, as may seem advisable for one reason or another. Until one has learned to copy (and construct) models in a lively and intelligent way, to a high standard, it is better not to copy too much. Such things as the cook's make-up or Mother Courage's costume do not have to be imitated. The models should not be forced too much.

Pictures and descriptions of a performance do not yield enough. You do not learn much by reading that a character moves in a particular direction after a given sentence, even if the tone of the sentence, the way of walking and a convincing motive can all be supplied – which is already difficult enough. Those who are prepared to undertake the imitation are not the same as those in the original model; with them it would not have come out the same way. All those who deserve the name of artist are unique; they represent the general in a particular way. They can neither be perfectly imitated nor give a perfect imitation. Nor is it as important for artists to imitate art as it is for them to imitate life. The use of models is therefore a particular kind of art, and only so much can be learned from it. The aim must be neither to copy the example exactly nor to depart from it too quickly.

In studying what follows – a number of considerations and contrivances emerging from the rehearsal of a play – the solutions proposed to certain problems should above all lead you to see the problems themselves.

Photography

Of the several thousands of photos taken during the productions there is a selection of around eight hundred that is lent out by the archive of the Berliner Ensemble. The photos in this book are extracted from this selection. As with most photos taken during a production, they are deceptive in one respect: the background appears dark, although in reality it was light and clear. The cyclorama, for example, was never dark but always light grey, almost white. However, the lighting apparatus of the Deutsches Theater is too weak to show the soft golden light that bathed the entire stage. Even the shadows in the foreground, which appear here and there in the photos and are caused by the irregular positioning of the lights, were weaker in the performance itself, indeed were barely noticeable.

Music

Paul Dessau's music for *Mother Courage* is not particularly catchy; like the stage set, it left something for the audience to contribute: in the act of listening they had to link the voices with the melody. Art is no land of idle plenty. In order to make the transition to the musical items, to let the music have its say, we lowered a musical emblem from the rigging whenever there was a song which did not spring directly from the action, or which did spring from it but remained clearly apart. This emblem consisted of a trumpet, a drum, a flag, and electric globes that lit up; a slight and delicate thing, pleasant to look at, even if it was badly damaged in scene 9. Some people regarded this as sheer playfulness, as an unrealistic element. But on the one hand playfulness in the theatre should not be condemned too harshly as long as it is kept within bounds, and on the other it was not wholly unrealistic, for it served to set the music apart from the reality of the action. It provided us with a visible sign of the shift to another artistic level – that of music – and allowed us to give the correct impression that these were musical insertions, rather than to lead people to think quite mistakenly that the songs 'grew out of the action'. Those who object to this are quite simply opposed to anything erratic, 'inorganic', pieced-together – chiefly because they object to any shattering of illusion. They ought to object not to the tangible symbol of music, but to the manner in which the musical numbers are built into the play, that is, as insertions.

The musicians were placed so that they could be seen, in a box beside the stage – thus their performances became little concerts, independent contributions made at appropriate points in the play. The box was connected to the backstage area, so that a musician or two could occasionally go backstage for trumpet calls or when music occurred as part of the action.

We began with the overture. Although it was rather thin, as it was performed by only four musicians, it nonetheless provided a suitably solemn preparation for the turmoil of war.

Stage design

For the production described here, at the Deutsches Theater in Berlin, we used the famous model devised during the war for the Zurich Schauspielhaus by Teo Otto. The model used a permanent framework of huge screens, made out of such materials as one would expect to find in the military encampments of the seventeenth century: tenting, wooden posts lashed together with ropes, etc. Buildings such as the parsonage and the peasants' house were produced in three dimensions, realistic both in terms of construction methods and material, but in artistic abbreviation, only showing so much as was necessary for the action. The cyclorama was covered in coloured projections, and the revolving stage was used to represent the journeys. – We varied the size and position of the screens and used them only for the camp scenes, so as to distinguish these from the highway scenes. The Berlin stage designer made his own versions of the buildings (in scenes 2, 4, 5, 9, 10 and 11), but according to the same principle. We dispensed with the background projections used in Zurich and hung the names of the various countries over the stage in large black letters. We used an even, white light, and as much of it as our equipment permitted. In this way we eliminated any vestige of 'atmosphere' that could easily have given the incidents a romantic tinge. We retained almost everything else down to the smallest details (chopping block, hearth, etc.), particularly the excellent positionings of the cart. This last was very important because it determined much of the grouping and movement from the outset.

Surprisingly little is lost if you do without complete freedom of 'artistic creation'. You have to start somewhere, with something; why not with something that has already been fully thought through? Freedom will be acquired through the principle of contradiction, which is always active and vocal in all of us.

Realistic theatre and illusion

Writing in 1826, Goethe spoke of the 'imperfection of the English boarded stage' of Shakespeare's day. He says: 'There is no trace here of the insistence on naturalness to which we have gradually become accustomed through the improvement in machinery, in the art of perspective and in costuming.' 'Who,' he asks, 'would tolerate such a thing today? Under such conditions Shakespeare's plays would become highly interesting fairy tales, merely narrated by a few people who have tried to increase their effectiveness somewhat by making up as the characters, by coming and going and carrying out the movements necessary to the story, but who have left it to the audience to imagine paradises and palaces on the bare stage, just as they please.'

Since he wrote these words, a hundred years of improvements have been made to the mechanical equipment of our theatres, and the 'insistence on naturalness' has led to such an emphasis on illusion that we latecomers may well be more inclined to put up with Shakespeare on a bare stage than with a Shakespeare that has ceased to require or provoke any use of the imagination at all.

In Goethe's day any improvements to the mechanics of illusion were relatively harmless, because the machinery was so imperfect, so much 'in the childhood of its beginnings' that theatre itself was still a reality and both imagination and ingenuity could still be employed to turn nature into art. The sets were still theatrical displays, in which the stage designer gave an artistic and poetic interpretation of the places concerned.

The bourgeois classical theatre occupied a happy halfway point on the road to naturalistic illusionism. Stage machinery provided enough elements of illusion to create a more perfect representation of certain natural elements, but not so much as to make the audience feel that they were no longer in a theatre; art had not yet come to signify the obliteration of all indications that art is at work. Because there was no electricity, lighting effects were still primitive; where poor taste decreed that sunset effects were necessary, poor equipment prevented total enchantment. The authentic costumes of the Meiningen theatre came a little later; they were usually magnificent, although not always beautiful, and they were at least counteracted by an inauthentic manner of speaking. In short, theatre remained the theatre, at least in so far as it failed in the business of deception. Today the restoration of the theatre's reality as theatre is a precondition for any realistic representation of how people live together. Too much heightening of the illusion in the setting, along with a 'magnetic' manner of acting which gives the spectator the illusion of being present at a fleeting, fortuitous, 'real' event, create such an impression of naturalness that we can no longer interpose our own judgement, imagination or reactions, and must simply conform by sharing in the experience and becoming one of 'nature's' objects. The illusion created by the theatre must be a partial one, so that it can always be recognized as illusion. Reality, however completely represented, must be altered by art, so that it may be seen to be subject to change and treated as such.

And that is why we are demanding naturalness today – because we want to change the nature of the way we live together.

Elements of illusion?

The sight of the cyclorama behind a completely empty stage (in the Prologue and in the seventh and last scenes) doubtless creates the illusion of the sky above a flat landscape. There is no reason to object to this simply on the grounds that there must be some stirring of poetry in the soul of the spectator for such an illusion to come about. It is easy enough to create such an illusion: the actors are able simply by their actions to suggest, at the beginning, an open landscape to the entrepreneurial spirit of the little sutler family, and an immeasurable wilderness to the exhausted fortune-hunter at the end. And we can in any case always hope that, mixed with the materiality of this impression, there will come an impression of a more formal nature: that the spectators will partake of that initial void from which everything arises if they first see just the stark, empty stage that is to be populated. They know that the actors have been working on this tabula rasa for weeks, testing first one detail, then another, coming to know the incidents of the chronicle by portraying them, and portraying them by passing judgement on them. Now it begins, and Mother Courage's cart comes rolling on to the stage. – If there is such a thing as a beautiful approximation in matters large of scale, there is certainly no such thing on a small scale. A realistic portrayal requires carefully worked-out detail in costumes and props, for here the imagination of the audience can add nothing. All the implements for working and eating must be most lovingly made. And the costumes, of course, cannot be as for a folklore festival; they must show signs of individuality and social class. They have been worn for a longer or shorter time, are made of cheaper or more expensive material, are well or not so well taken care of, and so on.

The costumes for this production of *Mother Courage* were by Kurt Palm.

What a production of Mother Courage and Her Children is primarily meant to show

That in wartime the big profits are not made by the little people. That war, which is a continuation of business by other means, makes human virtues fatal even to those who possess them. That no sacrifice is too great for the struggle against war.

[BFA 25, 171–7]

These are Brecht's introductory notes to the *Modelbook*. In defence of his own style, he ranges through theatre history, with references to Shakespeare, to Goethe's 1826 essay on 'Shakespeare as a dramatist', and to the Meiningen court theatre which was renowned in the second half of the nineteenth century for its creation of 'historically authentic' sets and costumes. There is an article on the work of the designer Kurt Palm in *Brecht on Theatre*. The formulation in the penultimate sentence is a variation on the famous remark by Clausewitz, that war is 'the continuation of politics by other means'.

What follows now are the more detailed notes on the Prologue and the first two scenes.

Notes and Scene-Photos for the Prologue, Scenes 1 and 2

Scene-photos are by Ruth Berlau, Hainer Hill and Ruth Wilhelmi from the productions at the Deutsches Theater, the Berliner Ensemble and the Munich Kammerspiele. Further Munich photographs by Hildegard Steinmetz and Willi Saeger.

PROLOGUE

By way of a prologue, Mother Courage and her little family were shown on their way to the theatre of war. Mother Courage sang her Business Song from Scene 1 (so that in Scene 1 her line 'In business' is followed immediately by the sergeant's question: 'Halt! Who are you lot with?'). After the overture, to spare the actor the exertion of singing against the rumbling of the revolve, the first stanza was played on a record to a darkened auditorium. Then the prologue began.

The long road to war

The linen half-curtain, on which the titles of the scenes are subsequently projected, opens and Mother Courage's cart is rolled forward against the movement of the revolve.

The cart is a cross between a military vehicle and a grocery shop. A sign affixed to the side of it says: 'Second Finnish Regiment' and another 'Mother Courage, Groceries'. On the canvas Good Swedish pork sausages are displayed next to a flag with a price tag for '4 florins'. The cart will undergo several changes

1. A canteen woman and her family on their way to the theatre of war

in the course of the chronicle. There will sometimes be more, sometimes less merchandise hanging on it, the canvas will be dirtier or cleaner, the letters on the signs will be faded and then again freshly painted, depending on the state of business. Now, at the start, it is clean and full of wares.

The cart is pulled by the two sons. They sing the second stanza of Mother Courage's Business Song. 'Captains, how can you make them face it – / March off to death without a brew?' On the box sit the mute Kattrin, playing the jew's harp, and Mother Courage. Courage is sitting in lazy comfort, swaying with the cart and yawning. Everything, including her one backward glance, indicates that the cart has come a long way.

We had conceived of the song as a theatrical entrance, lusty and cocky – we had the last scene of the play in mind. But Weigel saw it as a realistic business song and suggested that it be used to portray the long journey to the war. Such are the ideas of great actors.

Once this was settled, it seemed to us that by showing the business woman's long journey to the theatre of war we would be showing clearly enough that she was an active and voluntary participant in the war. But certain reviews and many discussions with individuals who had seen the play showed that a good many people regarded Mother Courage merely as a representative of the 'little people' who 'get caught up in the war', because they 'cannot do anything about it', are 'helpless victims of the war', and so on. A deeply engrained habit leads the theatregoer to pick out the more emotional utterances and overlook everything else. Like descriptions of landscapes in novels, references to business are received with boredom. The 'business atmosphere' is simply the air one breathes and as such requires no special mention. And so, regardless of all our efforts to represent the war as an aggregate of business deals, the discussions showed time and time again that people regarded it as a timeless abstraction.

Too short can be too long

The two stanzas of the opening song, plus the pause between them during which the cart rolls silently along, take up a certain amount of time, and this initially seemed too long to us in rehearsal. But when we cut the second stanza, the prologue seemed much longer, and when we prolonged the pause between the stanzas, it seemed shorter.

The Courage song in the Prologue

Weigel employed a dialect colouring throughout the whole play, but only for the new version by the Berliner Ensemble did she also use it in Courage's Business Song as well. The song came to life.

It must never be forgotten that our stage German is artificial. The actor's lines gain reality when they are practised in the vernacular, that is in local dialect. Few texts, really only those that are thoroughly wooden, lose something in the process. Some, of course, must be spoken in the poet's dialect, such as Schiller's and Hölderlin's in Swabian, Kleist's in the dialect of the Mark Brandenburg, and so on.

SCENE ONE

The business woman Anna Fierling, known as Mother Courage, encounters the Swedish army

Recruiters are going about the country looking for cannon fodder. Mother Courage introduces her mixed family, acquired in various theatres of war, to a sergeant. The canteen woman defends her sons against the recruiters with a knife. She realizes that her sons are falling prey to the recruiters and predicts that the sergeant will meet an early death. To make her children afraid of the war, she has them draw black crosses as well. Thanks to a small business deal, she nevertheless loses her brave son. The sergeant leaves her with a prophecy, too:

'Like the war to nourish you?
Have to feed it something too.'

Basic arrangement

2. The setting, 'SWEDEN', and the projection on the half-curtain: 'Spring 1624. The Commander-in-Chief Oxenstierna is raising troops in Dalecarlia for the Polish campaign. The canteen woman Anna Fierling, known under the name of Mother Courage, loses one son.'

3. Recruiters are going about the country looking for cannon fodder.

Recruiters are going about the country looking for cannon fodder. On the empty stage the sergeant and the recruiter are standing right front on the lookout, complaining in muffled voices of the difficulty of finding cannon fodder for their general. The city of which the sergeant speaks is assumed to be in the auditorium. Then Mother Courage's cart appears and the recruiters' mouths water at the sight of the young men. The sergeant cries 'Halt!' and the cart comes to a stop.

4. A sergeant inspects Courage's papers, while a recruiter inspects her sons.

5. Mother Courage introduces her mixed family, acquired in various theatres of war, to a sergeant.

Mother Courage introduces her mixed family, acquired in various theatres of war, to a sergeant. The professionals of commerce and of war meet, the war can start. At the sight of the military, the Fierlings may hesitate for a moment as though afraid: the soldiers of their own side are also enemies; the army gives, but it also takes. Mother Courage's 'Morning, sergeant' is spoken in the same curt, military monotone as his 'Morning, all.' Climbing down from her cart, she makes it clear that she regards showing her papers as a formality, superfluous among professionals ('All right, we'll run through the whole routine'). She introduces her little family, acquired in various theatres of war, in a jocular tone: she puts on a bit of an original 'Mother Courage' act.

The cart and the children are on the left, the recruiters on the right. Mother Courage crosses over with her tin box full of papers. She has been summoned, but she is also sallying forth to scout and do business. She describes her children from the other side of the stage, as though better able to take them in from a distance. The recruiter makes forays behind her back, stalking the sons, provoking them. The pivotal point is in the lines: 'I bet you could use a good pistol, or a belt buckle?' and 'I could use something else.'

6. The recruiters ascertain that the sons are fit for war.

7. The canteen woman defends her sons against the recruiters with a knife.

The canteen woman defends her sons against the recruiters with a knife. The sergeant leaves her standing there and goes over to the sons, followed by the recruiter. He knocks on their chests, feels their calf muscles. He goes back and plants himself in front of Mother Courage: 'Why aren't they in the

8. Courage realizes that her sons are falling prey to the recruiters and predicts that the sergeant will meet an early death.

army?' The recruiter has stayed with the sons: 'Let's see if you're a chicken.' Mother Courage runs over, thrusts herself between the recruiter and her son: 'He's a chicken.' The recruiter goes over to the sergeant (on the right) and complains: 'He was crudely offensive'; Mother Courage snatches her Eilif away. The sergeant tries to reason, but Mother Courage pulls a clasp knife and stands there in a rage, guarding her sons.

Mother Courage realizes that her sons are falling prey to the recruiters and predicts that the sergeant will meet an early death. Again she goes over to the sergeant ('Give me your helmet'). Her children follow her and look on, gaping. The recruiter makes a wide detour, comes up to Eilif from behind and speaks to him.

When after some hesitation the sergeant has drawn his black cross, the children, satisfied, go back to the cart, but the recruiter follows them. And when Mother Courage turns ('I've got to take advantage'), she sees the recruiter between her sons; he has his arms around their shoulders.

9. To make her children afraid of the war, she has them draw black crosses as well.

To make her children afraid of the war, Mother Courage has them draw black crosses as well. The rebellion in her own ranks is in full swing. She runs angrily behind her cart to paint black crosses for her children. When she returns to the cart's shaft with the helmet, the recruiter, grinning, leaves the children to her and goes back (right) to the sergeant. When the sombre ceremony is over, Mother Courage goes to the sergeant, returns his helmet, and with fluttering skirts climbs up on the seat of the cart. The sons have harnessed themselves, the cart starts moving. Mother Courage has mastered the situation.

10. On the recruiter's advice, the sergeant offers to make a purchase.

11. Because of a small business deal, she nevertheless loses her brave son.

Because of a small business deal, she nevertheless loses her brave son. But the sergeant has only been half defeated; on the recruiter's advice, he offers to make a purchase. Electrified, Mother Courage climbs down from the cart and the sergeant draws her off left behind the cart. While the deal is in progress, the recruiter takes the harness off Eilif and leads him away. Kattrin sees this, climbs down from the cart and tries in vain to call her mother's attention to Eilif's disappearance. But Mother Courage is deep in her bargaining. Only after she has snapped her moneybag shut does she notice his absence. For a moment she has to sit down on the cart shaft, still holding her buckles. Then she angrily flings them into the cart, and the family, with one less member, moves gloomily off.

12. The sergeant leaves her with a prophecy, too: Like the war to nourish you? Have to feed it something too.

The sergeant leaves her with a prophecy, too. Laughing, he predicts that if she wants to live off the war, she will also have to give the war its due.

A mistake

The cyclorama of the Deutsches Theater is flawed in that it offers no entry point, so it was necessary to set up a screen in the background to conceal the cart at the beginning. Otherwise the cart could have come out of a hole in the cyclorama. The stage designers gave the screen the vague form of a farmstead; we could have insisted that it have the form of a screen. But this would have been worse than a hole in the cyclorama for the cart to enter the stage, so we didn't nit-pick.

The recruiters

The empty stage of the prologue was transformed into a specific location by means of a few clumps of wintry grass marking the edge of a highway. Here the military men stand waiting, freezing in their armour.

The great disorder of war begins with order, the disorganization starts as organization. The troublemakers have troubles of their own. We hear complaints to the effect that it takes brains to get a war started. And so the military men are businessmen. The sergeant has a little book that he consults, the recruiter has a map to help him in his struggle against the landscape. The fusion of war and business cannot be established soon enough.

Grouping

There will be some difficulty in persuading the actors playing the sergeant and the recruiter to stay together and in one place until Mother Courage's cart appears. In our theatre, groups always show a strong tendency to break up, partly because each actor believes he can heighten audience interest by moving about and changing his position, and partly because he wants to be alone and to divert the audience's attention from the group to himself. But there is no reason not to leave the military men together; on the contrary, both the image and the argument would be impaired by a change of position.

Changes of position

Positions should be retained as long as there is no compelling reason for changing them; and a desire for variety is not a compelling reason. If one gives in to a desire for variety, any movement on the stage is rapidly devalued; the spectator ceases to look for a specific meaning behind each movement, he stops taking movement seriously. However, the full force of a change of position is particularly necessary at the pivotal moments in the action. Legitimate variety is obtained by ascertaining the pivotal moments and planning the arrangement around them. For example, the recruiters have been listening to Mother Courage; she has succeeded in diverting and entertaining them with her talk and so putting them in a good humour; so far there has been only one ominous circumstance: the sergeant has asked for her papers, but has not examined them – his only purpose was to prolong their stay. She takes the next step (physically, too: she goes up to the sergeant, takes hold of his belt buckle, and says: 'I bet you could use a belt buckle?'), she tries to sell them something, and that is when the recruiters spring into action. The sergeant says ominously: 'I could use something else' and along with the recruiter goes over to the sons at the cart's shaft. The recruiters examine the sons as they would horses. And the pivotal moment is underlined when the sergeant goes back to Mother Courage, plants himself in front of her, and asks: 'Why are they dodging military service?' (The effect of such movements should not be weakened by having the actors speak during them!) If changes of position are needed to make certain incidents clear to the audience, the movement must be utilized to express something significant for the action and for this particular moment. If nothing of the sort can be found, it is advisable to review the whole arrangement up to this point; it will probably be seen to be at fault, because the sole purpose of an arrangement is to express the action, and the action (it is to be hoped) involves a logical development of incidents, which the arrangement need only present.

On details

Every detail, even the smallest, must of course be acted out to the full on the brightly lit stage. This is especially true of incidents which are glossed over on our stage almost as a matter of principle, such as payment on conclusion of a sale. Here Weigel devised (for the sale of the buckle in 1, the sale of the capon in 2, the sale of the drinks in 5 and 6, the handing out of the burial money in 12, etc.) a little gesture of her own: she audibly snapped shut the leather moneybag that she wore slung around her neck. It is indeed difficult in rehearsals to resist the impatience of actors who are in the habit of trying to sweep an audience off its feet, and to work out the details painstakingly and inventively in accordance with the principle of epic theatre: *one thing after another*. Even minute details are very revealing, such as the fact that when the recruiters step up to her sons and feel their muscles as if they were horses, Mother Courage displays maternal pride for a moment, until the sergeant's question ('Why are they dodging military service?') shows her the danger their assets put them in: then she rushes between her sons and the recruiters. The pace at rehearsals should be slow, if only to make it possible to work out details. Determining the pace of the production is another matter and comes later.

A detail

Mother Courage shows no savagery in pulling a knife. She is merely showing how far she will go in defending her children. The actor must above all show that Mother Courage is familiar with such situations and knows how to handle them.

Mother Courage has her children draw lots

Only by a mild tirade and by pointedly averting her face when Swiss Cheese draws his slip from the helmet – in other words by a slightly exaggerated display of impartiality (see for yourself, no sleight of hand, no tricks here) does the actor show that Mother Courage knows she has been tampering with fate. For otherwise she fully believes what she says, namely, that in some situations certain of her children's qualities and defects could be fatal.

Mother Courage predicts that the sergeant will meet an early death

It turned out that Mother Courage had to turn towards Eilif before stepping up to the sergeant for him to draw his lot. Otherwise it would not have been understood that she does this to put her son, so eager for war, off the war.

The belt buckle deal

Mother Courage loses her son to the recruiter because she cannot resist the temptation to sell a belt buckle. After climbing down from the cart to bring the sergeant the buckle, Courage must at first show a certain amount of distrust by looking around anxiously for the recruiter. Once the sergeant has seized the string of buckles and drawn her behind the cart, so that the recruiter can work on the son, her distrust shifts to the area of business. When she goes to get schnapps for the sergeant she takes the buckle, which has not yet been paid for, out of his hands; and she bites into the coin. The sergeant is thoroughly disgruntled at her distrust.

If the distrust at the beginning were omitted, we would be left with a stupid, utterly uninteresting woman, or a person with a passion for business but no experience. The distrust must not be absent, it must merely be too weak.

Mime elements

To be acted out: how the recruiter removes the harness from Eilif ('women'll be after you like flies'). He is freeing him from a yoke.

He has forced a florin on him. Holding out his fist with the florin in it in front of him, Eilif goes off as if in a trance.

Proportion

Weigel showed a masterful sense of proportion in portraying Mother Courage's reaction to the abduction of her brave son. She showed dismay rather than horror. Her son is not lost by becoming a soldier, he is merely in danger. And she will lose other children. To show that she knows very well why Eilif is no longer with her, Weigel dragged her string of belt buckles, of which one had been sold, along the ground, sat on the shaft for a few moments' rest with the buckles in front of her between her legs, and then threw them angrily into the cart. And she does not look her daughter in the face as she puts her into Eilif's harness.

SCENE TWO

Before the fortress of Wallhof Mother Courage meets her brave son again

Mother Courage sells provisions at exorbitant prices in the Swedish camp. While driving a hard bargain over a capon, she makes the acquaintance of an army cook who is to play an important part in her life. The Swedish general invites a young soldier into his tent and honours him for his bravery. Mother Courage recognizes her lost son in the young soldier. Taking advantage of the meal in Eilif's honour, she gets a better price for her capon. Eilif relates his heroic deed and Mother Courage, while plucking her capon in the kitchen adjoining the tent, expresses opinions about rotten military leaders. Eilif does a sword dance and his mother answers with a song. Eilif hugs his mother and gets a slap in the face for putting himself in danger with his heroism.

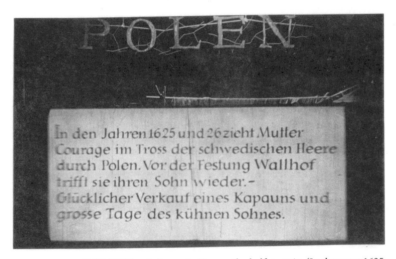

13. The setting, 'POLAND', and the projection on the half-curtain: 'In the years 1625 and 26 Mother Courage crosses Poland in the train of the Swedish armies. Before the fortress of Wallhof she meets her son again. – Successful sale of a capon and great days for her brave son.'

14. Mother Courage sells provisions at exorbitant prices in the Swedish camp. While driving a hard bargain over a capon, she makes the acquaintance of an army cook who is to play an important part in her life.

Basic arrangement

Mother Courage sells provisions at exorbitant prices in the Swedish camp before the fortress of Wallhof; while driving a hard bargain over a capon she makes the acquaintance of an army cook who is to play an important part in her life. In this scene the movement occurs at the pivotal moment ('You know

15. The Swedish general invites a young soldier into his tent and honours him for his bravery. Mother Courage recognizes her lost son in the young soldier.

what I'm going to do?'). The cook stops peeling his carrots, fishes the piece of rotten meat out of the garbage barrel and takes it over to the butcher's block. Courage's attempt at blackmail has failed.

The Swedish general invites a young soldier into his tent and makes a short speech commending him for his bravery. A drum roll outside the tent announces the arrival of highly placed persons. It need not be clear whether the general drinks in order to honour the soldier or honours the soldier in order to drink. Meanwhile in the kitchen next door the cook is preparing the meal. Courage stays right there with her capon.

Mother Courage recognizes her lost son in the young soldier; taking advantage of the meal in Eilif's honour, she gets a better price for her capon. Mother Courage is overcome with joy at seeing her son, but not too overcome to turn Eilif's reappearance to her business advantage. Meanwhile, the general gets the chaplain to bring him a spill to light his clay pipe.

16. Eilif relates his heroic deed and Mother Courage, while plucking her capon in the kitchen adjoining the tent, expresses opinions about rotten military leaders.

Eilif relates his heroic deed and Mother Courage, while plucking her capon in the kitchen adjoining the tent, expresses opinions about rotten military leaders. At first the mother beams as she listens to the story, then her face clouds over, and in the end she throws her capon angrily into the tub in front of her. She goes back to her work, all the while settling her scores with the general, and next door the general shows her son on the map what new heroic deeds he needs him for.

17. Eilif does a sword dance and his mother answers with a song.

18. Eilif hugs his mother and gets a slap in the face for putting himself in danger with his heroism.

Eilif does a sword dance and his mother answers with a song. Eilif does his sword dance at the front of the stage near the partition between tent and kitchen. Mother Courage creeps up to the partition to finish the song. Then she goes back to her tub but remains standing.
Eilif hugs his mother and gets a slap in the face for putting himself in danger with his heroism.

The capon deal

Courage and the cook's bargaining over the capon served among other things to establish the beginning of their tender relationship. Both showed pleasure in the bargaining, and the cook expressed his admiration not only for her ready tongue but also for the speed with which she exploited the honouring of her son for business purposes. Courage in turn was amused at the way the cook fished the chunk of beef out of the garbage barrel with the tip of his long meat knife and carried it, carefully as though it were a precious object – although to be kept at a safe distance from one's nose – over to his kitchen table. The actor Bildt masterfully showed the cook as a Don Juan, fired up by the new relationship, preparing the capon with theatrical elegance. It should be noted that this 'dumb show' was performed with restraint, so that it did not distract from the scene in the tent.

Bildt even took the trouble to acquire a Dutch accent with the help of a Dutchman.

Busch's army cook in the new version

In order to indicate the beginning of tender relations while fighting over a cheap price for a capon, Busch inserted an old Dutch ditty (Nit Betteres als de Piep). While singing he drew Courage on to his lap and, embracing her, reached for her bosom. Courage pushed the capon down into his hand. After the song he said drily into her ear: 'Thirty.' When she shook her head, he fished the stinking chunk of beef out of the barrel. (Courage gives him the cue for the song with 'Take the pipe out of your mouth when I'm talking to you.')

The general

Cliché was not wholly avoided in the portrayal of the general. It had something blustering and gruff about it, and showed too little about the ruling class. It would have been better to make him a raddled Swedish aristocrat, who honours the brave soldier as a matter of routine, absent-mindedly, so to speak. If this had been done, his very entrance – he is drunk, supports himself on the guest of honour, and heads straight for the wine jug – would have been more instructive. As it was, it amounted to little more than rowdy drunkenness.

A detail from the new version

The general was portrayed as a raddled aristocrat; nonetheless he roared his orders at the cook very loudly. In addition he turns his tribute to the marauding mercenary into a demonstration for the chaplain, whose religious propaganda does not further the war effort. After 'Hacked 'em to pieces, did you' he glances at the chaplain as he lets Eilif smoke from his pipe, and after 'You've the makings of a young Caesar' he passes him the wine jug, although only after having established that there is not much left in it.

The war of religion

The general's treatment of the chaplain is intended to show the role of religion in a war of religion. This was brought out most crudely. The general has him bring the burning spill for his pipe and at one point contemptuously pours wine over his cassock; with his eyes on Eilif, the chaplain wipes the hem of his cassock, half protesting, half taking it as a joke. He is not invited to sit down to table like the young murderer, nor is he given anything to drink. But what shows his position most clearly is the undignified way – a consequence of the indignity of his position in life – with which he then sits down at table and pours himself wine when the table is freed up and the general leads the young soldier, in whose presence all this is enacted, to the map on the tent wall. This position is the source of the chaplain's cynicism.

Eilif's dance

The short sword dance performed by the brave son must be executed with passion as well as ease. The young man is imitating a dance he has seen somewhere. It is not easy to make such things evident.

Costume: Eilif has a cheap, dented breastplate and is still wearing his frayed trousers. Not until scene 8 (the outbreak of peace) does he sport expensive clothing and equipment; he dies rich.

A detail

During her angry speech about rotten military leaders Courage plucks her capon violently, giving the plucking a kind of symbolic significance. Brief bursts of laughter from the amused cook interrupt her blasphemies.

Giehse's Courage

In the Munich production based on the Berlin model, Giehse, who had created the role of Courage in Zurich during the world war, showed how a great actor can make use of the arrangement and theatrical material in a model production to devise a unique and distinctive character. In doing so she invented ever finer changes, which also enrich the model. For example when she does a small triumphant march, holding the coin obtained for her capon by exploiting her son's triumph in her raised fist. Or when, as Eilif stumbles into the kitchen and greets her with a barbaric bellowing, obviously in the manner of the Fierlings, she answers her son with a bad-tempered mutation of that bellowing. In this way, the slap is set up. (Weigel had showed joy at the reunion and, suddenly remembering Eilif's heedlessness, had slapped him.)

[BFA 25, pp. 178–93 and 247–56]

Most of the rest of the detailed notes on each scene of *Mother Courage*, as in the *Modelbook*, are in an appendix to the play in *Collected Plays: Five*. The full sequence of photographs is only available in German publications.

Details from Scene 3

A gestic moment

During a raid by the Catholic troops the chaplain tries to hide his clerical garb ...

… while the camp prostitute prepares to start working again.

[BFA 25, p. 347]

Movement

Kattrin reports the arrest of Swiss Cheese.

Dumb Kattrin gesticulates too wildly in telling her mother that Swiss Cheese has been arrested, and consequently her mother does not understand her and says: 'Use your hands, I don't like it when you howl like a dog, what'll his reverence say? Makes him uncomfortable.' Here, Hurwicz had Kattrin pull herself together and nod. She understands this argument, it is a strong one.

[BFA 25, pp. 353–4 and 202]

Yvette's race

Three times the camp prostitute races to save Courage's son and the wagon. Her rage changes from simple anger at Courage's attempt to swindle her, by paying her out of the regimental cash box, to fury at Courage's betrayal of her son.

[BFA 25, pp. 354 and 203]

Sequence: The mute scream

The trader has haggled for too long

The mute scream

The expression of extreme pain after she has heard the volley of shots, the unscreaming open mouth with head bent back, are probably derived from a press photograph of an Indian woman crouched over the body of her dead son during the shelling of Singapore. Weigel must have seen it years before, although when questioned she could not recall it. That is how observations enter the actor's consciousness. – Incidentally, Weigel only assumed this attitude in later performances.

[BFA 25, pp. 317–20 and 203–4]

Variations in Berlin and Munich

The red shoes

The red shoes *Berlin*

Munich

Sitting huddled on the chest again, as she was during the drunken soldier's song, the injured girl touches her forehead gingerly once or twice to ascertain where the wound is exactly; otherwise, except for the willingness with which she lets herself be bandaged, she gives no indication of knowing what the scar will mean for her. Ignoring Yvette's red high-heeled shoes and creeping away into the cart are forms of protest: she blames her mother for her misfortune.

[BFA 25, pp. 374–5 and 216]

Courage and the cook sing

Berlin

A winter storm is blowing and in the early dawn Courage and the army cook, both in rags, drag the raggedy wagon to a stop in front of a parsonage. The cook reluctantly unharnesses himself and confesses to Courage that he has inherited a tavern in Utrecht and intends to make his way there. He invites her to join him [... but he refuses to take Kattrin along ...]. The cook and Courage sing the song of the refutations of the great. While they sing their

Munich

begging song, Courage desperately thinks over the cook's offer, presumably her last hope of settling down.

[BFA 25, 358–9 and 224]

These details and variations are by way of examples of the sort of material that Brecht thought worthy of closer analysis and included in the *Modelbook*.

Concluding Texts from the Model: Scene 12

The final image of Courage *Berlin*

Munich

Taking time

At the end as at the beginning it is necessary for the cart to be seen rolling along. The audience would of course understand if it were pulled off. If it goes on rolling there is a moment of irritation ('that's quite long enough'). But if it goes on still longer, a deeper understanding sets in.

The pulling of the cart in the last scene

For Scene 12 the peasants' house and the barn with roof (from Scene 11) were removed from the stage; only the cart and Kattrin's body remained. The word 'Saxony' in big letters was hoisted into the flies when the music started, and so the cart was hauled off a completely empty stage, recalling the first scene. Mother Courage described a complete circle on the revolving stage with her cart, passing the footlights a final time. As usual, the stage was brilliantly lit.

The discoveries of the realists

In giving the peasants the money for Kattrin's burial, Weigel quite mechanically puts one of the coins she has fished out back into her purse. What does this act accomplish? It shows that in all her grief the business woman has not wholly forgotten how to calculate, as money is so hard to come by. And it presents this as a discovery concerning human nature, which is moulded by various conditions. This tiny action has the power and suddenness of a discovery. To dig out the truth from the rubble of the self-evident, to make a marked link between the specific and the general, to capture the particular within a general process, that is the art of the realists.

A change in the text

After 'I'll manage, there isn't much in it,' Courage added, first in Munich, then in the Berlin production too: 'I've got to get back into business.'

Mother Courage learns nothing

In the last scene Weigel's Courage seemed to be eighty years old. And she understands nothing. She reacts only to remarks connected with the war, such as that one must not be left behind. She takes no notice when the peasants brutally accuse her of being to blame for Kattrin's death.

In 1938, when the play was written, Courage's inability to learn from war's unproductive character was a prophecy. At the 1948 Berlin production the wish was expressed that at least in the play Courage would understand.

To ensure that the realism of this play benefits the spectator, that is, to ensure that the spectator learns something, the theatres must work out a way of performing it which does not lead to audience identification with the principal character (heroine).

For example, judging by spectators' statements and press reviews, the original production in Zurich was artistically sophisticated but merely pictured war as a natural catastrophe and ineluctable fate, so confirming the belief of the petty-bourgeois members of the audience in their own indestructibility and power to survive. But even for the equally petty-bourgeois Mother Courage the decision 'to participate or not to participate' was left open throughout the play. It follows that the production must have represented Courage's business activity, her desire to get her cut and her willingness to take risks, as perfectly natural and 'eternally human' characteristics, so that there really was no way out for her. Indeed, in this day and age the petty bourgeois can no longer stay out of war, as Courage could have done. And a performance of the play can probably give a petty bourgeois spectator nothing more than a real aversion to war and a certain insight into the fact that the big business deals which constitute war are not made by the little people. A play is therefore more instructive than reality, because in a play the situation of war is set up more as an experimental situation, for the purpose of giving insight; that is, the spectator assumes the attitude of a student – provided the type of performance is right. The proletarians in the audience, the members of the class which really can take action against war and vanquish it, should be given an insight – which of course is only possible if the play is performed in the right way – into the relationship between war and commerce: as a class, the proletariat can do away with war by doing away with capitalism. Here, of course, a good deal depends on the growth of self-awareness among the proletariat, a process that is going on both inside and outside the theatre.

The epic element

As for the epic element in the Deutsches Theater production, indications of it could be seen in the arrangement, in the delineation of the characters, in the accurate execution of detail, and in the spirited rhythm of the entire performance. Moreover, the contradictions that pervade the play were not taken over ready-made, but worked out, and the parts, visible as such, fitted well into the whole. Nonetheless, the central aim of the epic theatre was not achieved. Much was shown, but the element of active showing was ultimately absent. It was only brought out clearly in a few rehearsals devoted to recasting. Here the actors 'marked', that is, they simply showed the new members of the cast certain positions and tones, and the whole took on a wonderfully relaxed, effortless, and unobtrusive quality that stimulates the spectator to think and feel for himself.

No one missed this fundamental epic element; and this is probably why the actors did not dare to offer it.

Concerning these notes

It is to be hoped that the present notes, indicating a few of the explanations and inventions of various kinds that are necessary for the performance of a play, will not give an impression of contrived seriousness. It is simply difficult in writing about these things to convey the carefree lightness that is essential to the theatre. Even in their instructive aspect, the arts belong to the realm of entertainment.

[BFA 25, pp. 384–5 and 240–3]

These are the last texts in the published *Modelbook*.

From *Theatre Work* (1952)

Introduction

In 1952 the Dresdner Verlag and the Berliner Ensemble brought out a lavishly illustrated, large-format volume, edited by Ruth Berlau, Bertolt Brecht and some of their younger colleagues (Claus Hubalek, Peter Palitzsch and Käthe Rülicke), describing, documenting and commenting on six of the recent productions at the Ensemble. It was called *Theaterarbeit* (*Theatre Work*). The productions in question were Brecht's own *Mr Puntila*, *The Mother* and *Mother Courage*, alongside versions of Maxim Gorky's *Vassa Zheleznova*, J.M.R. Lenz's *The Tutor*, and Gerhart Hauptmann's *Beaver Coat and Conflagration* (two plays conflated: *Der Biberpelz* and *Der rote Hahn*). The over-four-hundred pages include: extracts from the plays themselves and related material, relevant poems, theoretical essays by Brecht, extensive production notes and commentaries, sketches by Caspar Neher, photographs of the rehearsals and productions (the majority of them by Berlau), analyses of individual scenes, and a considerable number of essays by others close to or sympathetic to the project of the Berliner Ensemble. With the exception of the last category of texts, many of the pieces were also published elsewhere. There is some overlap with the *Modelbooks* themselves and with *Buying Brass*, not to mention with the contemporaneous *Versuche* volumes.

In the book itself, the texts are organized according to the plays and productions to which they refer, in the following order: *Mr Puntila and His Man Matti*, *Vassa Zheleznova*, *The Tutor*, *The Mother*, *Beaver Coat and Conflagration*, and *Mother Courage and Her Children*. These are then followed by fifty pages of *Models*, including illustrations and analyses of productions of *Mr Puntila*, *The Mother* and *Mother Courage*. The work is less detailed than in the published *Modelbooks*, but the reach is wider, so that, for example, alongside the familiar images of *Mother Courage*, we also have photos of a Dutch production. Finally there are another sixty pages on 'craftsmanship', with brief paragraphs by designers, make-up artists and costume makers, and above all contributions by actors and on acting. The juxtapositions and cross-connections between the pieces make for an exceptionally lively account. In the meantime, much of the material, and all the texts by Brecht himself, have also appeared in both the German and English editions (the texts on individual plays are mostly contained in the Notes to the *Collected Plays* volumes in the Methuen Drama series, with, for example, the detailed directorial notes to *The Tutor* in the volume of

Berliner Ensemble Adaptations). Nonetheless, *Theatre Work* remains an indispensable handbook for anyone interested in the production process and self-understanding of the early Berliner Ensemble, or indeed in the practice of a socially critical theatre anywhere. Like the *Modelbooks*, it is another sort of practical pendant to the *Short Organon*.

Theatre Work

Some Remarks on My Discipline

When we began to make theatre again after the 'Hitler war' had ended, perhaps the most difficult part was that neither the artists nor the audience seemed to be aware of the scale of destruction that had taken place. When it came to the factories that lay in ruins, to the houses without roofs, it was obvious that a great effort was demanded; but in the theatre, where more had really been destroyed than could be reconstructed by building alone, nobody seemed to demand much more nor to offer much more than a continuation, made somewhat more difficult by the lack of bread and stage sets. And yet the decline was monstrous. Brutality and stupidity triumphed, showing an iron will to live on beyond their time.

And they were particularly widespread in the portrayal of our most noble works of art. Yet the decline was not seen, because it was accompanied by an equally monstrous decline in the capacity of judgement.

The swift decay of artistic methods under the Nazi regime appeared to continue almost unnoticed. That the damage done to theatre buildings was so much more visible than that done to the type of performance is probably due to the fact that the former took place with the fall of the Nazi regime, but the latter during its rise. And so today people will actually speak of the 'brilliant' technique of the 'Göring theatre', as if such a technique could be adopted regardless of where that brilliance shone. As if a technique which served to mask social causality could be used to reveal it!

When we began to make theatre again after the 'Hitler war' had ended, theatre in the spirit of progress and experiment, with the purpose of changing society, as was so urgently needed, theatre's artistic methods, which require so long to develop, had been as good as destroyed by the spirit of regression and escapade. The poetic had degenerated into the declamatory, the artistic into the artificial. Outward appearances were all that mattered, and false inwardness. Instead of the exemplary there was representation, instead of passion came temperament. A whole generation of actors was selected according to false criteria, trained according to false doctrines.

How was one to put on new productions for the new spectators with such a depraved theatre, ruined both spiritually and technically? How was this to help create the new man, so necessary for this continent? How was the great fable to be unfolded, to reveal the pivotal moments of that so essential social change? How was the context of the world about us to be formulated – once a fixed quantity, now an unsteady variable? How was a dramaturgy of contradiction and dialectical processes to be established, a dramatics no longer claiming objectivity? How was the new positive critical attitude of the new audience to be constructed?

The question already contains the answer. The tasks required to give new strength to the decaying theatre would not be particularly easy, but rather the very hardest. Barely capable any longer of producing even the most super-ficial entertainment, it would have one last chance if it turned itself to tasks that it had never previously considered. Inadequate in itself as theatre, it had to strive to change not just itself, but the world around it too. From now on it could only hope to form its depictions of the world if it also assisted with forming that world itself.

In the part of Germany where some of you are at home and some are guests, great efforts are being made in the realm of theatre. Let me assure you that they are not only being made in that part of Germany. And let me assure you that we who are making those efforts know how fruitless they must ultimately remain without the efforts of the other parts of Germany. The catchphrase of the classical era still applies: we will have a national theatre, or no theatre at all. And I still have to speak of peace, as we all do, and unceasingly. My discipline, the theatre, is only one area of culture, not the most important one. What will happen to them all? In a Koreanized Germany, across which war passes back and forth and back and forth again, should we permit them all to be completely devastated?

[BFA 23, pp. 150–2]

Brecht wrote this speech for a congress 'On the Indivisibility of German Culture' which took place in Leipzig in May 1951. It was greeted with enthusiastic applause and part of it was broadcast by GDR Radio. The 'catchphrase of the classical era' refers to the efforts of German writers (Lessing, Goethe, Schiller) in the late eighteenth and early nineteenth century to throw off the influence of French court theatre and establish a German national theatre. The Korean War (1950 to 1953) had by this time already seen armies sweep south and north and south again before they settled into the stalemate of trench warfare around the 38th parallel.

Bertolt Brecht's Stage Direction

Bertolt Brecht sits in the auditorium during the rehearsals. His direction is inconspicuous. His interventions are barely noticeable and always with the 'prevailing wind'; he never disturbs the work, not even with suggestions for improvement. He does not give the impression of wanting the actors 'to create what he has in mind'; they are not his instruments. Instead, he works with them to find the story that the play is telling, and helps every actor to find his strength. He works with the actor like a child using a riding crop to direct little twigs out of a puddle on the bank and into the river, so that they begin to float.

Brecht is not one of those directors who always know better than the actors. The attitude he takes to the play is one of 'not knowing'; he waits and sees. It is as if he does not know his own play, not a single word of it. And he has no interest in knowing what the text says, but instead in how the text is to be shown by the actor on the stage. If an actor asks, for example: should I stand up at this point?, the typical Brecht answer frequently follows: I don't know. Brecht really does not know, but only finds out at the rehearsal.

For Brecht, everything – positions, walks, gestures – serves to show the play's story.

The story of *Mother Courage and Her Children*: The canteen woman Anna Fierling, named Mother Courage, travels into the war with her three children to do business. One by one she loses all three children and becomes destitute. Unteachable, she travels on alone. The twelve scenes of the play show this story. But every scene is again divided up into a series of incidents. Brecht directs as if it were possible to take any of these minor incidents out of the play and act it for itself alone. They are painstakingly drawn up, furnished with the most minute details.

Brecht once wrote: the poet's word is no more sacred than it is true. Theatre is not in the service of the writer, but of society.

On Brecht's stage everything must be 'true'. But he above all favours a particular kind of truth, that is, when truth appears as a discovery. During the play he often points, beaming, at one particular actor, who is at that moment showing something special or especially important about human nature or how human beings live together.

How human beings live together is studied in detail. At the beginning of the eighth scene of *Courage*, for example, a young farmer and his mother come to the camp to sell bedcovers. It is not just a case of showing that peasants sell their bedcovers. One must show that they are doing so in the fourteenth year of the war; they are not doing anything unusual. But they find it hard to commit this usual act, because the covers are the last thing that they have to sell, they are perhaps even indispensable. What will they cover themselves with in the evening? How does the mother look at the sack of covers, which are so important for her family? How does the son lift the sack with such important contents off his shoulder? And how does he sling it back on there, when he hears that peace has broken out and realizes that the covers no longer need to be sold?

The instruction given by theatre must also be entertaining. On Brecht's stage everything must be beautiful. Pelagea Vlassova's humble room should be just as beautiful as the arrangement of the workers in the factory yard or the coloured costumes of the petty-bourgeois women queuing at the copper collection point.

Of course, one does not always perceive all of this at a first glance. But Brecht stages his play in such a way that one discovers something new even in the tenth performance. The plays appear richer the more often one sees them. Even if one has known the play for a long time, the arrangement, gestures, colours etc. impart new enjoyment.

Brecht often acts things out himself, although only very short snippets, and he breaks off in the middle so that he never presents anything that is complete. He does not prescribe anything, but arouses the actors' imagination and creative capacity. He always imitates the actor to whom he is acting something out, although of course he does not play-act. His attitude is: people like this often do such a thing in such a way.

Moreover, all the actors must command the eye and ear of the spectator for at least a moment. Brecht explains: nobody goes through life unobserved, how can an actor be allowed to go across the stage unobserved? 'This is your moment', he calls to the actor, 'don't let it slip through your fingers. You're the focus now, to hell with the play.' Of course, this must be a moment at which the play demands or allows this focus. Brecht then says, 'It is in the interest of all the actors to bring out the common cause, but it is also in your interest. But then there is also your own interest, which contradicts it to some degree. Everything lives off this contradiction.' He never allows an actor, that is, a person in the play, to be sacrificed 'for the benefit' of the play, for its tension or tempo.

When it comes to his actors, Brecht is the most gratifying of spectators. The actor is entitled to recognition for a good performance. A joke remains a joke, even if it is told for the twentieth time. The actor still deserves to get a laugh. Otherwise he must assume that this time he has told the joke badly.

Brecht always finds something to give to the actor at the right moment. There is never embarrassment because something is missing, there are no empty minutes because something needs to be considered. The actor is kept busy, even if the solution is not final. The rehearsal flows without interruption.

Brecht knows how to respond to the actors. They don't need to adapt to his mood, instead he sounds out each of their moods. If the actor is having a 'good day', Brecht is insatiable; he draws everything he possibly can out of him, but in a way that is almost imperceptible and effortless for the actor. If the actor is in a bad mood, Brecht leaves him in peace; he never insists on anything that cannot be easily produced.

Brecht works with concentration, but not strain. His cheeriness at the rehearsals passes to the actors. It is obvious that he intends to enjoy himself.

His enjoyment of beautiful gestures and true attitudes provokes the actors; they show more in the expectation of his amusement.

Brecht hates long discussions during the rehearsals, particularly those of a psychological nature. In over two hundred rehearsal hours for *The Tutor* there were in total no more than fifteen minutes of discussion between the auditorium and the stage. Nonetheless, he tries out every suggestion. 'Why give the reasons, just show us the suggestion' and 'Don't talk about it, act it out' are the basic ideas. If a suggestion is good, it is adopted. A lack of applause is more apt than long arguments to turn the actors off a bad suggestion.

Brecht always speaks loudly and calls out his suggestions to the actors, mostly from down in the auditorium, so that everyone can hear them. That does not prevent his interventions from remaining inconspicuous. While he directs he is surrounded by pupils. He immediately passes successful suggestions on, always naming the person who suggested it: 'X says, Y thinks'. In this way, the work becomes everyone's work.

He explains to his directorial pupils: 'If we cannot eke out of a play or a scene what is within it, then we must beware of stuffing something into it that does not belong there. Plays and scenes must not be overstrained. If something is of minor importance, then it is still important. If you lend it too much, then you destroy the minor (but genuine) importance. There are weak scenes (and weaknesses in general) in every play. If the plays are on the whole halfway good, then there is often an equilibrium that is hard to discern and easy to disrupt. For example, the playwright often draws a particular strength for one scene out of the weakness of the previous one. Sometimes the weakness of a scene also serves to make visible something other than what is said. It is to be presumed that Shakespeare intended the speech by Coriolanus's mother, when she confronts her son as he crusades against his home city, to appear feeble – he did not want Coriolanus to be held back from his plan by real reasons or by deep emotion, but by a certain inertia, yielding to an old habit. It would therefore be wrong to give Volumnia better arguments to make the speech more convincing. On the other hand, our actors often have too little faith in the play, in an interesting historical moment that is being narrated, in a powerful utterance, etc.; in that case, they do not allow whatever is interesting "anyway" from having its own effect. Moreover, a play must also have its less effective moments. No spectator is able to follow a whole performance with the same degree of tense attention; this must be taken into account.'

[BFA 23, pp. 162–6]

This text was written especially for *Theatre Work*, apparently on the basis of a sketch by Ruth Berlau.

Phases of a Stage Direction

1. *Analysis of the play*

Consider which socially valuable insights and impulses the play offers. Boil the plot down to half a sheet of paper. Then divide it into separate incidents, establishing the pivotal moments, i.e. the important events that carry the plot a stage further. Then examine the relationship of the incidents to one another, their structure.

Think of ways and means to make the plot easily narratable and to bring out its social significance.

2. *First discussion of the stage set*

Basic ideas for the set. Study: is there a uniform solution? Scenery for the individual scenes or acts. Creation of stage sketches which supply elements of the plot, groupings, individual attitudes of the main characters.

3. *Casting*

Preferably not irrevocable. Consider that it is in the actor's interest to be used in a variety of ways. Avoid theatrical convention wherever it contradicts reality.

4. *Reading rehearsal*

The actors read with the least possible expression and characterization, chiefly to acquaint themselves with the play. Present the analysis of the play.

5. *Blocking rehearsal*

Positions and movements are roughly and provisionally mapped out for the main incidents. Various possibilities are tried out. The actors get a chance to test their own ideas. Emphases, attitudes and instances of gestus are indicated. The characters can begin to emerge, although without any attempt at continuity.

6. *Set rehearsal*

The experiences gained in the blocking rehearsals are used to transfer the designer's sketches to the stage, so that work can start on them straight away; for the sooner the actor can perform in the completed set, the better. However, from now on everything essential to the acting must be provided in a form fit for use (walls, flats, doors, windows, etc.). Nor should any rehearsing take place without props.

7. *Rehearsal of details*
Each detail is rehearsed individually, ignoring the final tempo. The actors establish their characters' behaviour towards the other characters and get to know what their characters are like. Once the main incidents are more or less in shape, the 'linking passages' are rehearsed with particular care.

8. *Run-throughs*
Everything that was pulled apart during the rehearsal of details is now pulled together again. It is not a matter of tempo but of continuity and balance.

9. *Discussion of costumes and make-up*
Once the groupings can be seen as a whole and the characters emerge individually, then costumes and make-up are discussed and work on them begins. High heels, long skirts, coats, spectacles, beards, etc., have already been experimented with in the early rehearsals.

10. *Checking rehearsals*
An additional check to see whether the play's socially valuable insights and impulses are coming across, whether the plot is being fully and elegantly told, and whether the pivotal moments are working. It is now a matter of probing, inspecting, polishing.

At this point it is wise to make a check of the groupings by taking photographs.

11. *Tempo rehearsals*
The tempo is now set. Lengths of scenes are settled. It is as well to conduct these rehearsals in costume, as this slows things down.

12. *Dress rehearsals*

13. *Rapid run-throughs*
The play is run through very rapidly without a prompter. Gestures are indicated.

14. *Previews*
To test audience reaction. Where possible the audience should be one that enables discussion, such as a factory or student group. Between previews there are correction rehearsals, to apply the lessons learned.

15. *First night*

Without the director, so that the actors can move without feeling that they are being watched.

[*Theaterarbeit*, pp. 256–8]

This text was first published in *Theatre Work*. It presumably derives from notes made by Brecht's assistants at the Berliner Ensemble.

Five Notes on Acting

If you want to master something difficult, you have to make it easy for yourself

Irrespective of whether the actors on stage are supposed to lose themselves or hold themselves in check, they must know how to make the acting easy for themselves. First an actor must conquer the stage: that is to say, he must acquaint himself with it as the blind acquaint themselves with their surroundings. He must divide up his part, modulate it and thoroughly savour it until it suits him. Whatever they are meant to express, he must 'arrange' his movements so that he enjoys even their rhythm and substance. These are all tasks for the senses, and an actor's training is of a physical kind.

If the actors don't make it easy for themselves, they don't make it easy for the audience either.

Control of 'stage temperament' and cleansing of stage diction

Before we can arrive at a realistic style of acting we have to combat certain affectations that have developed on our stage. There is for instance that so-called stage temperament which, quite independent of the meaning of any scene, is mechanically switched on as soon as the curtain goes up, and which represents a largely unconscious attempt on the actor's part to excite the audience by means of his own excitement. This mostly takes the form of unnecessarily noisy or artificial declamation, blanketing the emotions of the character with the emotions of the actor. You seldom hear any genuine human tones, and you get the impression that life must be exactly like the theatre, instead of the theatre being just like life. Such purely external temperament is necessary neither to interest nor involve the audience. Then there is so-called stage diction, which has ossified into an empty form. Far from aiding intelligibility, overly articulated speech hampers it. And High German only comes to life when it is suffused with local dialects. Actors must always work hard to keep their language close to everyday life, they must never cease to 'look ordinary people in the mouth'. Only in this way can they speak verse truly as verse or deliver heightened prose without destroying the character and situation of their role. The pathos in attitude and language that was appropriate for Schiller and the productions of Shakespeare, and which we owe to his era, is detrimental to our own playwrights and now detrimental to Schiller himself, too, as it has ossified into routine. Great forms can only take on a new lease of life if they are continually nourished by a continually changing reality.

Taking the tone

Many elements of the actor's craft risk falling into decay, including the ability to respond to a partner's tone. An actor needs to take the lines served to him like a tennis player receiving a ball. This is done by catching the tone and passing it on, so that rhythms and cadences develop which run through entire scenes. If the tone is not returned in this way, then it sounds like the aural equivalent of a group of blind men talking to each other without ever looking at the person addressed. There is something to be said for replacing the word 'lines', which we use for the various remarks and replies that make up a role, by the word 'rejoinders', because that indicates that each remark or reply contains an element of opposition. Even when a line expresses agreement it still nearly always contains some correction of what we have just heard, where particular interests make themselves heard. Complete agreement, a simple, unqualified 'yes', means removing some doubt on the part of the questioner or else establishing an alliance against third parties.

These all-embracing conflicts between the characters must be developed through very close cooperation within the ensemble. This cooperation, however, may also take the form of competition. Failure to respond to the tone may arise simply from an unmusical ear or from an incomplete understanding of the sense, but it may sometimes also indicate a general unsuitability for cooperation. Not always unconsciously, actors may perform entirely for themselves, beginning each line afresh and simply negating their partner's preceding remark. This sort of actor is also liable to insert those small and deadly gaps into the dialogue, often tiny hesitations which follow the partner's line and cut off the new line from the rest, emphasizing it, underlining it and giving its speaker a monopoly of the stage.

General tendencies which actors should guard against

Gravitating to the centre of the stage.
Detaching yourself from groups to stand alone.

Moving towards the person you are talking to.
Always looking at the person you are talking to.
Not looking at the person you are talking to.
Always standing parallel to the footlights.
Getting louder as you get faster.
Playing one thing out of another instead of one thing after another.
Obscuring contradictory character traits.
Failing to explore the playwright's intentions.
Subordinating your own experiences and observations to what you imagine
the playwright's intentions to be.

Training new actors

The Berliner Ensemble does not believe in keeping new actors in monastic
seclusion, away from real life and the public theatre. Newcomers with talent
are taken on immediately after their basic drama training. They must,
however, have talent, and discovering talent is not terribly easy. Furthermore,
they have to be strong personalities, and tracking them down is not terribly
easy either. It is no good looking for 'actor types', handsome or grotesque
figures, equipped with the standard actor's methods, obvious 'Gretchens',
born 'Mephistos', patent 'Martha Schwerdtleins'. And we must discard the
conceptions of beauty and character formerly applied by our court theatres
in selecting actors and now mass-produced in Hollywood (along with
UFA). The paintings of the great masters show a very different and valuable
conception of beauty and character. These young – or not so young, for that
matter – actors should then be immediately incorporated into the full life of
a working theatre and should appear before an audience as soon as possible.
They see the masters at work during rehearsals, and they act with them. And
the audience provides the most essential part of the education.

[BFA 23, pp. 168–71 and 174–5]

> These short texts by Brecht were all brought together for *Theatre Work*.
> It was Martin Luther, the translator of the German Bible and one of
> the founding fathers of the modern German language, who coined the
> expression about 'looking ordinary people in the mouth'. Gretchen,
> Mephisto and Martha are all characters in Goethe's *Faust*. UFA was the
> great German film company.

The Berliner Ensemble Models

The Berliner Ensemble produces *Modelbooks* for some of its productions.
So far there are models for *Mr Puntila and His Man Matti*, *The Mother* and

Mother Courage and Her Children. *The Tutor* is currently being prepared. They consist of four hundred and fifty to six hundred photographs of the production as well as notes on the experiences and discussions during rehearsals of the plays. The *Modelbooks* can be passed on to other theatres on request.

The Berliner Ensemble recommends the use of models like this in general.

The performance can be photographed in full over two evenings using two Leicas. The equipment must be placed on tripods and have shutter release cables, so that many images can be taken quickly and securely.

The scenes must be recorded from the same angle, as otherwise the model users will be unable to orient themselves as to the positions of the figures.

The photographic equipment is located on the balcony, not in the middle but at the side; if there is no balcony, a platform must be constructed so that the stage can be recorded from above. In this way, the images gain certain depths, and the arrangement can emerge vividly. (The *Modelbooks* show quite how much is missed by the spectators whose seats are not above the level of the stage.) Twenty films are taken in one evening; every film has thirty-six exposures. Two evenings produce around one and half thousand pictures.

Initially all the pictures showing entrances, exits and changes of position are assembled. Then come the finer touches, the selection of movements and instances of gestus that have a characteristic nature. Subsequently we ascertain whether the action is told in the pictures: the plot must be visible. The pivotal moments are brought together. Finally the points that are still missing are photographed. A director's assistant or the director sits with the photographer and specifies the precise moments. The key words for every scene have been noted down beforehand.

For the production of the model, the director's assistants make notes during the rehearsals: on the choreography (positions and groupings), on the emphases, the director's suggestions, the playwright's remarks, the pivotal moments, the socio-critical points, on the comic, tragic and poetic moments. These notes are processed by the dramaturgs and form part of the *Modelbooks*, so that along with the pictures there are explanations for a particular position, grouping, spacing etc. Studies of the pictures often result in corrective rehearsals.

Next, 'beauty' photographs are taken: from which side should this scene be photographed? How close can one get with the camera? In other words, how much does the picture need to show so that it is not only beautiful but also narrates the incident? When is it worth taking 'movement pictures'? Detail pictures are taken following considerations as to which gesture or expression shows the character of the figure, and in particular their contradictions.

Our *Modelbooks* also contain pictures of costumes and masks: all the actors are photographed in costumes and masks against a white background. These (and the pictures of each figure) are our only posed photographs. The actors are requested to stand expressionless before the camera. The photographs are taken from the front, right, left and behind.

The model also requires pictures of the set design: scenery with projections; also pictures of the props; historical props or particularly beautiful props, such as Galileo's instruments, Antigone's board of masks and the gong in its frame.

All of this is very instructive for directors and directors' assistants, and dramaturgs can also learn from the production of models. It helps them to identify exaggerated gestures, untrue expressions, false attitudes, good expressions and characteristic gestures. Thus the finished *Modelbook* is not only valuable for the user but is also of value for the work and instruction of the producer.

It is clear that this work is only worthwhile if a production is worthy of imitation as a whole or at least in certain details. It is also of value because something can be recorded for later ages; be it the acting style, set construction or the taste of our age. Every performance shows something instructive – one can even learn from the bad ones.

[BFA 25, pp. 535–7]

This and the next essay were written by Ruth Berlau for *Theatre Work* and then edited by Brecht.

Theatre Photography

Working conditions

As theatre photography has developed, it has become possible to produce reasonably exact models. At present theatre photography is rarely taken seriously: the theatre allows some photographers to take mainly posed photos in the breaks during general rehearsals, which they need to advertise the production. The principal actors are crowded together into some kind of effective position, which is often not lifted from the production at all.

For these 'posed' pictures the actors use exaggerated mime to make up for the lack of animated acting.

Posed photographs mean that the object is killed for the purpose of the photograph. Only photographs taken during the production can convey true impressions.[1]

The photographer must be permitted to be present at rehearsals so that he can ascertain which are the key moments. The fees for the pictures must also be increased, to take account of the amount of work involved.

It must, after all, be important to the directors that their productions are recorded, and they should therefore talk things through carefully with the photographer. Every theatre should set up a photo archive with pictures of both good and bad performances: for critics, for actors, for those building the sets, for future generations.

Photographability as a criterion

It is barely possible to photograph naturalistic and highly stylized performances. In these cases, the pictures appear either over-stuffed or empty. Where there is disorder or arbitrariness, the basic process cannot come to the fore. We often use our photos to check the sense and beauty of the arrangements. In the photos, the word or the movement cannot give the lie to a scene that is lacking something. Neither the actor's performance nor the suspense as the action progresses can prevent an observer of the pictures from overlooking the details: the sloppy little scene in the background, the meaningless chair constructed without love. During a rehearsal even a director can overlook a secondary character who is contributing nothing to the scene, because he is focusing on the actor leading the scene. It is often enough simply to show an actor a picture for him to correct a mistake. And the pictures always recall details which were forgotten during the long series of performances. – Photography says a lot in particular about lighting. The lens discovers what strains or tires the eye of the spectator. The bright spotlight that wipes out the actor's face on the photograph also turns it into a speck for the spectator. Badly lit details that do not achieve their effect on the photograph are also without effect for the spectator.

Artistic theatre photography

Theatre photography is in its infancy. It will develop its own laws, according to its aims. The sharpness of an image, for example, is not always the priority. Our actors are hardly performing for spectators with opera-glasses these days. It is no longer so much about the mimed expression which a situation elicits from a figure, but about the situation itself, the particular incident

---

[1] However, as the lighting is inadequate for this purpose, the pictures cannot show back projections and do not reveal how the stage of the Berliner Ensemble was always flooded with bright light.

between these particular people. Photographs can only reproduce the artistic atmosphere of a performance if they have a genuine effect as images. Art can only be reproduced in an artistic way. Consequently, the 'graininess' that is otherwise so feared can become an artistic method. The blurring caused by a great deal of movement should not cause too much concern either. What will remain decisive is how much of the sense and character of the production is captured.

Theatre photography, a new possibility

Unlike Asiatic theatre, European theatre has not yielded a sister art. There are only a few, disparate portraits of actors and depictions of scenes. The theatre would gain much if it could and was obliged to expect its performances to be recorded as images. The actors would find new delight in the true-to-life and significant figures that they shape, knowing that later eras would learn of their knowledge and effect.

[BFA 25, pp. 531–3]

Does Use of the Model Restrict Artistic Freedom?

Questions from the Wuppertal theatre director Erich Winds

Winds: When we produced *Mother Courage* here you made available to us all the material from the Berlin performance to help plan the production. Your representative Frau Berlau informed myself, the producer, the scene designer and the actors in detail as to your wishes, and these were illustrated by a large number of stage photographs together with explanatory texts and also by your written stage directions. Because it is hardly usual in the theatre for an author to influence a production in such detail, and because we in Wuppertal are trying the experiment for the first time in this highly developed form, it would be interesting to know your reasons for issuing an exemplary production and setting it up as a defining model for other productions.

Brecht: As it stands, *Mother Courage* can also be staged in the old way. (Indeed our theatre can stage anything – from *Oedipus* to *Beaver Coat*, not because it has an individual style strong enough to melt down the products of so many different authors, but because it lacks any style of its own.) But this would certainly mean losing the quite specific effects of such a play, and its social function would fail. The first thing a hackney coach-driver would have said if left alone with the motor-car would have been: So what's so new about that? Whereupon he would have harnessed eight horses to it and driven off. There is no purely theoretical way of approaching the modern epic theatre; the best thing is practical copying, along with a wish to find out the reasons for groupings, movements and gestures. One probably needs to have made a copy before one can make one's own model.

By representing humanity and its development in artistic terms literature makes its extraordinary contribution to human self-knowledge. Here the new can be made visible in the first stage of its development. This great independent role for art can only befit a genuinely realistic art. So realism is not a matter for esoteric literary discussion, but is the basis of art's own enormous social significance, and thereby of the artist's social position. Our books, our pictures, our theatres, our films and our music can and must contribute decisively to solving our nation's vital problems. Scholarship and art take such a pre-eminent place in our republic's social order because this is the place that befits the significance of progressive scholarship and realist art. A cultural policy of this sort demands creative cooperation from our intellectuals on a level with its aims. It is led by a literary, theatrical and cinematographic movement which helps thousands to understand past and present and to recognize the future: by those painters, sculptors and musicians in whose art something of the essence of our time can be felt, and whose optimism is an aid to thousands.

Winds: Is there not a danger that a model production in your sense may lead to a certain loss of artistic freedom in the stage performance that is derived from it?

Brecht: Complaints about a loss of freedom in artistic creation are to be expected – in an age of anarchic production. But even in this age there is a continuous thread of development, in science and technology for example this is the passing-on of knowledge gained, the standard. And the 'freelance' artists of the theatre are not particularly free when you take a closer look. They are usually the last to be able to rid themselves of century-old preju-dices, conventions, complexes. Above all they are quite ignominiously dependent on 'their' audience. They have to 'hold its attention'; to 'thrill' it at all costs – that is, to set up the early scenes so that the audience will 'buy' the later ones, to give it spiritual massages; to ascertain its taste and take that as a guide. In short, it is not they who have to be entertained by their own activities; they must follow the dictates of others. Our theatres are essen-tially still in the position of merchants purveying to the public – how much freedom can there be left to lose? At most the freedom to choose the way in which the audience is to be served.

Winds: And is there not a danger that the model theory may lead to a certain routine and rigidity, and that the production may amount to no more than just a copy?

Brecht: We must free ourselves from the general contempt for copying. It is not the 'easy option'. It is not a shameful failure, but an art. Or rather it needs to be developed into an art, to the point where there is no question of routine and rigidity. Let me put forward my own experiences as a copyist: as playwright I have copied the Japanese, Greek and Elizabethan drama; as director the arrangements by music-hall comedian Karl Valentin as well as Caspar Neher's stage sketches; yet I have never felt my freedom restricted. Give me an intelligent model of King Lear, and I will find my fun in recreating it. What difference does it make whether you find that the text shows Courage handing the money for Kattrin's burial to the peasants before leaving, or turn to the model and then discover that she counted it out and then put one coin back in her purse? In fact you will find only the former in the text, and the latter with Weigel in the model. Should you register the former and forget the latter? After all, we give the theatre nothing but copies of human behaviour. If they are anything at all, then the groupings and the groups' movements are statements about that behaviour. Our theatre is already unrealistic in that it underestimates the value of observation. Our actors look into themselves instead of out at the world around them. They treat the incidents between human beings, on which all depends, simply as vehicles for a display of temperament, etc. Directors use plays, even new plays, as a stimulus for their 'visions', which are not so much visions as adjustments to reality. The sooner we put a stop to this the better. Of course artistic copying has to be learned, just as the construction of models does. In order to be imitated, a model has to be imitable. The inimitable must be distinguished from the exemplary. And there is slavish imitation and masterful imitation. Although it is worth noting that the latter involves no less 'resemblance' in quantitative terms. To put it practically, it is enough if the arrangement that is used to tell the story in the model is taken as a starting point for the rehearsals. Quite apart from the fact that our directors are not used to arrangements telling stories, and that they are neither familiar with nor in favour of the social function that the stories in these new plays have – it is high time for the theatre to develop a method of working that suits our age, a collective method drawing on all possible experiences. We must work towards an increasingly precise description of reality, and this means, aesthetically speaking, an increasingly delicate and powerful one. This can only come about if we make use of the knowledge that has already been gained, without of course stopping there. The changes to the model, which must be designed exclusively to give greater precision, differentiation, imaginativeness and charm to the process of representing reality with a view to influencing it, will be all the more expressive in that they represent a negation of what currently exists – this for connoisseurs of dialectics.

Winds: Your instructions for the staging of *Mother Courage* also speak of epic theatre, or the epic style of acting. Might I ask you to explain this to me briefly, as doubtless not only those who work in the theatre but all who are interested in it would like to know more details, especially as it seems to involve a new formal style?

Brecht: It is extremely difficult to give a brief description of the epic style of acting. Most attempts to do so have led to highly misleading vulgarizations. (Giving the impression that it was a matter of suppressing the emotional, individual, dramatic, etc. element.) Fairly detailed accounts can be found in the *Versuche*. I should like to add that this mode of acting is still developing, or more precisely is in its infancy, and still needs many people's collaboration.

Winds: Do you feel that the epic style of acting is relevant only for *Mother Courage*, as a chronicle, or is it of practical value for all our contemporary work in the theatre, to be applied also to the classical age, the Romantics and the *fin-de-siècle* dramatists?

Brecht: An epic acting style is not equally valid for every classical work. It seems to be most easily applicable, that is to hold most promise of results, in works like Shakespeare's and in the earliest works of our own classical writers (including *Faust*). It depends on how the social function figures in these works – the representation of reality with a view to influencing it.

Winds: May I say at this point that I have every hope that the epic form of acting will liberate performance from the bonds of individualistic under-standing and acting, and that this new objectification will revitalize the artistic work of the theatre? For there is no doubt that the spectator and listener in today's theatre are no longer prepared to adhere to the full 'as if' illusion that is demanded of them, in other words subjectively to perceive the actor and the role as identical. What the stage needs is doubtless a new force for illusion, that it might above all speak convincingly to those who are simple yet receptive. It seems to me that it is not only a question of the material but of the theatre's right to exist in our age. It is to be welcomed if the stage is given new impulses by the writer's and dramatist's practical suggestions, which can help the theatre out of its crisis, if such a thing can exist in the artistic realm.

[BFA 25, pp. 386–91]

This text came about when the artistic director of the Wuppertal theatre, Erich Alexander Winds (not the actual director of the production of *Mother Courage* there), requested that Brecht write something with which to counter the criticism levelled against the theatre for undertaking a production on the basis of the model. There was no actual conversation; rather, Brecht imagined the questions, to which he then provided 'answers'. It first appeared in the regional newspaper published in Wuppertal, the *Westdeutsche Rundschau*, in September 1949. It was then republished, first by the GDR journal *Aufbau* and then in *Theatre Work*.

How Erich Engel Uses the Model

Copying is an art in and of itself, one of the arts that the master must himself master. He must do so precisely because he is otherwise incapable of producing anything that can be copied. Let us observe how a great director goes about making a copy.

Erich Engel only very rarely brings a fixed idea for the arrangement to the rehearsal. Generally he indicates a few provisional positions; then he studies them and begins to 'go into' them, that is, to suggest improvements that will bring out the meaning of the plot with greater purity and elegance. With this kind of inductive rehearsing a template can hardly prove to be a hindrance, but simply serves as the provisional idea to be studied and corrected. (Although under some circumstances it may have to be dropped completely.) The master proves himself in the use of such templates, recognizing their value. He handles a model arrangement like this as carefully as a great violin maker does a Stradivarius, in whose hands the curves, the varnish, the body of the instrument appear almost as new. He does not make any changes before he has fully understood the intention of the existing arrangement. However, this means that he must be in a position to recreate the template first, loosely, as something that is provisional yet significant. He wrings out the template completely, gleans from it indicators of the scene's pivotal moments and the interpretation. He minutely scrutinizes the advantages and disadvantages of the arrangement for his actors. When he first has them assume the positions and movements of the template, he appears not to pay much attention to the actors' distinctive features; but that is only how it appears, for it is precisely in their efforts that he occasionally notes how the template is suitable for them: the template is not always unsuitable, if the effort is great. If he then begins to make changes, he does so where he discovers a particular feature of the scene that is not inherent in the arrangement, or a particular feature of the actor that cannot be expressed in it. How consistently he investigates the before and after when such a case arises! And how assuredly he brings new tension and new balance to the character and to the scene. The modifications arise when these changes are incorporated into the template. The modifications that arise in this way may then be so substantial that something completely new arises. But the master finds flaws in the template itself, which have occurred during the preparation of the template, and he senses the balance in which the irreconcilable contradictions are held. He knows how often a truth appears to be disruptive during the work, appears not to fit into the concept, and how much he would like to leave it out because it disrupts the line. At this point a character who is being persecuted unjustly does something nasty – will it not seem that he is justly persecuted if it is properly signalled? At that point the clever character acts stupidly in this or that respect, the beloved is disagreeable – ought this to be kept secret? And the flaws in the development – should we paper over them? The contradictions – should we resolve them in favour of one side or the other? The master discovers these things in the template, he is able to find his way back to the difficulties that have been overcome.

[BFA 25, pp. 391–3]

This text was first published in *Aufbau* in 1950. Brecht knew Engel from before 1933, when he had been involved, for example, in the direction of *The Threepenny Opera* (1928). In 1949 he assisted Brecht in the direction of the Deutsches Theater production of *Mother Courage* and then went on to stage *Mr Puntila and His Man Matti* at the Berliner Ensemble, after the 'model' of the 1948 Zurich premiere.

How the Director Brecht Uses His Own Model

Brecht produced *Courage* in Munich according to his Berlin model. When it came to groupings and above all spacing, he examined the pictures in the *Modelbook*. He sought what was visually effective and beautiful, but he never slavishly followed his own model. He allowed the new production to develop in an unconstrained manner: a new solution might suggest itself, but that new solution had to be at least on a level with the old, tried and tested solution in the model. He studied the *Modelbooks* to find out why he had arrived at a particular solution, position or gesture. Soon the actors noticed the director's intention and were not disgruntled: model or no model, they were able to show what they wanted to show; if it was good, it was taken up straight away. Brecht immediately gave up an old solution if the actors delivered another that reproduced the general idea, the gestus, the content and further narrated the chronicle. If Brecht was made aware of things that were lost in the new solution, he built them in and made absolutely certain that nothing of value was lost. The only immovable element was the position of Mother Courage's canteen cart. It provides a fixed place in the arrangement, a good foundation.

[BFA 25, p. 394]

This seems originally to have been a draft by Ruth Berlau, which Brecht rewrote for publication in *Theatre Work*.

From the Correspondence of the Berliner Ensemble about the Model

Questions from the directors' collective of Döbeln

Question: How can the canteen cart be shown to be permanently rolling along the stage if there is no revolve?

Answer: It should first be investigated whether it is possible to install a manual revolve, to be pulled by a few stage hands. If not, then the prologue can represent a departure: Courage's family are packing up the last few items. The sons sling the harness around their waists, while Courage and Kattrin climb on to the cart. They continue to sing through all this activity. When the curtain falls, the cart rolls the short distance permitted by the stage. It seems to us most important to show that everything is in motion. The same applies for the seventh scene. In the final tableau Courage can pull the cart around twice – this solution is possible on large stages with no revolve, at any event. If there is no cyclorama, the cart should only start rolling as the curtain falls.

There is another possible solution, however, which requires some experience of mime. Those who are pulling the cart perform the movements of walking and pulling without actually moving forward with the cart. Two of the wheels can be turned from the inside of the cart, using ropes.

Question: How can scene changes be made shorter on stages without revolves?

Answer: The lengths of scene changes are hugely important even for stages without revolves. You cannot expect an audience to wait half an hour for scene changes in a play like *Mother Courage*. The play has fifteen tableaus, and the scene changes must last no longer than two minutes. The revolve cannot be used for quick scene changes, because the stage has to be empty in several scenes.

Scene changes must be rehearsed just as scenes are. It is part of the directing process: every stage hand must be given a role. What will they carry on? What will they take off when they leave? How much light can the stage hands be given if the projection has to remain clear on the curtain? Do the stage hands need to be given straw shoes, to keep the noise on the stage to a minimum?

The director must make use of a stop-clock. The duration of scene changes can only be monitored if the time is constantly monitored.

Question: How can one achieve the best mode of expression for the mute Kattrin?

Answer: This can be achieved if the actor playing Kattrin begins the rehearsal process by fully articulating what she will later have to express using gestures and tiny sounds. For example in the first scene: 'The recruiter is taking Eilif off with him! Do something – come on! The devil is stealing Eilif away from us – come on, please!' In the third scene: 'Two soldiers have enquired after a soldier from the Second Finnish Regiment – they have seen Swiss Cheese – one of them had only one eye. Swiss Cheese understood nothing and went off with the strongbox ...' It must be spoken in a rapid tempo, because Kattrin is agitated, but it must contain everything. Only when the mother chides her for howling like a dog does Kattrin repeat everything slowly and clearly.

During the rehearsals the clarity of these words is gradually reduced, so that only sounds remain. Every actor is free to invent her own sounds.

Question: Do Courage's children know that the mother swindles the sergeant in the first scene when she asks him to draw the black cross?

Answer: No. Courage predicts the sergeant's early death in the field in order to warn the children, above all her brave son Eilif, who now wants to become a soldier. Unfortunately the model does not include a picture showing how Courage turns towards Eilif, and whether he is watching her before she has the sergeant draw the lot. Our pictures answer the question 'Are the children amused by the trick?': the brave son Eilif takes it in sulkily – he no longer wants to pull the cart and to have his mother run his life; the upright Swiss Cheese is delighted when the sergeant has drawn his cross: 'Drawn a black cross, he has. Write him off.' Kattrin responds with great seriousness, and only grins when Swiss Cheese starts to beam.

Question: In the model, the final moment of the fifth scene (On the Battlefield) shows Kattrin beaming as she lifts the child that she has rescued up into the air. Before the curtain closed we had Courage rolling up her booty, a fur coat that she has stripped off a soldier who could not pay for his schnapps. At this moment the chaplain says, 'There's still someone under there.' The directors' collective made this the end of the scene, to show the contrast between the one who is plundering and the one who suffers.

Answer: The solution found by the Döbeln directors' collective is an interesting example for how the model may be used freely. Our solution is an example for how the text may be used freely. (We cut the last sentence in the script.)

Question: In the second scene the field kitchen is located next to the general's tent in the open air. Eilif and the general enter the field kitchen through a slit at the back left. We had them go along the apron. Possible?

Answer: This does not seem possible to us. Not because it would destroy the illusion for the spectator. But the separation between the tent and the kitchen must be taken as real and emphasized as such, as it has a social significance. The appearance of the general in the kitchen is an event: the cook salutes, the canteen woman curtseys.

Question: Does Courage know that she lost her son Eilif because she wanted to sell a belt buckle?

Answer: Yes. She shows it by angrily hurling the bundle of buckles and belts into the cart before she moves off.

[BFA 25, pp. 395–7]

> Döbeln is a little town in Saxony between Leipzig and Dresden. The local production of *Mother Courage* was premiered on 24 February 1951 under the direction of Gert Beinemann and his theatre collective. Brecht was particularly interested to see how the model could be adapted for such a relatively under-resourced town theatre.

Creative Evaluation of Models

Pictures and descriptions of a performance do not yield enough. One cannot learn much by reading that a character moves in a particular direction after a given sentence, even if the tone of the sentence, the way of walking, and a convincing motive can be supplied – which is very difficult. Those who are prepared to imitate are not the same as those in the template; with them it would not have come into being. All those who deserve the name of artist are unique; they represent the general in a particular way. They can neither be perfectly imitated nor give a perfect imitation. Nor is it as important for artists to imitate art as it is for them to imitate life. The use of models is therefore a particular kind of art, and a certain amount can be learned from it. The aim must be neither to copy the example exactly nor to depart from it too quickly. In the study of models – explanations and inventions that emerge from the rehearsal of a play – one should above all be led by the solutions of certain problems to consider the problems themselves. While meant to simplify matters, models are not simple to use. They are designed not to make thought unnecessary, but to provoke it; not to replace but to compel artistic creation. Imagination is necessary not only to modify the template but also to accept it.

[BFA 25, pp. 397–8]

From the *Katzgraben Notes 1953*

Introduction

In 1952 Brecht was introduced to Erwin Strittmatter, and they worked together on some scenes of rural life in the GDR that Strittmatter had written to make the comedy *Katzgraben*, which Brecht intended to produce at the Berliner Ensemble. At the time Strittmatter (born 1912) was just establishing himself as a writer and had come to work at the Ensemble as an assistant; he went on to become one of the best known literary figures of the GDR.

Katzgraben is a fictional village in the GDR, in the Lausitz (an area of Lower Silesia, on the Polish border), and the play tells of the class differences and economic struggles within a small community of farmers. The main debating point is the construction of a new road to the nearby town, which will bring benefits to some, but which others see as disturbing the status quo. The social strata are represented by Kleinschmidt (literally 'little smith'), Mittelländer ('mid-lander') and Großmann ('big man'), whom Brecht and Strittmatter describe respectively as *Kleinbauer* (small farmer, smallholder), *Mittelbauer* (medium farmer) and *Großbauer* (big farmer, landowner). They are joined by their wives, the mayor and other officials, young farm workers and others, and, importantly, Kleinschmidt's daughter Elli, who is the mayor's secretary, then a student, and finally a qualified agronomist. The action takes place over several years. The new road is built in the end, but not without many a set-back. In the final scene, a village fete, Kleinschmidt describes his vision of the future; and Großmann drives his cart into a ditch, to everyone's amusement.

Brecht, always on the lookout for new talent, saw the play as a valuable opportunity to bring the class struggles of the contemporary GDR to the stage. He valued the language of the play, which is written in loose iambic verse and an elevated version of the local Lausitz dialect. Apart from the contemporary social resonance, however, the production was also an opportunity to test the ideas of the *Short Organon* against the rival theatre doctrine of Konstantin Stanislavsky, whose work, officially favoured in the GDR, was the subject of a big conference in Berlin in April 1953, that is, during the rehearsal period for the new play, which ran from February.[1] Fearing an assault on his own epic theatre and on the Berliner Ensemble, Brecht was careful to stress the things his approach had in common with Stanislavsky's.

---

[1] On the rivalry with Stanislavsky, see *Brecht on Theatre*, Part Three.

He asked his team to help keep a detailed protocol of the rehearsal process, to record the problems they encountered and the solutions they found. He used their notes as a basis for his own, or revised them, and began to plan a publication. Many of the short pieces are presented as dialogues, a form long favoured by Brecht. 'B' is of course Brecht himself, in this case one can assume that 'P' stands for Peter Palitzsch, a valued young colleague at the Ensemble, and others of the team are mentioned by name; but even if real conversations provided the starting point, Brecht was free and easy with what opinions are ascribed to whom.[2]

The play itself opened on 23 May 1953, directed by Brecht, with music by Hanns Eisler and designs by Karl von Appen, and with a great many of the most famous Brechtian actors: Friedrich Gnass, Angelika Hurwicz, Erwin Geschonneck, Helene Weigel, Regine Lutz, and the young Ekkehard Schall (who was to become Brecht's son-in-law). The production was revived in a new version, and in the new home of the Berliner Ensemble, the Theater am Schiffbauerdamm, in the following year. However, *Katzgraben* was no great success, and for the time being nothing further came of the plans for the rehearsal protocol. A very few of the notes were published in the play programme at the time, or in periodicals, but the publication of a substantial part of the whole series had to wait until 1958 when it saw the light of day in the East German periodical *Junge Kunst*, and then subsequently in editions of Brecht's works. In 1994 a fuller version of the *Katzgraben–Notate* was published in volume 25 of the new Berliner und Frankfurter Ausgabe of Brecht's works, but there are still a great many other notes by other members of the team, preserved in the Brecht and the Berliner Ensemble Archives, which remain unpublished. As was by now standard at the Ensemble, numerous scene photos were taken, but they were never integrated into the *Notes*. We include a small selection here just by way of illustration. Our extracts are otherwise organized in approximate chronological order of the rehearsals to which they refer.

The *Katzgraben Notes* are not a *Modelbook*, not a documentation of a production, rather they are Brecht's one and only attempt to make an official record of the entire rehearsal process. They give a fascinating insight into the nature of rehearsals at the Berliner Ensemble, against the politically charged context of debates about Stanislavsky and Socialist Realism.

---

[2] There seem to have been, even among the closer circle of actors and co-workers on the production, decidedly critical opinions of the text and the play as a whole (see Manfred Wekwerth, *Erinnern ist Leben*, Leipzig, 2000) but there is little trace of these in the *Notes*.

Katzgraben Notes 1953

Epic Theatre

P.: How is it that one comes across so many accounts of your theatre – most of them hostile – which give no idea at all of what it is really like?

B.: It's my own fault. These accounts, and much of the hostility too, apply not to the theatre I practise but to the theatre my critics read into my theoretical writing. I can't resist letting readers and spectators in on my techniques and my aims, and that takes its toll. Where theory is concerned, I offend against the iron law (one of my favourite laws, as it happens) that the proof of the pudding is in the eating. My theatre – and this can hardly be held against me, in and of itself – is a philosophical one, if the term is understood in a naive sense. I take it to imply an interest in people's behaviour and opinions. All my theories are actually much more naive than people think or than my way of expressing things would lead them to believe. In my defence I could perhaps point to the case of Albert Einstein, who told the physicist Infeld that since boyhood all he had done was think about the man who ran after a ray of light and the man who got trapped in a falling lift. And look at the complexity that gave rise to! I wanted to apply to the theatre the principle that it is important not only to interpret the world, but to change it. The changes, whether big or small, that ensued from this intention – an intention which I myself only gradually came to recognize – were only ever changes within the framework of theatre, and so 'naturally' a great many old rules remained completely unchanged. That one little word 'naturally' was where I went wrong. I hardly ever thought to mention these unchanged rules, and many who read my suggestions and explanations assumed that I wanted to abolish them too. If the critics were to look at my theatre the way spectators do, rather than attaching such importance to my theories first and foremost, then they would probably just see theatre – a theatre imbued with imagination, humour and meaning, I hope – and not until they began to analyse its effects would they be struck by certain innovations which they would then be able to find explained in my theoretical writings. I think the root of the trouble was that my plays need to be performed correctly to be effective, meaning that for the sake of a non-Aristotelian drama (alas!) I had to give a description (alack!) of an epic theatre.

[BFA 25, pp. 401–2]

This is the first of the texts in the *Katzgraben Notes*, echoed in form by the closing *'New Content – New Form'*, another dialogue with 'P', Peter Palitzsch. The anecdote about Einstein is told in Leopold Infeld's book on Einstein (1953) which Brecht had clearly been reading. The remark about 'not only interpreting the world, but changing it' goes back to Karl Marx and the eleventh of his *Theses on Feuerbach*.

Rehearsal Methods

Rehearsals took place before lunch, from ten o'clock until two, in full daylight and in the presence of various interested parties, including foreign visitors such as the great Polish director Schiller. Most of the time Brecht called out his instructions to the actors from his chair, which was placed a good ten metres away from the stage. Discussions at the director's table, always very brief, were recorded in writing. If ever two different approaches were suggested, both were rehearsed.

There was a deliberate contradiction in the way Brecht, without referring to his copy of the script – allowing the script to surprise him, as it were – blocked the play in the most pictorial way possible, but at the same time encouraged the actors to act, at first, in as naturalistic a way as possible. If the director's task, said B., is to make the meaning of the incidents instantly clear through the blocking of positions and movements, the actor's first priority is to make the reality depicted in the play as true to life as possible. B. took the verse into account only when vetoing any nuances which would have interfered with it, and when referring to it at those points where it dictated intonation.

[BFA 25, p. 404]

Leon Schiller was the director of the first production of *The Three-penny Opera* (1929) and was in Berlin at the time of the *Katzgraben* rehearsals.

Scenery

The first question was: how can the contemporary historical character of this comedy be expressed?

B.: The set has to look authentic. We are showing events in the countryside to people in the cities. I deliberately do not say 'conditions in the countryside'. This play deals with contemporary history, i.e. things that are happening right now, things that were different yesterday and will be different tomorrow. We need to 'hang on to' it all – it will be difficult to reconstruct in future, and it is historically significant.

It was decided that the images should have a documentary feel, so they were painted so as to resemble photographs. And, of course, real subjects were used. The set designer von Appen and Palitzsch went with Strittmatter to the Lausitz region to select the subjects. Several different elements were combined to achieve the essence that pure photography alone cannot provide.

B. attached great importance to exposing the dark, ugly, poverty-stricken side of Prussian village life, the 'uninhabitability' of these regions, which both the landed gentry [Junkers] and government had bullied and sucked dry. This was the land which the farmers, under the leadership of the Communists, had to make habitable – the old, hostile environment with the new people.

It was decided to use backcloths, in front of which furniture could be placed. Backcloths made rapid changes of scenery possible, and allowed the play to make detours into the countryside more easily. The association with documentary photography was to be reinforced by constructing a frame for the backcloths, similar to a mount.

The costumes were designed to serve the same purpose. Their colours had to be drawn from the tones of a certain style of photography, one with a sepia or greenish-black or similar tint. Of course, it was imperative that the costumes be designed using entirely naturalistic basic models. Only once these had been created could the artistic process of typification get underway.

[BFA 25, pp. 404–5]

Crises and Conflicts

B.: In highlighting the crises and conflicts in our play, we are committed to the dialectical thinking of the revolutionary proletariat. Dialecticians highlight what is contradictory in any phenomenon or process; they think critically; in other words, their thinking brings phenomena to their point of crisis so as to be able to grasp them.

Examples: During the German workers' movement of the last century, the Lassalleans viewed and treated both bourgeoisie and aristocracy as a single reactionary mass. They did not recognize the profound differences between these ruling classes. Marx and Engels then pointed out that the working class could not make political progress without taking advantage of the conflicts between its oppressors and exploiters and distinguishing between progressive and reactionary currents, even within the bourgeoisie. Lenin taught the Russian working class to view and treat the peasants not simply as a homogeneous mass but as a vast group of people divided into its own very different classes, each of which had very different attitudes to the bourgeoisie and the landed nobility. Adopting this perspective enabled the working class to pick out allies from among the peasantry whose interests corresponded to its own interests, or could be brought into line with them. As for thinking in crises, the German Social Democrats saw development as something steady, continuous and inexorably progressive; they believed that the ever expanding proletariat would, by 'democratic means', achieve ever greater influence within the state, and endeavoured (as 'doctors of capitalism') to help the bourgeoisie extricate itself from the crises it found itself in – imperialistic wars or economic depressions, for example. Marx, Engels and Lenin, on the other hand, tried to expose these crises in the sharpest focus possible and to take advantage of the bourgeoisie's difficulties to further the interests of the proletariat.

Our play is a dialectical play. We need to bring out contradictions, differences and conflicts of a social nature (and other kinds as well, of course). Take the Kleinschmidts, a small family of new farmers who, in comparison with their neighbours, certainly seem to be very harmonious. But even they have their conflicts. Sending her daughter to school means extra work for the farmer's wife. Nor is her husband's inventiveness a source of unmitigated delight to her. The chopping of the corn stover makes a mess in the house, and the neighbours laugh. The husband, in turn, gets no encouragement from his wife for his experiments – instead he has to put up with being mocked, even in front of visitors. The daughter has to hide the fact that she is in love with the big farmer's foster-son, for her father sees him as a toady (to the big farmer). And there are internal conflicts too: the daughter going to school is a bad thing in terms of the housework, but a good thing in terms of opposing the big farmer, for whom she works her fingers to the bone. The farmer is torn between wanting to vote for building the new road, and being afraid to get on the wrong side of the big farmer, upon whom he is financially dependent. Contradictions among the medium farmers: the farmer's wife is in favour of the FDJ when it protects the young farm girl from the farmer's advances, but she is against the FDJ when it protects the girl from attempts to extend working hours unreasonably. Etc., etc.

Crises arise for the new farmer when he has to decide how to vote on the new road, when he has no feed for the ox he has finally acquired, and when the ground-water level drops. For the medium farmer when he has no fresh seed and when he has to choose between big farmer and small farmer. For the big farmer, when the party secretary gives oxen to the small farmers, when the tractors arrive, etc., etc.

In our production actions, attitudes and intonations must be identified for each crisis and conflict, in order to make each one clearly visible and understandable.

[BFA 25, pp. 416–18]

The followers of Ferdinand Lassalle, in the mid-nineteenth century, were reformists, who came in for strong criticism from Marx and Engels. The FDJ (Freie Deutsche Jugend) was the 'Free German Youth', the official communist youth movement of the GDR.

Politics in the Theatre

B.: It is not enough merely to demand insights from the theatre, to look to it for instructive depictions of reality. Our theatre has to make people *desire* insight; it must illustrate the *pleasure* to be had in changing reality. Our spectators must not merely hear how the bound Prometheus is to be freed – they must also be filled with the desire to free him. Our theatre must teach people to feel the desires and pleasures of inventors and explorers, and the liberator's sense of triumph.

Following the rehearsal of 23.3

[BFA 25, p. 418]

It is clear that most of the notes were meant to be dated to particular moments in the rehearsal process, but in practice many of these dates are incomplete or altogether missing.

III, 2 Constructing a Hero

While working out the crises and conflicts of the play, one of the things we focused on was the party secretary's reaction to the news that the village is facing a shortage of ground water and that the farmers do not intend to continue with the building of the road until a solution to this fundamental problem can be found. B. urged Willi Kleinoschegg, the actor playing the miner, to portray Steinert as feeling genuinely helpless.

Kleinoschegg: But he's not the sort of man to be so easily rattled by a bit of bad news!

B.: I'm afraid this is not the moment in the play to demonstrate the secretary's unflappability.

K.: What use is a helpless secretary? What kind of a role model is that?

B.: The man is faced with the collapse of a political operation in which he has invested a great deal of effort and in whose importance for the village and for the village's class struggle he passionately believes. If he wasn't concerned about it at all he would merely show himself to be a fool. If he was only pretending not to be concerned – in which case you would still have to act his concern! – he would simply lose the trust of the farmers who were on his side.

K.: But he knows what to do straightaway.
    Then we need machines.
    Tractors, diggers. As soon as we have machines
    We'll be out of this mess.

B.: If you want my advice, those are precisely the lines you should use to show how deep his helplessness runs. Just as the drowning man clutches at straws, so the old worker clutches at machines. Machines will put everything right, there's nothing they can't handle! Machines are the way the working class tries to overcome its difficulties, instinctively, 'a priori'.

K.: I'm afraid I might not be able to play this new type of character properly. I don't think every functionary has to be a hero, you understand, but part of the story our play tells is that the big positive changes which take place in Katzgraben couldn't have come about without Steinert.

B.: Yes. But I don't think you should see yourself as playing a hero who then goes around doing heroic deeds of one sort or another. Just have your character do the deeds written for him in the script and he will show himself to be a hero. Constructing a hero out of any other material than concrete actions and the sort of behaviour that the play makes available to you – constructing him out of popularly held opinions about heroism, for example – could cause false opinions about heroism to hold us back. A weak man, for example, is not a man who fears danger or who cannot hide his fear from others, but a man who fails in practice when confronted with danger. Let's not forget which class our hero belongs to! The ideal of the man with the poker face is a capitalist or perhaps a feudal ideal. There are certain transactions which require the trader never to reveal that he has been affected by an opposing argument; the slightest sign of uncertainty would undermine his credit, etc. The oppressor, likewise, whether capitalist or feudal, must never betray any anxiety. But Steinert, a leader of the workers' movement, stands in the midst of the people – their fate is his fate, and his fate their fate; he does not need to hide anything, he just needs to be quick to act, together with these people whose common interest he shares. It's true that under capitalism the faces of the people have also taken on a blank, inscrutable expression, the expression of those who have to hide their thoughts and reactions or for whom it is not worth expressing them, because they are not thought to matter. Under socialism the human face must once again be a mirror for feelings. In this way it will once again become beautiful.

No – portray Steinert as genuinely shaken and show how he takes action and where necessary persuades others to take action too – and then we will have our proletarian hero.

[BFA 25, pp. 418–20]

Is Katzgraben *a Proselytizing Play?*

B.: I don't see it as one. Wolf's *Cyankali* is a proselytizing play, and a very good one, incidentally. It was written during the Weimar Republic, and in it the author demands the right to abortion for working-class women under capitalism. That's a proselytizing play. Even Hauptmann's *The Weavers*, a play full of beautiful things, is a proselytizing play, in my opinion. It is an appeal to the humanity of the bourgeoisie – although a sceptical appeal, admittedly. *Katzgraben*, however, is a historical comedy. The author depicts his era, and comes down on the side of progressive, productive, revolutionary forces. He makes certain suggestions as to the actions the new class should take, but his aim is not to right a particular wrong, rather to demonstrate his new and infectious sense of life. That's why his history is a comedy. He is narrating part of the story of his class as a story of surmountable difficulties, corrigible ineptitudes, which he laughs at but never takes too lightly. And this is how we must perform the play – we must infect a proletarian audience with the desire to change the world (and supply it with some of the knowledge necessary to do so).

[BFA 25, pp. 423–4]

The other plays referred to here are Friedrich Wolf's *Cyankali*, a 1929 play about abortion legislation, and Gerhart Hauptmann's *The Weavers* (1892), the greatest classic of German Naturalism.

The Verse Form

B.: What purpose is served by the verse form? A political purpose, first and foremost: it furthers the class struggle. The verse form elevates incidents in the lives of simple, 'primitive' people like farmers and workers – who in previous plays have only ever been roughly sketched – to the higher level of the classical plays, and it demonstrates the nobleness of these people's ideas. Once merely 'objects of history and politics', they now speak like Coriolanus, Egmont or Wallenstein. With the verse form much that is incidental, irrelevant or undeveloped disappears – only that which helps to convey the bigger picture is incorporated into the verse. In this respect the verse form is like a great sieve which filters out non-essential material. In addition to this, it makes every utterance and expression of emotion clearer, just as good blocking makes the incidents between the people in the play clearer. And it makes many individual lines catchier and more memorable, and the onslaught on people's feelings harder to resist.

Following the rehearsal of 8.4

[BFA 25, p. 426]

Verfremdung

P.: The reason it's difficult to learn from you is that you make everything look so easy; the moment you give an instruction it immediately seems like the only possible course of action.

B.: I'm probably not doing a very good job of demonstrating the modification process, or perhaps you're not paying enough attention to my 'Not like that, but like this' – in other words, you're too quick to forget what was in favour of what is now. The process of developing a production must be seen not as one of growth but as one of assembly – a kind of engineering.

P.: It's not a process of assembly. The play has to grow organically or it will be a failure.

B.: All right then – let's just say it's useful to think of my role, while I'm developing a production, as that of an engineer rather than that of a gardener.

P.: So what do you do to move the production on?

B.: Every time I look again at a scene I ask myself not only whether it achieves my aims but also whether I have aimed high enough. Could I not potentially say even more about the behaviour of the people in the play, something more precise about the incidents, something more instructive, something funnier, something that would prompt an even stronger desire to adopt a certain kind of behaviour or elicit an even greater horror of another, asocial kind of behaviour? When I think I have identified something that embodies a particular principle, I try to bring out very clearly how that principle is manifested.

P.: How do you do that?

B.: Using *Verfremdung* – i.e. by portraying it as something which is 'this way and no other'.

P.: But you don't use actual *Verfremdung* techniques like the ones you recommend in your *Short Organon*?

B.: No. We're not at that stage yet.

P.: How would you go about it, if you wanted to use *Verfremdung*?

B.: I would have to completely re-educate the actors and I would need both them and the audience to have quite a high level of awareness about certain things – they would have to have an understanding of dialectics, etc.

P.: How did it come about that the blocking could be used 'to convey the plot'? Could you give a little example?

B.: All right, one, and a little one! The transitions into the main incidents, for example, which I wanted to subject to *Verfremdung*, I would clearly identify as transitions (as is the case in opera) – they would be briefer, less accentuated, more peripheral, so that here too the essential elements would be distinguished from the non-essential ones. And I would give the incidents an illustrative character, without detracting from their vitality, realism or roundedness, of course.

P.: Why not just go ahead and do it?

B.: The theatre is like a swimmer who can only swim as quickly as the current and his own strength allow. In a situation where the audience still thinks that a realistic portrayal means a portrayal which gives the illusion of reality, we will not achieve any of our desired effects.

Before the rehearsal on 11.4.53

[BFA 25, pp. 429–30]

The 'not – but' principle mentioned here in B's first response is outlined in the *Short Organon*, §57 (see *Brecht on Theatre*).

Brecht (arms raised) rehearses his actors in *Katzgraben*.

II, 3 Revelation and Justification

B. has the actors play the scene all the way through. Then he takes a break and consults with Strittmatter and the directors.

  He has a table placed in front of the director's chair and asks the actors to come and sit with him.

B.: The scene is finished. I don't know what else to say about it. Not a single nuance is missing. But the scene is wrong. Neutralizing the medium farmer in the class struggle is a big deal, a difficult political operation, and all we're getting out of it is a little merriment. You, Geschonneck, are so against your character, you expose him so mercilessly to ridicule, that your big farmer is little more than a bogeyman. He couldn't lead the class struggle for five minutes, behaving that way. You need now to think about his subjective justification. Show him to be an intelligent man and a cunning negotiator, who has just got a bit rattled by the new state of affairs. The heated argument that ensues between the medium farmer and the big farmer in this scene shows that even between these two classes, who for a long time acted together in oppressing and exploiting the small farmer, there are old scores to settle. In a sense, the ox given to the small farmer frees the medium farmer too from subjugation (subjugation to the big farmer). He doesn't take part in the struggle, but even he is sickened by the act he has to put on to the big farmer and the small farmer, pretending to have toothache so as to get out of going to the meeting. I'd like you, Bienert, to say the last line, 'Make the bed, missus!' in a sullen, listless voice.

The actors ran through the scene once at the table, and then twice on stage, with the positions and intonations unchanged but with everything more serious. The effect was astounding.

Strittmatter: I've got no worries at all now.

Rehearsal of 14.4.53

[BFA 25, pp. 435–6]

Empathy

A Stanislavsky conference was being organized, so B. invited the directors, dramaturgs and a few of the actors to come to his house. He had a whole pile of Stanislavsky literature lying on a table, and quizzed the actors on what they knew about Stanislavsky.

Hurwicz: I read his *The Secret of Acting Success* – the book only came out in Switzerland and that was the title it had over there (I think it was the wrong one). A lot of it seemed a bit extravagant to me at the time, but I also found sections which immediately struck me as being very important, and some of what's in there I've been using for years. He talks about how for the portrayal of emotions you need to have very concrete ideas, which means switching on your imagination. Just privately, for yourself. But you're anti-empathy, Brecht.

B.: Me? No. I'm in favour of it, at a certain stage of rehearsals. It's just that something else is needed as well, namely an attitude to the character you're empathizing with, a social evaluation. I advised you yesterday, Geschonneck, to empathize with the big farmer. It seemed to me that you were conveying only criticism of the character, rather than the character himself. And Weigel, as she sat by the tiled stove today shivering fit to burst, must have felt some degree of empathy.

Danegger: Will you let me write this down so I can repeat it next time the subject comes up? You know people accuse you of rejecting empathy entirely and of not wanting to see rounded human beings on the stage at all.

B.: Fine. But then I'd also like you to add that empathy doesn't seem to me to be enough – except perhaps for naturalistic plays where the complete illusion of nature is produced.

D.: But Stanislavsky allowed – or indeed encouraged – complete empathy for realistic portrayals as well.

B.: That's not the impression I got from the publications I had access to. He talks constantly about what he calls the super-objective of a play, and decrees that everything is to be subordinated to the Idea. I think that a lot of the time he only stressed the importance of empathy because he hated the despicable habit certain actors have of humbugging the audience, duping it etc., instead of focusing their representation on the character they're meant to be playing, and on the ideas – on what he so sternly and impatiently calls 'the truth'.

Geschonneck: There's never complete empathy during the performance. You have the audience in the back of your mind the whole time. At the very least.

Weigel: The audience is watching you play a person who is different from yourself. That's the process, and why shouldn't we be conscious of the process? And as for Geschonneck's 'at the very least' – how am I supposed to say the line 'I have to get back in business' at the end of *Mother Courage*, for example, after 'business' has cost me the last of my children, if I am not myself genuinely shocked by the fact that the person I am playing is incapable of learning?

B.: And consider this, as well: how could I possibly say to you, Geschonneck, if the situation were different, that in the final scene of *Katzgraben* you should play the big farmer in a completely unnuanced way, almost as a caricature, as the author wants you to?

[BFA 25, pp. 439–40]

The New Farmer, the Medium Farmer, the Big Farmer

X.: Won't people say that a writer who presents us with a small farmer called Kleinschmidt ['Littlesmith'], a medium farmer called Mittelländer ['Midlander'] and a big farmer called Großmann ['Bigman'] is being overly schematic?

B.: Yes, people might say that.

X.: You yourself have never written a play like that, or directed one.

B.: No. If I understand you rightly, what bothers you is not the naming of the characters in itself: that's perfectly legitimate in comedy. As for your objection to schematism: I've thought about that too, naturally. I examined the play very carefully to see whether the characters – as is usually the case with schematism – were faceless, bloodless, no more than formulas for social types; what I found, however, were distinct individuals, real roles, farmers from among Strittmatter's acquaintance, so to speak. They are representatives of their class like the ones found in the old folk tales. Or in Raimund's plays.

X.: That's all well and good, but there's just something about the play that doesn't quite …

B.: Indeed.

X.: We like to class realism as being very close to Naturalism.

B.: And there's nothing wrong with that. I've never been a Naturalist, I've never really liked Naturalism, but I can see that, despite its flaws, it has enabled the breakthrough of realism into modern literature and modern theatre. It's a fatalistic realism: it's overrun with elements that are unnecessary from an evolutionary point of view, it offers an image of reality that isn't practicable, its poetic aspect is rather stunted, etc., etc. – but it does bring reality into view, and it does contain raw material that hasn't been idealized to saturation point. Despite everything, an important epoch in literature and theatre – surpassable only by an epoch of Socialist Realism!

X.: And *Katzgraben*?

B.: Socialist Realism will either take many forms or it will continue as a single style and quickly wither and die of monotony (because it meets too *few* needs). We must pay close attention to what emerges. What does emerge, we must develop. There is no point in thinking up an aesthetic, contriving one, cobbling one together from familiar elements and expecting that playwrights will then deliver what the aesthetes have thought up. The worst thing you can do is sit at a desk concocting an ideal of *the* work of art. Because then the only thing people look for in works of art is whether or not they embody the ideal.

X.: Does that mean we just have to accept what the playwrights come up with?

B.: No.

[BFA 25, pp. 441–2]

Ferdinand Raimund was a Viennese author of magical comedies in the 1820s. On Brecht's responses to Socialist Realism, the official Soviet aesthetic of a practice of art from the perspective of the revolutionary proletariat, see especially *Brecht on Art and Politics*.

What Are Our Actors Actually Doing?

P.: I'm not sure whether the actors really know enough about your intentions – the aims you have in mind for the production, I mean.

B.: Can you see what the aims are?

P.: To show the changes to life in the countryside (as part of the life of our republic) in such a way as to enable the spectator to play an active part in those changes.

B.: And?

P.: And to make people want to play an active part.

B.: Yes, it's important to mention that. Our artistic representation of the reality of village life must generate certain impulses in the spectator – socialist ones. At which points do we create such impulses?

P.: In the final scene, for a start! There you have the young people's dream of the development of socialism, and Steinert's speech denouncing stupidity and prejudice. (Learning and changing!) That's the scene of increasing prosperity.

B.: Or increasing possibility, you might say! But in every scene we have to communicate impulses to the spectator, right from the beginning, otherwise the ones in the final scene won't come off.

P.: In the first act (i.e. in 1947) there's nothing but difficulties.

B.: Yes. Which makes for excellent impulses. You have the small farmer Kleinschmidt renouncing his political ideals because he's dependent on the big farmer. And the miner and Party Secretary Steinert gets left in the lurch by the poor farmers and told he doesn't understand the way things are in the countryside.

P.: What sort of impulses does that produce?

B.: Somebody who takes an intelligent view of Kleinschmidt may begin to want to be a subject of politics instead of an object – in other words, to be able to determine politics instead of being determined by it. Steinert's defeat might inspire people to get involved in such ventures themselves. The best people are motivated by problems, not solutions.

P.: And seeing Kleinschmidt's wife and her hatred of the oppressor Grossmann might also produce an impulse.

B.: Those are a few specific points; might you be able to bring out any others? And can we come up with any insights we want our performance to convey?

P.: It almost feels a bit uncomfortable, dissecting a work of art like this. After all it's not as if we establish such points theoretically first and only then realize them in 'artistic form'. That would make us an alchemist's laboratory.

B.: But when questions arise, we don't brush them aside just because we don't immediately know the answers.

P.: But that's what others usually do.

B.: Well, let's carry on: which opinions are we trying to refute?

P.: But just now you wanted to know which insights we're trying to convey!

B.: Yes. I've just gone one step further. Realistic art *fights* – it fights unrealistic perceptions. We must depict not only how reality is, but how reality really is. Let's start with the image most of our audience have of a farmer.

P.: Are we starting with the small farmer Kleinschmidt?

B.: No, that would be going too far ahead. We'd be assuming then that in our audience's view of the world a small farmer appears as a small farmer. But in fact he appears as a farmer. Distinguished from other farmers, of course, by certain characteristics that God gave him.

P.: Physically and intellectually speaking he is slow, plodding, dull, etc. The liberal bourgeoisie despised him for it, and the Nazis respected him for it – and mythologized him. We see small farmers, medium farmers and big farmers.

B.: With specific characteristics.

P.: Derived from their class affiliation!

B.: Among other things.

P.: But the kinds of behaviour which are important in practice, i.e. the ones you need to know about if you want to help change social existence, come to light in our case as part of the class struggle.

B.: Absolutely. Now let's try and find some examples!

P.: There's the casting, for a start. You chose the actor Gnass over the actor Gillmann, who would have made a very good Kleinschmidt, so that Kleinschmidt's talent for invention would not appear to be an innate 'quirk' or God-given characteristic of his.

B.: One insight we provide is how differently progress can impact upon different people. The fact that Elli Kleinschmidt is able to attend the agricultural college is viewed by her father almost exclusively as justice for his class, but by her mother almost exclusively as an injustice to herself. The new cropping plan inspires not only approval in the progressive small farmer Kleinschmidt but also resistance – to the coercion inherent in any plan. At the end of the scene we witness a tableau that resembles a tensile test on metal. Kleinschmidt is pulled in one direction by his fear of incurring the anger and economic reprisals of the big farmer, and in the other direction by the fear of surrendering his new economic prospects (a road in the town) and losing face in front of his neighbours and family. But you have to experience those sorts of things in order to conduct the class struggle properly. Even many of our own politicians are unable to correctly predict the consequences certain measures will have – all the consequences, that is. (And in the theatre these sorts of plays address us all as politicians!)

P.: You mean that Steinert, for example, must have neglected something, because there was something he didn't taken into account when sending Kleinschmidt's daughter to school: namely that this would inevitably cause difficulties for her mother. He hasn't talked to her about it, it seems, or argued it out with her. And so she is cold towards him. ('Did Steinert talk her into it?')

P.: It's strange, but the more clearly we define our tasks and the more apparent the value of our efforts becomes, the less I feel that these tasks are necessarily the job of art, or that the special nature of art amounts to nothing more than the performance of these tasks.

B.: They are tasks whose significance is debated or not yet understood. The themes in and of themselves do not yet inspire poetic ideas and are not reminiscent of such ideas inspired by other, similar themes. But exploring the inner life of human beings and calling upon them to build a humane society are fitting functions for poetry. The domain of insights and impulses undergoes a considerable, decisive change in art, in that the pleasure the insights provide goes beyond that of their usefulness, and the impulses also become pleasurable, in the most noble way.

P.: And is that what our actors are doing? And do they know it?

B.: They are doing it as well as they know how.

Discussion in Buckow on 26.4.

[BFA 25, pp. 447–51]

The Positive Hero

Berlau: The argument goes that spectators should be able to empathize so strongly with a character on stage that they end up wanting to emulate him or her in real life.

B.: Empathy on its own may generate the desire to emulate the hero, but not the ability to do so. If the attitude is to be an effective one, it must be adopted not only impulsively but also rationally. In order for people to imitate a certain (correct) type of behaviour, they first need to understand that the principle can be applied to situations that are not exactly the same as those portrayed. It is the theatre's job to present the hero in such a way that he stimulates conscious rather than blind imitation.

Berlau: Isn't that extremely difficult?

B.: Yes. It isn't easy to get heroes.

Between rehearsals

[BFA 25, p. 456]

Second Dress Rehearsal

There was a run-through of the play, and minutes were shaved off individual scenes thanks to improved pace (final rehearsals are always timed.) At every point the directors try to frame the plot more and more clearly by amplifying the gestus.

At the evening rehearsal Besson suggested to the actor playing the young miner (Fiegler), that he should speak his lines very loudly, almost in a shout. He had always spoken too quietly and unintelligibly and – in order to appear manly in spite of it – in a sort of bass. B. was quick to give a reason for the increase in volume: he works in the mine all day with a very loud drill, which forces him to speak loudly. The character was miraculously transformed.

Rehearsal of 13.5

[BFA 25, pp. 468–9]

Brecht met the young Swiss actor and director Benno Besson in Zurich in 1947, and in 1949 he joined the Berliner Ensemble and became one of Brecht's more important 'students'.

Criticism of Elli

In the discussion with cultural officials following the second preview, Regine Lutz came in for criticism: her Elli, it was said, came across as 'stupid'. B. asked whether Elli seemed 'stupid' in the first scene, when discussing the cropping plan with her father. No, he was told – it was in the love scene with Hermann (I, 3). Laughing, B. explained that it had been the actress's idea to portray Elli as being extremely gauche when it came to love. It is love, in Lutz's view, that turns her 'stupid'. Everyone laughed, but said that this did not really come across.

Weigel suggested putting it in the script. Strittmatter therefore gave Erna the line: Someone only has to mention love and you get all silly and awkward.

22.5.

[BFA 25, pp. 478–9]

Criticism of Elli 2

Almost every discussion with politically educated spectators resulted in harsh criticism of Lutz's portrayal of the small farmer's daughter. B. suggested that in the scene outside the pub (I, 3), the girls should also discuss organizational questions in a sensible and witty manner, which would throw into sharp relief the old-fashioned 'stupidity' where love was concerned. He suggested similar changes with regard to III, 3. Apart from that, he reassured the actress.

B.: At the turn of the century, the dream of a great actress was to influence the latest fashion in hats. Now she is called upon to educate our youth. Spectators are constantly on the lookout for false depictions of 'representative youth'. It is no small matter to hold up the mirror to a nation's youth, when this youth is regarded with such love and devotion and trust. Your every movement is noted, your every inflection listened to closely. The actor of the classical Chinese theatre, whose every single gesture was scrutinized by his audience, carried much less responsibility than you do now! At the end of the day all he had to do was reproduce (undistorted) the familiar traits of characters from legends. You are in the position of exhibiting – and inviting judgement of – the traits of the young people who are to develop Socialism.

[BFA 25, pp. 479–80]

New Content – New Form

P.: Won't the audience first need to come to grips with the new form that *Katzgraben* embodies?

B.: I think the new form will help the audience to come to grips with *Katzgraben*. The most alien thing about this play is the subject matter and the Marxist perspective.

P.: Do you think those things account for everything that is unfamiliar about the play?

B.: For the most part.

P.: You don't think that the way Strittmatter constructs his plot is influenced by the fact that he's a novelist?

B.: No. Most of the more unfamiliar artistic techniques he uses in this play would be unusual in a novel too. Take the way the play is divided up into years, for instance. Not that they are exactly years – it's just that in the countryside a year and its harvests represent a useful way of measuring time. But it's the way we keep coming back to Katzgraben at intervals – like Rückert's Chidher, the eternal wanderer who always returns after a certain amount of time, always to find something new.

P.: You mean the audience suddenly finds an ox on the small farmer's plot, then a tractor?

B.: Not only that, of course.

P.: All right then – first a powerful big farmer, then a less powerful one?

B.: Not only that. It finds a different Kleinschmidt, a different Kleinschmidt's wife, a different Party Secretary Steinert etc. Different people.

P.: Not completely different.

B.: True. Not completely different. Certain characteristics have developed in them and others have died away. But we have to remember that what we're looking at are not so much people who have changed but people who are changing. The playwright always selects those points in time when things are developing at a particularly rapid pace. Let's stay with Kleinschmidt as an example: we come across him when his dependency on the big farmer is hitting him especially hard and when he finds himself, because of the new cropping plan, compelled to exercise all the creative powers he possesses. And we come across him in the depths of a psychological crisis: his self-awareness is already so highly developed as a result of the new conditions in the countryside that the humiliation of having to bow to the big farmer feels particularly bitter to him. In the following year too (in the second act) we find him in a situation which propels him even further on in his development, so to speak.

P.: Can't situations like that be placed closer together in time and made to flow more continuously, to avoid those jumps in time that we're not used to seeing in the theatre?

B.: I don't really hold with retaining old habits in an era when so many new ones are being created. Strittmatter needs the jumps in time, quite simply, because the developments in the consciousness of his characters depend on the development of their social existence, and this development doesn't progress all that quickly.

P.: Speaking of which, it's interesting what some of the farmers who saw the play said after one of the performances. They found the overview of a period of several years very useful. 'We lived through it all, but it's only now that we've seen it presented like this, at a glance, as an overview of an extended period of time, that we can really see everything that went on. You do experience it all from day to day, of course, but not so intensely.'

B.: They were witnessing, you might say, the powerful momentum of events and actions, which in its turn provides the powerful momentum for the future. In short, this Chidher-technique – however unusual it may seem at first – is extremely advantageous for this play in particular, and Strittmatter makes use of other artistic techniques for different reasons. He's just like his new farmer, driven by a socially necessary, progressive project to explore new avenues, new techniques.

P.: Such as?

B.: Such as the play's characterization, which incorporates specific character traits of historical significance. And the inclusion of people who are significant in terms of the class struggle. And the plot – a plot which allows the hero (Kleinschmidt) to be replaced in the last act by a different hero (Steinert). And the way the actions are subject to different motivations from those in earlier plays.

P.: Many people feel the lack of great passions in the new theatre.

B.: They don't realize that they are only missing those passions they found and still find in the old theatre. In the new theatre they find, or would find, new passions (alongside old ones), which have developed since or which are still in the process of developing. Even when they feel these passions themselves, they don't yet feel them when they are put on stage, because the modes of expression have also changed and continue to change. Everyone is still capable of identifying jealousy, ambition or greed as passions. But the passion for getting the fields to yield more crops, or the passion for bringing people together into working collectives – the passions that inspire the small farmer Kleinschmidt and the miner Steinert – are, even today, more difficult to feel and to share. What's more, these new passions create completely different relationships between people from those created by the old passions. Which means that their disputes will be different from what spectators are used to seeing in the theatre. The forms which disputes between people take (and these disputes are central to the drama) have changed a great deal. According to the rules of the old form of drama, for example, the conflict between the new farmer and the big farmer would be greatly intensified if the big farmer were to set fire to one of the new farmer's barns. This might still grab the audience's attention, even today, but it would not be typical. What would be typical would be the big farmer demanding the return of a horse he had loaned to the new farmer. This too would amount to an act of violence, but would be unlikely to whip our audience into a frenzy. When the new farmer combats the big farmer by giving the medium farmer a discount on seed potatoes, even this is a way of doing battle, using new tactics; but again it may make much less of an 'impact' than the new farmer marrying his daughter to the medium farmer's son. Our audience's political eyesight is sharpening only gradually – for the time being the new plays gain less from it than it does from them. The big farmer claps a hand to his head in despair and says 'Six oxen for the village! That's quite a blow!' I laugh when I hear that, but who else does? And who takes any interest in the fact that the big farmer immediately understands the political significance of oxen being given to the small farmers, while the small farmer who has been given an ox simply despairs because he has no feed for it?

P.: I've heard spectators say that they 'can't see how it fits together': in other words, they don't understand how one thing relates to another, why the play tells you about this or that thing without then taking it any further. Take the second scene of the first act, where it emerges that the medium farmer has been harassing the young farm girl. One critic, and an intelligent one, a man with a sense of humour, said to me: 'There are guns being loaded all over the place, but they're not being fired.'

B.: I understand. We generate expectations which we then don't fulfil. The spectators, informed by their experience of theatre, expect the relationship between the farmer and the young girl to be followed up in some way, but in the next act (and year) there is no further mention of it. The very fact that there is no further mention of it is comical, I find.

P.: The comedy is reinforced by having the farmer shake his head sadly in agreement when his wife complains about the increasing insubordination of the farmhands.

B.: Unfortunately, this will only be perceived as comical by spectators whose attention during the first act has mainly been focused on the way the patriarchal relationships are dissolving and the fact that the farmer's wife is happy about this, because the FDJ protects the farm girl from her husband. In the second act, these spectators expect to see the continuation of this process of emancipation and so they laugh when they find the farmer and his wife aggrieved and united, with the farm girl by now energetically demanding time off. Spectators cannot achieve such a perspective, of course, if their experiences have not prepared them for it.

P.: For those spectators who haven't had such experiences, the enmities depicted in *Katzgraben* won't seem particularly stageworthy either.

B.: Probably. In our reality it's harder and harder to find opponents for bitter disputes on stage, opponents whose enmity would be perceived by the audience as self-evident, intuitive, fatal. Any conflict to do with possession is perceived as natural and interesting. Shylock and Harpagon each possess money and a daughter, which 'naturally' gives rise to marvellous disputes between them and the opponents who want to take from them money or daughter or both. Kleinschmidt's daughter is not his possession. He fights for a road that he is never going to possess. A whole host of anxieties, emotional dilemmas, disputes, jokes and strong emotions that were typical of the old era and its plays either cease to matter entirely or are sidelined, while effects typical of the new era become more important.

P.: You're talking about the new type of spectating again – the one that requires a new kind of theatre.

B. *(guiltily)*: Yes, I should stop doing that so often. We really have to blame ourselves more than the spectators when we don't achieve the effects we intend. But that means I must be allowed to defend certain innovations which are necessary for us to 'get the audience on our side'.

P.: But these innovations can't be introduced at the cost of the human factor. Or do you think the audience should also have to relinquish its demand for red-blooded, rounded characters?

B.: The audience doesn't need to relinquish any demands at all. All I ask is that it combines them with new ones. Molière's audience laughed at Harpagon, his Miser. The usurer and hoarder had become risible in an era when big merchants were on the rise, taking risks and borrowing money. Our audience would be better able to laugh at Harpagon's greed if this greed were not portrayed as a character trait, as a quirk, as something 'all-too-human', but rather as a kind of class-related disease, as a kind of behaviour that has only just become risible – a social vice, in short. We need to be able to portray what is human without treating it as something intrinsic to humanity.

P.: You're implying that what's particularly radical for the new style of playwriting is the suggestion found in the classical writers that people's consciousness is determined by social existence.

B.: Which they create. Yes, that's a new perspective which is not taken into account in the old style of playwriting.

P.: And yet you keep stressing how necessary it is to learn from the old plays?

B.: Not the elements of their techniques that are bound up with an outdated perspective! What needs to be learned is the boldness with which the earlier playwrights created things that were completely new for their era; what needs to be studied are the devices by which they were able to adapt traditional techniques to serve new purposes. We must learn from what is old how to create what is new.

P.: Am I right in thinking that some of our best critics harbour a certain mistrust of new forms?

B.: Yes, you are. People have had very bad experiences with innovations – which were not in fact genuine innovations. Bourgeois drama and bourgeois theatre, in their inexorable and ever accelerated decline, tried constantly to make reactionary, unvarying content more palatable for audiences by frantically cycling through different fashions in terms of external form. These entirely formalistic endeavours – pointless formal gimmicks – led our best critics to advocate the study of classical plays. And it is true that there's a lot to be learned from them. The way they came up with socially significant stories and mastered the art of telling them in dramatic form, the interesting people they created, the way they cultivated language, the big ideas they made accessible and the way they promoted what was socially progressive.

Between rehearsals

[BFA 25, pp. 480–6]

In Friedrich Rückert's 1829 poem 'Chidher' a legendary wanderer returns to the same spot every five hundred years and finds it completely changed.

Despite the recalcitrance of the material of this particular play, Brecht contrives to end the *Notes* by situating his own work in that pre- and post-bourgeois tradition of 'socially progressive' classics.

'Acting is Not Theoretical'

by
Di Trevis

Let's face it. The *Buying Brass* essays are a difficult read. I have been working on Brecht plays, plays about Brecht, cabarets of the songs of Brecht and recitals of the poetry of this great writer for over forty years and I will freely admit, these theoretical writings baffle and frustrate me. For readers of German I am assured the writing is lively and engaging. I am told in explanation that they were not finished and were bundled together rather hurriedly and at times mistranslated or poorly organized, but even so ... I was not looking forward to a group of actors battling through opaque prose instead of getting up on the floor and using their practical skills.

So it was from this starting point that I invited a group of six actors to spend a few days exploring some of Brecht's acting exercises. We met, as I like it, not as pupils and academic expert but from the first sitting in a circle, in honest dialogue and on the level.

Who is Brecht beyond the clichés and myths? What kind of acting can we learn from him? What did he call for?

Acting is the antithesis of theory. Those who can talk most about it are notoriously poor at actually doing it. Actors enter the space bringing their bodies, their emotions, imagination and biographies with them. Acting is about action, not cerebral activity. But actors also have an innate sense of the world about them and highly honed powers of observation. They know disappointment, unemployment and poverty. They travel to the rehearsal room through the jungle of the cities, the vicissitudes of public transport, able to observe on train, bus, tram and teeming street the objects of their study and their potential audience – fellow men and women trying to survive in the world. Then this world of work, struggle and exploitation has to be filtered through their bodies into their mouths and their words and become their craft. It is sensuous and their work flows, if it goes well, through muscle, breath and vocal cords.

Theoretical talk paralyses an actor's impulse, and no single theoretical word confuses them more possibly than the only one they have ever heard talk of when discussing Brecht ... 'alienation'. In this respect the *Modelbooks*, with their eloquent silence about *Verfremdung*, are a refreshing pendant to

Buying Brass. How many times have I had to explain to actors that their job is not in fact to … 'alienate' the audience! Even the simpler phrase 'show that you are showing' needs elucidation and practical examples on the rehearsal room floor.

> … before you show the way
> A man betrays someone, or is seized by jealousy
> Or concludes a deal, first look
> At the audience as if you wished to say:
> Now take note, this man is now betraying someone and this is how he does it.
>
> (BFA 15, p. 166; *Poems*, p. 341)

So my actors that spring morning in Soho, London, were no different from any others I have met in my working life. Their ages ranged from sixty-five to twenty-two. They had one thing in common: they were interested in improving their skills. The youngest was about to embark on training, the oldest a veteran of the Royal Shakespeare Company with four decades of experience behind him. In between were four actors expertly trained over three years by top British drama schools and already making their way in the profession.

Then I made my first startling discovery. With the exception of me and the veteran actor, none had acted in a professional production of a Brecht play and no one had investigated the theatre of Brecht in any depth at their respective schools. With the fall of the Wall and the fracture of the Soviet bloc and a surge towards global capitalism, how many times in the last fifteen years have I seen artistic planners grimace at the suggestion of a Brecht production or young directors declare they are going to do a Brecht play … but not with the politics or the music!

These actors, like most of their peers, are trained through immersion in Stanislavsky technique: they start from personal emotional response, from naturalism. Fortunately, however, the modern actor is also trained thoroughly in movement and, when taught well, this is not only intended to serve the actors' physical versatility in naturalism but also to take the actor into a more heightened expressive style. Many actors are thus encouraged to work non-verbally, through animal study and through the use of mask. And such is Brecht's often unacknowledged influence on contemporary staging that the basic ingredients of his theatre are completely familiar to them. Taken in the context of the overblown, sentimental German theatre against which Brecht reacted, his views were startlingly innovative, but nowadays the stripped-back set, visible changes of scene, actors moving in and out of character, the use of song and poetry, the address to the audience, the absence of the 'fourth wall' – all this is seen and practised by actors night after night on our modern stages and in fact refers back to a theatre from which Brecht drew many ideas: the theatre of the sixteenth and seventeenth centuries.

So what kind of exercises did Brecht give his actors?

A basic requirement for any actor tackling Brecht is that they should be minutely aware of the nuances of social class and be able to express this through 'gestus' or outward physical characteristic. A useful opening exercise to get the actors thinking along the right lines is to send them before they read a word of theory out on to the street. There, as Brecht would say, outside the doors of the theatre is both their audience and the material world and the economic forces they seek to depict.

> You artists who perform plays
> In great houses under electric suns
> Before the hushed crowd, pay a visit some time
> To that theatre whose setting is the street.

(BFA 12, p. 319; Poems, p. 176)

They must find on the streets and in shops, cafés and restaurants someone at work and study them carefully so that on their return they can show us in their words and outward gestures, their particular physical and social characteristics. How do their tasks affect their bodies? What does endless repetition do to a person? How does time wear them down? What are their work tools? How do they personalize them and handle them? What can be expressed about their economic position? What place do they occupy in the immediate pecking order? What value do they feel society assigns to them? 'I show ...' Brecht writes in his poem 'The playwright's song',

> What I have seen. In the man markets
> I have seen how men are traded. That
> I show, I, the playwright.
> How they step into each other's room with schemes
> Or rubber truncheons, or with cash
> How they stand on the streets and wait
> How they lay traps for one another
> Full of hope
> How they make appointments
> How they hang each other
> How they make love
> How they defend their loot
> How they eat
> I show all that.

(BFA 14, pp. 298–9, Poems, pp. 257–8)

It is important for the actors to imitate carefully what they observe and experience in real life and to avoid clichés. This was especially evident in the playing of class. When, for instance, I asked the actor Peter C to show me an English upper-class man making conversation with an unemployed working-class youth he, albeit expertly, reverted to a clichéd, drawling, upper-class English accent, nose in the air, almost soldierly in posture. The youth, well observed by Geoffrey B, was monosyllabic, frustration in his barely audible words, bashing his fist into his hand compulsively but revealing a terrible repressed anger, no eye contact.

– What d'you do?
– Nuffink.
– But can't you go and find a job?
– Unemployment, innit.

Then I asked Peter to show us upper-class gestus as it is in the early twenty-first century, to try and show us how we actually see it and experience it. Royal princes, Old Etonian members of the political class, for instance, are currently speaking in a kind of softened Cockney which we call 'Estuary', as it seems to have travelled a few miles down the Thames estuary and slightly softened in the process. It indicates an effort, albeit unconsciously, by the upper classes to appear levelled down to a more socially acceptable position of equality. It was chilling to see in action the body language and speech patterns of the modern ruling class: what the Old Etonian Prime Minister David Cameron likes to call 'conservatism with a human face'. Peter's accent relaxed and, exuding bonhomie, he said,

Hi! My name's Will …

And later,

Let's go to a boozer.

This was a perfectly enacted royal prince whom we see driving his own car and employing a glottal stop while his peers in the Cabinet with precisely the same informal style and accent cut benefits and vilify the unemployed. The audience thus observe not a familiar cliché but what clothing the wolf presently employs to bamboozle them.

To develop this sense of gestus or realistically observed social behaviour evinced through the whole body, one of Brecht's exercises suggests actors behave according to a list of adjectives, near in meaning but subtly different:

Note the difference between *strong* and *crude, relaxed* and *loose, quick* and *hurried, imaginative* and *digressive, thought out* and *elaborate, deeply*

felt and *blissful, contradictory* and *nonsensical, clear* and *emphatic, useful*
and *profitable, high-flown* and *loud-mouthed, ceremonious* and *pompous,*
delicate and *feeble, passionate* and *uncontrolled, natural* and *accidental.*
(*Buying Brass,* B75, p. 68, above)

A word of warning, however: an exercise is often only good in its author's
hands; when mechanically reproduced by another director or teacher it can
become commonplace and dull. The clue in this exercise is that these words
are to be understood adverbially – they refer to action. So it is important, as
it was for Brecht in all his work, to put props into an actor's hands so that
the exercise involves expression through gesture and object, not just inner
feeling. In other words, these are not adjectives referring to unchangeable
individual characteristics but words describing action in a particular circumstance with a particular object. I should remind you that costumes and props
were ever present in Brecht's rehearsal rooms. Brecht's actors never relied on
mime but on a physical reaction to a material object or garment:

... The pewter spoon
Which Courage sticks
In the lapel of her Mongolian jacket, the party card
For warm-hearted Vlassova and the fishing net
For the other, Spanish mother ...
(BFA 12, p. 330; *Poems,* p. 427)

Give the actors an object to handle and they will have the opportunity
for minute cultural observation in this exercise. I asked Anna T to pretend
to use a mirror and put on a hat 'delicately' and Claire 'feebly'. One was full
of social and sexual insecurity, the other vanity and superiority. 'Quickly'
and 'hurriedly', when enacted in the putting on of a coat, gave one actor
deft swiftness, the other desperate fumbling haste. This exercise made the
actors focus carefully on meaning and social nuance and how that can be
expressed. I did not give them time to talk about meaning but to enact it
impulsively. I also encouraged them to concentrate less on an inner psychological feeling – for exercises with objects are important too in Stanislavsky
training – and more on an outer physical quality, allowing the object to
inform the full physical expression. When James H put on his coat hurriedly,
we began to see an actor showing us how a man in desperate haste interacts
with a coat he cannot control. Brecht placed enormous emphasis on how his
actors used props, not interested in theatrical skill but in a revealing human
situation. The actor not only handles the prop; the object, in turn, dictates
the movement of the actor. It can almost become another character. He was
emphatic about the portrayal of the workman or craftsman in relation to the

tools of his trade and went to great lengths to find the correct prop for his actors – material, craftsmanship, age, wear and patina all taken into consideration. When playing Mother Courage, Helene Weigel had to learn how to pluck a chicken. Soldiers learned exactly how the gun was assembled with unhurried indifference before shooting down Kattrin.

These adverb lists can be extended by a thoughtful director, and the actor could be asked to find three adverbs that might apply to an activity and discover which one is most useful to the narrative. As an exercise in developing observation and physical expressiveness throughout the whole body, I felt we had stumbled upon 'a kernel of brilliance'. Most of all the actors started to have fun, not because they were trying to be funny but they were pushing the adverb often to its furthest extreme without losing truthfulness. *Spass* (fun) was the word Brecht used for this most vital ingredient, and I wish it was the word immediately associated with him, not *Verfremdung*.

On the second day, the actors worked with movement director Jane Gibson. Here she wanted to try an approach to character from the outside to the inside, rather than from inner contemplation outwards. Actors chose outfits from an array of rehearsal clothes and then found what the clothes did to their bodies, first as they stood still, then as they walked. Finally each actor picked up a prop and, letting it dictate their movement, found a voice and social type. Here we saw an immaculate couturier answering the phone to a customer, a stout embarrassed woman trying on a coat that did not fit, a working-class boy in driving gloves clasping imaginary weights between his hands in a display of machismo.

All the actors found this approach to character liberating in that it took them into their bodies and relied upon impulse instead of paralysing thinking and character analysis. 'So much of my work just locks me in my head,' said Geoff, 'this is such a relief.'

All the exercises we had explored so far were quite accessible to the Stanislavsky-trained actor, but the yes/no exercise took them into a real political consideration of their work. This is an exercise where Brecht asks actors to show a moment of crucial decision in character development where one decision might lead to inhumanity, the other to humanity, political consequences and perhaps danger. He suggests the audience must be aware that there are two directions in which a character can move: towards the forces of reaction or revolution. This presupposes a view of history where there can be no stasis: 'Everything changes', Brecht wrote, 'You can make / A fresh start with your final breath' (BFA 15, p. 117; *Poems*, p. 400).

To elucidate a position where an ordinary 'non-political' character is forced to move over some sort of political line, I used a moment in Christabel Bielenberg's compelling memoir of Berlin during the Second World War, *The*

Past is Myself, when a neighbour asked her to take in a Jewish couple who were on the run from the Nazis. This would have meant a death sentence if she were caught. I had to encourage Anna to move from the thought 'shall I/ shan't I?' to a depiction of the struggle to decide and the competing feelings running through her body. She stood in a doorway and moved backwards with a tiny shake of the head, then looking towards the couple standing defenceless in the street, she moved slightly towards them. Then her body seized up with fear, she looked furtively around, then longingly towards the safety of her house, her feet rooted to the spot, eventually moving back to her door. Still we could not guess what she would do. Finally she called the couple forward and hustled them into her house despite all her anxiety. This exercise fascinated the actors because they had rarely been called upon to depict this kind of decision making: there is no escape at this particular historical point. One small action will put you irrevocably on one side or the other. We all like to think we would make the humane decision, but how many of us really would?

In the ensuing discussion we decided that most actors would be capable of enacting this moment, but it would be the *director's* task to draw it out and give it its dramatic importance. And this is where so much theory becomes merely abstract because the actors cannot achieve this kind of work alone. They form part of a collaborative effort, of a collective vision, and much of the dynamic and emphasis of a scene is in the director's, not the actor's hands – a point I have made again and again to actors when they ask if a new kind of acting is called for in Brecht. Most modern actors are perfectly capable of emphasizing the political development of their characters, but in the end it is the director through the overall political understanding of the narrative who can give space and attention to such moments and who can call for a simple clear enactment of it on the part of the performer.

It is in the director's hands too that the question of dramatic context can be examined. Here we explored what the actor's contribution might be to a scene where a simple action can be completely charged with meaning if placed in a particular context. To demonstrate this, I devised a scene with a copper bowl of water on a table, an imaginary mirror, a rough towel and a piece of paper with writing on it. I asked a non-actor in the room to approach the table slowly, to dip her face in the water with her eyes open, dry her face on the towel and then try and memorize the words pinned up on the wall next to the mirror. I specifically asked that she evince no emotion and try not to construct an emotional narrative. What Alvin Nikolai the dancer called 'motion not emotion'. I then asked her to repeat the scene several times until the timing became steady. Finally I asked her to repeat the action while I read the following poem:

When years ago I showed you
How to wash first thing in the morning
With bits of ice in the water
Of the little copper bowl
Immersing your face, your eyes open
Then while you dried yourself with a rough towel
Reading the difficult lines of your part
From the sheet pinned to the wall, I said:
That's something you're doing for yourself; make it
Exemplary.
Now I hear you are said to be in prison.
The letters I wrote on your behalf
Remain unanswered. The friends I approached for you
Are silent. I can do nothing for you. What
Will your morning bring? Will you do something for yourself?
Hopeful and responsible
With good movements, exemplary?

(BFA 14, p. 360; Poems, p. 290)

The effect in the room was profound as the onlookers realized they were looking at the actress Carola Neher, prisoner in the Soviet Gulag, for whom Brecht could 'do nothing'. In the ensuing discussion, the actors realized that trying to bring emotion into this image would militate against its power. Its starkness and simplicity together with the dramatic revelation of context in slogan, song or poem had immeasurable power. The same startling use of contextual information occurred when Helene Weigel, as Mother Courage, silently screamed, as the audience heard the drum roll announcing that her son had been executed.

Perhaps, however, the most thrilling part of our workshop came with Brecht's suggested exercises for classical texts, Schiller's *Maria Stuart* and Shakespeare's *Hamlet*, *Macbeth* and *Romeo and Juliet*. These consisted of scenes which Brecht wrote for the actors to perform as rehearsal pieces, rather in the manner of his designer Caspar Neher, who often composed moment drawings of scenes that did not actually occur in the plays but which helped Brecht to develop a vision of the world he and the actors were trying to create. All these rehearsal scenes were designed to reveal a hidden side of the characters' lives. In *Macbeth* we explored life in the porter's lodge with messengers arriving and deliveries being made; in *Romeo and Juliet* a scene between Juliet and her nurse which showed Juliet's peremptoriness with her servant. In *Maria Stuart* a scene between the two queens was rewritten as a fight between two fishwives on a dockside.

The work on the Schiller play gave us one of those wonderful moments in a rehearsal room where an actor goes from a stumbling, stilted reading of classical language to a passionate fluency in the space of a quarter of an hour. Claire B moved from her fishwife harangue into the text with hardly a moment's hesitation, and the emotional investment of both monarchs was revealed as they violently protested their rights and grievances with the gusto of fishwives.

This use of rehearsal scenarios was what the actors enthused about most. The modern actor or director does not need these scenarios written out as Brecht does for us, but each situation in a potential production can be examined carefully, and scenarios of previous action, of the hidden world of servants or inferiors, of queens as brawling neighbours or princes as yobs picking a fight can be outlined and improvised. The actors can move from scenario to written scene and explore the discoveries of one in the formality of the other. A great deal can be gleaned from this trick of turning class, situation and character as if it were a sculpture, to view it from another angle. And that, put at its simplest, is what Brecht asks theatre makers to do.

The workshops described here took place in January 2013 and were the subject of a short film by May Abdalla http://www.bloomsbury.com/brecht-on-performance-9781408154557/

Brecht wrote a large number of poems about acting and the theatre, some of which are referenced in this account. They include a small group which Brecht would subsequently publish as 'Poems from Buying Brass' (in *Versuche* 14, 1955, and now in BFA 12, pp. 317–31) although they did not at all originate in that context. The first and last of these, 'On everyday theatre' and 'Weigel's props', are quoted above, along with 'The playwright's song', 'Everything changes' and 'Washing'. All of these are in *Bertolt Brecht, Poems 1913–1956*, edited by John Willett and Ralph Manheim (London: Methuen, 1976).

Select Bibliography

The standard German edition of Brecht's writings (*Werke*) is the:
Große kommentierte Berliner und Frankfurter Ausgabe (Berlin and Frankfurt: Aufbau/Suhrkamp, 1988–2000), abbreviated as BFA, on which the selection of texts in this edition is based.

The standard German reference work on Brecht's non-literary writings is:
J. Knopf (ed.), *Brecht Handbuch: Band 4. Schriften, Journale, Briefe* (Stuttgart: J. B. Metzler, 2003).

In English, the major publications on Brecht's non-literary writings are:
Brecht on Art and Politics, edited by Tom Kuhn and Steve Giles (London: Methuen, 2003).
Brecht on Film and Radio, edited and translated by Marc Silberman (London: Methuen, 2000).
Brecht on Theatre, edited by Marc Silberman, Steve Giles and Tom Kuhn (London: Bloomsbury, 2014).
Journals 1934–1955, translated by Hugh Rorrison and edited by John Willett (London: Methuen, 1993).
Letters 1913–1956, translated by Ralph Manheim and edited by John Willett (London: Methuen, 1990).

In addition, a wide range of important material, above all as it pertains to individual plays, is contained in the volumes of *Collected Plays 1–8*, edited by John Willett, Ralph Manheim and Tom Kuhn.

Useful further literature in English includes:
Althusser, L., *For Marx* (London: Verso, 1982).
Barnett, D., *A History of the Berliner Ensemble* (Cambridge: Cambridge University Press, 2014).
—*Brecht in Practice: Theatre, Theory and Performance* (London: Methuen, 2014).
Barthes, R., *Critical Essays* (Evanston: Northwestern UP, 1972).
—*Image, Music, Text* (London: Fontana, 1979).
Benjamin, W., *Understanding Brecht* (London: New Left Books, 1973).
Brooker, P., *Bertolt Brecht: Dialectics, Poetry, Politics* (London, Croom Helm, 1988).
Giles, S., *Bertolt Brecht and Critical Theory: Marxism, Modernity, and the 'Threepenny Lawsuit'* (Bern: Peter Lang, 1998).

Giles. S. and R. Livingstone (eds), *Bertolt Brecht: Centenary Essays* (Amsterdam: Rodopi, 1998).

Jameson, F., *Brecht and Method* (London: Verso, 1998).

Lunn, E., *Marxism and Modernism: An Historical Study of Lukács, Brecht, Benjamin and Adorno* (London: Verso, 1985).

Parker, S., *Bertolt Brecht: A Literary Life* (London: Bloomsbury, 2014).

Screen (special issue, 15, 2, summer 1974: *Brecht and a Revolutionary Cinema*).

Suvin, D., *To Brecht and Beyond: Soundings in Modern Dramaturgy* (Sussex: Harvester, 1984).

Taylor, R. (ed.), *Aesthetics and Politics: Debates between Bloch, Lukács, Brecht, Benjmain and Adorno* (London: Verso, 1977).

Thomson, P. and G. Sacks (eds), *The Cambridge Companion to Brecht* (Cambridge: CUP, 1994).

Weber, B. N. and H. Heinen (eds), *Bertolt Brecht: Political Theory and Literary Practice* (Manchester: MUP, 1980).

Wekwerth, M., *Daring to Play: A Brecht Companion* (London: Routledge, 2011).

White, J. J., *Bertolt Brecht's Dramatic Theory* (Rochester: Camden House, 2004).

—*The Theatre of Bertolt Brecht: A Study from Eight Aspects* (London: Methuen, 1977).

The annual publication of the International Brecht Society, *The Brecht Yearbook*, provides a further resource of current scholarly articles.

Index